TECHNICAL STANDARDS

An Introduction for Librarians

by Walt Crawford

Knowledge Industry Publications, Inc.
White Plains, N Y
London

Professional Librarian Series

Technical Standards: An Introduction for Librarians

Library of Congress Cataloging-in-Publication Data

Crawford, Walt.
    Technical standards.

    Bibliography: p.
    Includes index.
    1. Library science--Technological innovations--
Standards. 2. Library science--Standards. 3. Technology
--Standards. 4. Information science--Standards.
I. Title.
Z678 .85.C7   1985   025   85-23782
ISBN 0-86729-192-3
ISBN 0-86729-191-5 (pbk.)

This book has been printed on acid-free paper.

Printed in the United States of America

10   9   8   7   6   5   4   3   2   1

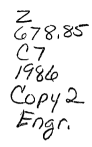

Table of Contents

List of Figures

Foreword

Standards aren't sexy. Probably the best thing we can say about standards is that they are usually transparent. Indeed, as Walt Crawford successfully demonstrates in the first chapters of this book—and the American National Standards Institute (ANSI) illustrates in its promotional materials—the major function performed by standards is to allow us to go about our business and personal lives without concern for our environment. We assume that our homes and offices are safe and that the devices we use—from toothbrushes and toasters to eyeglasses, lead pencils and calculators—will function. We feel that we are "entitled" to home and office environments that allow us to concentrate our energies on "meaningful" thoughts and activities—not on the basics of survival or comfort.

Not until we start planning visits to foreign countries do we become aware that the physical form of the plugs on our electrical appliances, as well as the electrical current on which they function, makes them inoperable outside of the United States without the correct conversion equipment. It is only when we find ourselves reading metric units in an instruction manual or inadvertently cutting off the top or bottom when photocopying correspondence from abroad, that we realize that American National Standards exist and are not a universal "given."

THE NEED FOR PARTICIPATION IN STANDARDS DEVELOPMENT

Most Americans do not usually consider the possibility of influencing the standards-development process. The lack of general knowledge about that process, therefore, is understandable. Like it or not, there are two base sizes for light bulbs and you must know which one you want or the bulb you purchase may not fit. Similarly, when existing standards interfere with our professional activities, or when the lack of a standard forces duplication or problems in our professional life, most of us retain the belief that we must grin and bear it.

Some individuals attempt to overcome the problem by inventing standards that can, they hope, be imposed on others in their profession. This, as Crawford points out, is the basis for "pseudo-standards" or internally developed standards specific to one organization. The broader the scope of influence of those individuals or organizations adopting pseudostandards, the more apt they are to attempt to impose their "standard" on others in their field.

In this era of automation, information overflow and dependency, and resource sharing, it is most important that those who need standards and those who find existing standards inadequate or inappropriate gain an understanding of their ability to influence the standards-development process. Bad standards impede the success of individuals and organizations. If we are to have the appropriate standards to function properly, we must have the input and help of those who know what is needed.

Standards-development is a tedious, time-consuming and often frustrating task. Reaching consensus on proposed standards simply repeats the frustrations of the development process. Why, then do people spend their time developing standards? Because, quite often, they experience more frustration from missing or inadequate standards than from the constructive task of designing workable standards.

Despite the tedium and frustration of the standards-development process, there are also benefits to becoming involved. The primary one, of course, is your ability, through participation, to assist yourself, your organization and your profession by developing a standard that will enable everyone to function more efficiently and effectively. But, be careful: you just might get hooked. The satisfaction of participating in the development of a widely accepted and frequently used standard can be comparable to that of being the author of a best-seller. Imagine Henriette Avram's excitement the first time that she heard the Library of Congress MARC standard referred to by library school students as *M*rs. *A*vram's *R*emarkable *C*atalog!

One final and often overlooked benefit of such participation is that standards development forces you to meet individuals outside of your own area of expertise and to understand their perspectives. In an era of specialization, we often find ourselves communicating primarily with those involved in our own small, specialized area of the profession or with those who can provide the information needed to solve a specific problem of immediate concern. The standards-development process demands that *all parties* influenced by the standard meet, think, argue and develop consensus. This brings you into working contact with your counterparts across the country, your suppliers, your customers and the technicians responsible for developing the tools you use to effect your goal. For more than 10 years, my own involvement in the standards field has enabled me to meet some of the people I respect most both here in the United States and abroad.

LIBRARIES MUST FIGHT FOR THE STANDARDS THEY WANT

Once you do get involved in developing American National Standards for libraries, information science and publishing (a process well-described by Crawford in this book), you discover that these standards result from the toil and expertise of individuals who give of their own personal time to meet, think, discuss and act. On the other hand, you also find that in developing computer systems standards, major corporations perform development-related tasks on company time, supported by company money.

In fact, the IBMs and AT&Ts of this world actually hire and pay individuals to represent their interests in the standards-development arena on a full-time basis. For example, if a standard is scheduled for discussion at a meeting in Washington, Paris or Tokyo, these individuals are sent to the meeting on company time and on company funds.

The computer has taken on an increasingly important role in our lives—from turning off an iron lying flat without movement for too long a period of time; to detecting a problem in a car engine and flashing the appropriate message on the dashboard; to allowing those in libraries, information science and publishing to communicate electronically. However, this increased dependence on computer standards has provided additional power to large computer systems standards developers. They seem to be having an increasingly difficult time differentiating generic hardware- and software-specific standards from application-level standards—particularly when the application involves the very information being processed by their hardware and software.

For example, computer systems standards developers objected to recent interest expressed by the library community in developing (1) a standard software descriptor for the outer package and the magnetic media and (2) a standard location for certain data elements on bibliographic databases offered to libraries on CD-ROMs (Compact Disk–Read-Only Memory). The library community, represented by NISO, fought and won both battles, but still faces a fight in the area NISO called "Text and Office Systems." Here, computer companies are attempting to develop broad general standards for what we would call electronic publications.

When this book was written, standards for computer applications within libraries, information science and publishing were on an equal footing with basic computer hardware and software standards in the national and international standards-developing organizations. Crawford offers an excellent description of ANSI and ISO—the International Organization for Standardization. However, steps have already been taken to move computer standards out of this counterpart relationship in the international arena. Soon, computer standards activities will report to an international super agency made up of ISO and the International Electrotechnical Commission (IEC). Once that move is completed, we can expect the same relationship to develop nationally. It will take an increased amount of volunteer participation by the library community to continue winning battles for its own standards in the face of such imposing competition.

Even if libraries successfully battle for control of their own computer applications standards within the United States, they still face an increasingly sophisticated international library community. ISO participants call many more standards-development meetings in Europe than U.S. delegates can afford to attend. In the international arena, many delegates are government-funded and their national standards are implemented by government decree rather than by the voluntary acceptance of the library community.

Thus, the final benefit of involvement in the standardization process ensures that future American National Standards will meet the needs of the American library community as it sees fit, not by compromising with standards established elsewhere.

In this book, Walt Crawford points out the standards we ignore in our day-to-day dealing with the environment and highlights the specific standards that affect the library community. We have not seen as readable a reference work and critique as Crawford skillfully presents in this book. He is a hard taskmaster in his criteria for the utility of standards and cites problems created by standards. He performs an important service in bringing information about these specific standards and an understanding of the standardization process to the library, information science and publishing community at a time when this area cannot be ignored.

Sandra K. Paul, President
SKP Associates

ACKNOWLEDGMENTS

Many of my friends and colleagues helped make this book possible, directly or indirectly. A few played specific roles and deserve credit for much of what's right about the book. Assertions, errors, clumsy wording and poor organization are all mine. Ideas in the first few chapters come from reading, thinking and ten years of discussions on standards issues.

Two people instigated this project: Adrienne Hickey, my former editor at Knowledge Industry, and Ruth C. Carter, then chair of LITA TESLA, the Technical Standards for Library Automation Committee. My wife, Linda Driver, supported the idea and provided her usual support and good advice; my boss, Glee Harrah Cady, also provided critical support.

Susan Schwartz was my editor at Knowledge Industry during the preparation of the manuscript, and provided cogent, insightful criticism which eased the route from rough draft to final submission. Karen Sirabian, my new editor at Knowledge Industry, brought a keen eye to bear on the final manuscript and suggested several significant improvements; Liz Harvey did a fine job of copy editing, polishing the rough spots without changing my intent or tone. Joan Aliprand, Robert Beebe, Wayne Davison and Charles Stewart of RLG all gave helpful review comments; Kathleen Bales, also of RLG, provided critical review of the indexes. Sandra K. Paul of SKP Associates, chair of the National Information Standards Organization (Z39), went out of her way to do a careful review of the manuscript. Paul Evan Peters of Columbia University, ALA LITA's representative on ASC X3, provided careful review and current information on ASC X3 and ISO TC 97. My thanks to them all.

Two colleagues in the library field are indirectly responsible for this book and for *MARC for Library Use.* David Weisbrod was unable to prepare an article on MARC for *Library Trends* and suggested my name instead. That article started a series of events leading to *MARC for Library Use;* I would never have started this book without the experience of that one. Brian Aveney, then editor of *Information Technology and Libraries,* prodded me into active writing for publication at a time when I found such writing difficult. Neither should be held accountable for the results.

John Kountz deserves some of the blame for my interest in technical standards. When I first joined ALA in 1975, Kountz was running TESLA with a flair that made the committee meetings fascinating. Somehow, my fascination with the early meetings resulted in long-term involvement with TESLA and, through TESLA, with technical standards.

Finally, there's the matter of mechanics. This manuscript was written using WordStar on a Morrow MD2 CP/M floppy disk microcomputer. Chapters were formatted using The FinalWord on an IBM PC/XT, and printed on the RLG Xerox 9700 laser printer (attached to an Amdahl 5860 computer). A new addition to the home front speeded editing by at least a month or two. Most editing was done using NewWord on a Morrow MD11, a CP/M machine with hard disk. The improvements in NewWord over WordStar (the two are compatible), the improvements in the Morrow terminal, and most of all the speed improvements of CP/M+ (3.0) and the Morrow hard disk, made an almost unbelievable difference in speed and ease of editing.

Comments and corrections are welcome and should be sent to me at The Research Libraries Group, Jordan Quadrangle, Stanford, CA 94305.

Walt Crawford
Menlo Park, September 1985

1

Introduction

We all rely on technical standards; most of the time we don't worry about those standards. When you plug in a television set, add oil to your car or use a Library of Congress record on OCLC or RLIN, you're relying on one or more technical standards. Technical standards for libraries can help you as a librarian, writer or researcher. You don't need to know every detail of every standard, but you can use technical standards better if you understand them.

People and companies use technical standards without necessarily paying attention to them. As shown below, we sometimes get by too well without paying attention: problems can arise when a standard is assumed but not verified.*

THE "STANDARD-SIZED" CATALOG CARDS

The Research Libraries Group (RLG) produces large numbers of catalog cards for users of the Research Libraries Information Network (RLIN). Until early 1982, RLG produced cards using an IBM line printer. Cards were printed two at a time on special continuous-form card stock with perforations between each pair of cards. When RLG acquired card stock, we specified continuous-form library catalog card stock meeting all applicable standards.

In 1982, RLG decided to use a Xerox 9700 laser printer to print catalog cards. The "cards" were prepunched sheets of card stock, each of which would contain four catalog cards. The producer certified that the material itself met applicable standards, and that the

---

*The example is used with the kind permission of my employers, The Research Libraries Group, Inc., who are always willing to admit a mistake.

holes were punched in appropriate places for standard catalog cards. RLG/RLIN staff would cut the sheets into individual cards after they were printed.

Production of cards began beautifully. We purchased a good character set, tested the programs and started shipping laser-printed cards. RLG followed standards at all steps along the way—including, of course, the 3-inch x 5-inch standard for library catalog cards. A few weeks later, RLG/RLIN began to get complaints: the catalog cards wouldn't fit in some catalog drawers. The production staff was troubled by the reports. The card stock was manufactured to standard, the holes were punched to standard and the cutting machine was carefully adjusted to precisely 3-inch x 5-inch. The "three-by-five" catalog card is a well-known standard: those dimensions occur repeatedly in library literature, even in the specialized literature of library standards.

After some consideration and research, we found the problem: we had relied on a common but false simplification of the standard size for a catalog card. It isn't three-by-five, even though everybody calls it that. The standard dimensions for a library catalog card are 75mm x 125mm. That's almost three-by-five, but not quite: the actual standard card is 2.95 inches high and 4.92 inches wide. If a catalog card drawer is precisely 5 inches wide, it will hold standard catalog cards nicely—but it won't hold 3-inch x 5-inch cards. RLG readjusted the card cutter, reran the oversize catalog cards and solved the problem, which could have been avoided by explicitly checking the standard.

RLG used a standard without referring to the standard, as we all do most of the time. This time, relying on memory and oral tradition created problems, which RLG solved at some expense and with some difficulty. The standard was misused through inattention. This particular standard has been steadily corrupted by years of casual reference to three-by-five library cards.

The Standard In Question

Library suppliers know how to make standard catalog card stock: the color, the thickness, where the holes should be punched and how big the holes should be. Suppliers follow a voluntary technical standard, originally established in 1969; ANSI Z85.1-1980:

American National Standard for Permanent and Durable Library Catalog Cards.[1] When RLG printed catalog cards on perforated stock, the organization didn't worry about ANSI Z85.1. Suppliers have no motive to produce nonstandard cards: there are no real markets for library card stock other than libraries and library suppliers.

Z85.1-1980
PERMANENT AND DURABLE LIBRARY
CATALOG CARDS

Like most ANSI standards, ANSI Z85.1-1980 includes a scope and purpose note, an explicit standard and a foreword that is not actually part of the standard. Unlike many other standards, ANSI Z85.1-1980 does not include practice guidelines, appendixes or an abstract. ANSI Z85.1-1980 is a short standard: explicit, unambiguous and clearly written.

Foreword

The foreword provides background for the standard:

> A de facto standard for the dimensions of catalog cards used in American libraries was established in the nineteenth century by Melvil Dewey. For the past fifty years, at least, almost every card catalog cabinet manufactured in the United States has been designed to accommodate cards of those dimensions.[2]

Z85.1 was originally approved in 1969. The 1980 version specifies hole placement more precisely and adds test methods for ink feathering and erasing qualities. Committee Z85, the *American National Standards Committee on Standardization of Library Supplies and Equipment,* never issued any other standards. Z85.1 is now maintained by the National Information Standards Organization, NISO (Z39).

Scope and Purpose

A technical standard should have a well-defined scope; many

problems with technical standards arise because standards are used beyond their intended scope. Z85.1 states a clear, straightforward scope and rationale:

> This standard establishes performance standards for permanent and durable library catalog cards. It specifies the size, caliper, hole size and location, and other characteristics of these cards.
>
> Although requirements for permanence and durability of library catalog cards differ according to the type of library, the standard specifies the minimum factors necessary to meet the needs of the research library. Research libraries ordinarily retain the majority of their acquisitions permanently. Catalog cards for such acquisitions must be durable library cards made from stock which will not deteriorate more rapidly than the books due to either (1) the composition of the paper or (2) the relatively heavy use conditions they must endure in the card catalog.[3]

In this case, what's good for the research library is certainly good for the public library as well. Even public libraries that must discard one book for every book added will keep some books for decades. No library should be concerned that catalog cards will cease to be useful before the books are discarded. More to the point, no library should have to worry that the catalog card drawers purchased from Highsmith won't hold cards provided by Baker & Taylor.

Details

The standard specifies 17 explicit dimensions and characteristics of catalog cards, including:

• Size: 75mm x 125mm, with a tolerance of +0 to −0.5mm;

• Cutting: If cards are guillotined (knife-cut) rather than cut by a rotary blade, the knife must be sharp, the cards back-trimmed to be free of burr;

• Hole: the hole must be centered in terms of width, 7.9mm in diameter, with a lower edge 4.8mm from the bottom of the card: the bottom placement has a tolerance of −0, +0.8mm. (These dimensions all make more sense in common measure: a 5/16 inch hole, 3/16 inch from the bottom of the card, with a 1/32 inch tolerance.) This section also says why the hole must be placed properly;

• Finish, Surface, Color: Smooth, lint-free, white or cream-white;

• Weight and thickness: Lightweight cards 0.020cm (0.008 inch) thick, weighing 200 grams per square meter (110-pound stock); medium-weight cards 0.025cm (0.010 inch) thick, weighing 235 grams per square meter (130-pound stock). In other words, medium-weight cards should pack 100 to the inch;

• Writing, Printing, Erasing Qualities: Explicit test methods to assure that cards take ink cleanly and that pencil marks can be erased cleanly;

• Acidity: pH of no less than 5.5, "measured by the hot extraction method described in TAPPI T 435 os-77";

• Endurance: the card must stand up to 800 double folds with 1 kilogram tension using a standard test method;

• Stock: card stock must not contain ground wood, unbleached fibers, or optical brighteners, and can contain only 2% fluorescence due to natural properties.

Technical standards build on other technical standards. Z85.1 refers explicitly to four standards established by the Technical Association of the Pulp and Paper Industry (TAPPI), including TAPPI T 435 os-77: *Hydrogen Ion Concentration (pH) of Paper Extracts—Hot Extraction Method,* and ANSI/TAPPI T401 os-74: *American National Standard for Fiber Analysis of Paper and Paperboard.*
   This summary doesn't include all pertinent aspects of the standard. If you're planning to produce (or cut) catalog cards, or want to check on your suppliers, you should spend $5 for a copy of ANSI Z85.1-1980. If you're buying catalog card stock, you need only

specify that it must be produced in accordance with ANSI Z85.1-1980. Typically, you'd simply call for "Library Catalog Cards (Permanent and Durable)" or "catalog card stock meeting applicable standards."

DEFINING TECHNICAL STANDARDS

In "Organizations Contributing to Development of Library Standards,"[4] Henriette Avram, Sally McCallum and Mary Price set forth some basic varieties of standards:

> Standards themselves take a variety of forms. They may be guidelines or models against which services, etc., are to be compared. Library service standards fall into this category. Other standards take the form of rules for activities that should be applied as consistently as possible but which, by their nature, will not necessarily produce the identical results even when followed. Cataloging rules are of this type. A third class of standards are specifications or "technical" standards for which strict observance is necessary if sharing is to take place. Format structure, character sets, and code list standards fall into this class.[5]

Technical standards are definitions or specifications; they communicate agreements on sharing techniques. Technical standards can:

• Record agreement on specifications;

• Extend the agreement beyond the original parties, as other parties obtain and follow the standards;

• Communicate to others that a set of specifications has been followed: reference to a technical standard is a brief way of referring to the specifications contained in that standard.

Chapter 3 discusses varieties of technical standards. For most of this book, two different definitions of technical standards are used, one broad and one fairly narrow. As a broad definition:

> A *technical standard* is an explicit definition that can be

communicated, which is not subject to unilateral change without notice and which, if properly followed, will yield consistent results.

THE NEED FOR STANDARDS

Complex societies require technical standards. Industrial and postindustrial societies depend on technical standards for everyday life and long-term progress. Technical standards provide the common bases from which individual developments may emerge. To quote Ken Dowlin, then president of the Library and Information Technology Association, "without technical standards, systems cannot grow."[6]

We may notice a need for technical standards:

• When technical standards are ignored or misused, as in the example of the catalog cards;

• When technological developments are stymied or made more difficult because many incompatible paths are taken in the absence of technical standards;

• When an area fails to develop quickly or economically because people working in the area have no common basis from which to proceed.

Tens of thousands of people devote hundreds of thousands of hours a year, and millions of dollars each year, developing, considering and maintaining technical standards.

The Problems and Dangers of Standards

Standards aren't always helpful. Technical standards can hamper innovation, when standards become established before a field has matured. Technical standards can lock out the most creative and efficient people in a field. Most technical standards in the United States are voluntary, but when all standard contracts call for compliance with all pertinent technical standards, nonstandard solutions may not be practical.

Technical standards can cause real damage. Efforts devoted to standards development can detract from efforts for innovation. Standards can keep old technology dominant beyond its time, harming everyone through inefficiency and inflexibility. Standards may not be developed with sufficient objectivity or balance and may favor some suppliers at the expense of others, or at the expense of users. Standards can be used to impose trade barriers or to suppress technologies.

Many standards aren't ANSI standards. Standards arise through various means: licensing preemptive innovations, "de facto standards" based on successful marketing and "industry standards" based on ill-understood "agreements" among competitors, in addition to standards formally developed and approved through ANSI. Things are referred to as "industry standards" which are not technical standards as defined in this book, failing primarily in that they can be changed unilaterally by a single agent, without consultation or negotiation. (Chapters 3, 4 and 6 discuss varieties and problems of standards and pseudostandards in more detail.)

TECHNICAL STANDARDS FOR LIBRARIES

Libraries rely on complex sets of related technical standards from other fields, and have a set of standards developed specifically for the library, information science and publishing industries. These standards, largely developed by the National Information Standards Organization—or NISO (Z39)—and its predecessor American National Standards Committee Z39, cover a range of topics from the structure of machine-readable bibliographic records (Z39.2) to a system for the romanization of Armenian (Z39.37). Library automation directly uses the range of standards established by Accredited Standards Committee X3 (Information Processing Systems).*

The Fall 1982 issue of *Library Trends,* which includes ten articles on the theme of "Technical Standards for Library and Infor-

---

*Library automation also uses standards developed by other organizations such as IEEE (Institute of Electrical and Electronics Engineers) and EIA (Electronic Industries Association), but this book will focus on ASC X3.

mation Science,'' provides good background. Most of the authors
are authorities in their specialties and present useful perspectives on
issues of technical standards for libraries.

This book is a basic introduction to technical standards with
particular focus on libraries and automation. The first six chapters
treat the general field of technical standards. Some examples come
from the library field, some from everyday life. Later chapters focus
on the narrower set of technical standards established by recognized
voluntary standards-making bodies. The most significant organization in the United States for establishing and coordinating voluntary
technical standards is the American National Standards Institute
(ANSI); the most significant international organization is the International Organization for Standardization (ISO). The latter half of
the book is a current reference to ANSI and ISO standards
specifically relating to libraries and automation, with little attention
to other fields.

DEFINITIONS

Most special terms used in this book are defined when they first
appear; many appear in the glossary. Five abbreviations used
throughout the book are defined below.

> **ANSI:** American National Standards Institute. The overall
> organization for voluntary standards in the United States,
> and the U.S. member of ISO. ANSI does not develop stan-
> dards; ANSI standards are created by various standards orga-
> nizations following ANSI guidelines. Many of these standards
> are published by ANSI, and all are available from ANSI.

> **ASC:** Accredited Standards Committee. The simplest suc-
> cessor to a former ANSC, American National Standards
> Committee. ANSI now requires that standards-creating agen-
> cies be separate bodies; a number of ANSCs, including X3,
> have become ASCs.

> **ISO:** International Organization for Standardization. The
> international body for voluntary standards, with represen-
> tatives from national standards organizations.

> **NISO:** the National Information Standards Organization,
> called NISO (Z39), formerly ANSC Z39. The ANSI-accredi-
> ted standards organization preparing standards for library

and information science and related publishing practices. NISO-developed standards continue to be numbered beginning Z39, as in Z39.2-1979.

Z39: Earlier name for NISO (see above). The organization changed names in 1984; most citations are likely to use the earlier name.

NOTE: All citations from ANSI standards are made with the permission of the American National Standards Institute; copies of all such standards may be purchased from the American National Standards Institute at 1430 Broadway, New York, N.Y. 10018. ISO standards are also available through ANSI. There are thousands of ANSI and ISO standards: at least 8000 ANSI, at least 6000 ISO. Catalogs of ANSI and ISO standards are available from ANSI: Chapter 9 includes ordering information.

FOOTNOTES

1. Available, as are all ANSI standards cited in this book, from the American National Standards Institute, 1430 Broadway, New York, NY 10018.

2. ANSI Z85.1-1980, p. 3. This material is reproduced with permission from American National Standard Z85.1-1980, copyright 1980 by the American National Standards Institute. Copies of this standard may be purchased from the American National Standards Institute.

3. *Ibid.,* p. 5

4. Avram, Henriette D.; McCallum, Sally H.; Price, Mary S. "Organizations Contributing to Development of Library Standards." *Library Trends.* 31(2): 197-221; 1982 Fall.

5. *Ibid.,* p. 198

6. Ken Dowlin, caption on ALA LITA poster, 1984

7. Available for $5 from the Journals Department, University of Illinois Press, 54 E. Gregory Drive, Box 5081, Station A, Champaign, IL 61820.

2

Technical Standards in Action

Technical standards affect each of us every day, starting even before we awake and continuing throughout the day. Depending on your interests, you may also be affected by the lack of technical standards in some areas.

A MORNING'S WORTH OF STANDARDS

Tens of thousands of technical standards have been established in the United States, including over 10,000 standards established by ANSI-accredited standards agencies. (See Chapter 3 for a discussion of this and other varieties of technical standards.) The following examples represent only a few of the technical standards that directly affect your everyday life.

Standards Before Work

Before you wake up, you're probably in bed. ANSI Z357.1-1981: *Bedding Products and Components,* may have influenced your sleep. If you are wakened by an electric clock, that clock is probably covered by ANSI/UL 826-1980: *Safety Standard for Household Electric Clocks,* one of the many ANSI standards developed by Underwriters Laboratory, Inc. ANSI/UL 499-1978: *Safety Standard for Electric Heating Appliances,* covers your electric space heaters; gas heaters have their own standards.

If you turn on a light, you're relying on some of the 18 ANSI standards for electric lamp bases, and 106 for electric lamps. One of these is ANSI C78.375-1973 (R1978): *Guide for Electrical Measurements of Fluorescent Lamps.* Those standards and guides mean that you can buy a lamp from one maker to put in another maker's fixture: the fixture is designed for a specified size and variety of lamp, and any current or prospective lamp manufacturer can determine the dimensions and characteristics required for a lamp to work in a standard fixture.

Some of you use electric shavers; some use electric hair dryers. ANSI/UL 1028-1980 provides a *Safety Standard for Hair Clippers and Shaving Appliances,* while ANSI/UL HD1-1980 states a *Method for Measuring Performance of Household Electric Hair Dryers.* You plug appliances into outlet boxes covered by ANSI/UL 514-1980: *Safety Standards for Outlet Boxes and Fittings;* the plugs and wiring follow standards and codes such as ANSI/NFPA 70-1984: *National Electrical Code* and ANSI C2-1984: *National Electrical Safety Code.* Household and other wiring is based on other standards developed by various agencies, including ANSI/IEEE C37.13-1981: *Low-Voltage AC Power Circuit Breakers Used in Enclosures* and a dozen standards for electric line construction.

On your way to work, you depend on hundreds of technical standards relating to cars, fuel, roads and traffic control. ANSI/ASTM D1120-78: *Method of Test for Boiling Point of Engine Antifreeze* affects the well-being of your car, as do ANSI/ASTM D2699-82: *Test for Knock Characteristics of Motor Fuels by the Research Method* and ANSI/ASTM D2602-75 (1980): *Method of Test for Apparent Viscosity of Engine Oils at Low Temperature Using the Cold-Cranking Simulator.* When you buy a specific grade of oil or a specific octane of gasoline, you rely on grading standards as specified in formal consensus standards such as those above. Your trip to work is also probably affected by an entire group of technical standards for "CAMAC," *Computer Automated Measurement and Control* of traffic. Seven CAMAC standards are grouped together as ANSI/IEEE Camac-1982.

Standards in the Library

When you arrive at work, you're still surrounded by technical standards, including many of those mentioned above and a number of others. Some of these are standards related to public places, some are related to general business and some are specific to libraries; many others affect non-print materials within the library.

The latter half of this book examines the 40-odd library and publishing standards in some detail, together with some related standards. In a typical day, you may be affected indirectly by a few of these:

1. ANSI Z39.7-1983: *Standards for Library Statistics*

2. ANSI Z39.9-1979: *International Standard Serial Number (ISSN)*

3. ANSI Z39.15-1980: *Title Leaves of a Book*

4. ANSI Z39.32-1981: *Information on Microfiche Headings*

5. ANSI Z39.45-1983: *Claims for Missing Issues of Serials*

If you deal with computers at all, even to search Dialog, you depend on ANSI X3.4-1977: *Code for Information Interchange,* which defines ASCII, the American Standard Code for Information Interchange. ANSI/IES RP1-1982: *Practice for Office Lighting* may have been used in specifying lighting for your offices. If your library entrance was recently modified, the architects probably used ANSI A117.1-1980: *Specifications for Making Buildings and Facilities Accessible to, and Usable by, Physically Handicapped People.* This simple listing of standards that affect your daily life could go on for many more pages; the standards above are only some of the more obvious ones in the ANSI catalog. These are examples of formal consensus standards which may affect you every day.

Other Types of Technical Standards in Library Life

If you work for one of the 5000-odd libraries that use OCLC, RLIN, WLN or UTLAS for cataloging, you're relying on a web of technical standards, some of them from Z39 or X3 and some of them from other sources. Among the ANSI standards involved are ANSI Z39.2-1977: *Bibliographic Information Interchange on Magnetic Tape,* used in all MARC record interchange, and ANSI X3.4-1977, the definition of ASCII.

All cataloging in USMARC formats is based on the *MARC*

Formats for Bibliographic Data, a community technical standard established and maintained by the Library of Congress in cooperation with other agencies. Each bibliographic service establishes additional definitions, constituting extended technical standards for that cataloging environment. Most current cataloging uses ISBD punctuation, an international standard established by the International Federation of Library Associations and Institutions (IFLA).

The American Library Association has established some technical standards used in everyday library life. One familiar standard is the ALA *Standard Interlibrary Loan Form,* a standard methodology for communicating an Interlibrary Loan (ILL) request and response, together with a printed form to embody that communication.

LIVING WITH STANDARDS

You should be able to rely on technical standards without being aware of them. Technical standards should be in the background except when you're developing something that directly depends on their application.

Consider the simple act of writing a brief business letter. You take a sheet of standard letter paper, probably acquired citing standard paper weight specifications and certainly using a standard size, and an "all purpose" envelope, which may be identified as a "#10" envelope. The envelope and the paper may have come from different suppliers, but you'll confidently assume that you can fold the paper into thirds and it will fit neatly into the envelope, as though they were made for each other. So far, you're relying on at least three standard specifications, possibly more.

You take the paper over to an electric typewriter. It may not be the typewriter you normally use, but you're confident that you can use it, since the keycaps will be in the standard "QWERTY" order. You also assume that the plug will fit into any convenient wall socket, and that the typewriter will run on the current available from that socket. You're relying on several additional standards: ANSI X4.23-1982: *Keyboard Arrangement for Alphanumeric Machines;* various standards for electrical connections; national consensus on voltage and frequency for current delivered through standard connections; and others.

In each case, technical standards allow you to carry on normal activities with ease because you can make assumptions. You assume that your paper will fit in the envelope; as a touch typist, you assume that your fingers will find the right keys. You assume that the plug will fit in the socket and that you won't electrocute yourself or fry the typewriter.

LIVING WITHOUT STANDARDS

Civilized life without technical standards would be difficult at best, and nearly impossible on any large, organized or industrialized scale. Consider trying to write that business letter without technical standards. The typewriter (if it existed) would be quite expensive. The manufacturer would have to negotiate with each supplier of materials as to what would be meant by "a large enough sheet of hard enough steel"—and define what "steel" means in this case—and do his or her own materials testing. Then the manufacturer would have to hand-craft each part of each typewriter, and would certainly have to decide where keys should go and what forms of paper might be used. Salespeople or customers would need to be shown what this particular machine was and what it could be used for. The typewriter wouldn't be electric; establishing electrical distribution systems without a complex web of measurement, safety and specification standards would be unthinkable.

This is only one aspect of your problems in sending a business letter in a world without standards. In any case, you wouldn't need to; most business would be carried on with people you could talk to directly or through associates, since you'd constantly be negotiating what it was you were buying or selling.*

LIVING WITH CONFLICTING STANDARDS

The above example could never happen, for when people begin to act outside their immediate circle, they create standards. Larger and more complex societies need larger and more comprehensive

---

*While early civilizations certainly carried out business over long distances without electric typewriters, such civilizations did have technical standards for weights and measures.

sets of standards. Industry requires detailed and formalized technical standards; technology rests on a basis of standards. When some of the standards aren't developed in time, or when different groups develop different (and conflicting) technical standards, problems arise. Two examples follow: one from consumer electronics, one from bibliography.

Quadraphonic Sound

High fidelity specialists have long been aware that two speakers cannot provide a fully accurate rendering of a "musical space," such as a concert hall. Two sound sources simply don't provide enough information for accurate reproduction, although our minds fill in much of the missing information. Quadraphonic sound provides a possible solution to the problem: four speakers, two in front of the listener and two behind, make a much more accurate musical space possible.

After years of experiments with four-channel quadraphonic sound on tapes, quadraphonic records began in the early 1970s. Initial reports were good: the new medium opened up the acoustic space, providing a potentially much more realistic listening environment. Despite good early reports, quadraphonic sound died a slow and economically painful death in the marketplace.

Rear speakers are difficult to place in most living rooms. Quad was expensive: two speakers, another stereo amplifier and the circuitry to decode quadraphonic information from two-channel recordings. Perhaps most important, three different standards for quadraphonic recording appeared, with no dominant early standard.

Columbia/CBS developed a matrixing system called "SQ," for Stereo/Quadraphonic. Sansui developed another matrixing system called "QS," for Quadraphonic/Stereo. RCA developed "CD-4," a discrete four-channel stereo-compatible system. Each system was clearly and unambiguously defined, used by more than one agency and not subject to unilateral change. Equipment manufacturers released amplifiers supporting one, two or all three of the quadraphonic systems. Millions of LP records were produced in quadraphonic sound.

Three different standards competed in the consumer marketplace. Record stores weren't sure what to stock and how to stock it, and many of the quadraphonic versions had more noise than straight stereo versions, even though all three systems were compatible with stereo. More time was spent considering *which* quadraphonic standard to follow than considering *whether* quadraphonic was worth the trouble. Equipment stayed expensive, partly because manufacturers had to include not one decoding circuit but three different decoding circuits. In the long run, the entire enterprise failed.

While quadraphonic sound was sufficiently disruptive to living rooms and budgets that it might not have succeeded in any case, the three-way split may have prevented quad from getting a fair trial.*

Bibliographic Citations

"There is no common agreement among scholars, editors, bibliographers, or publishers concerning the exact forms to be used in making either footnote citations or bibliographical references to books, articles, or other printed works."[1] Peyton Hurt's statement was true in 1968; it was true in 1977, when ANSC Z39 developed ANSI Z39.29-1977: *American National Standard for Bibliographic References.* It is still true today. (See Chapter 10 for a description and full citation for Z39.29.)

The problem is not a lack of recommended standards, but too many different sets of standards. *Bibliography and Footnotes,* cited above, presents two recommended formats (one for bibliographies, one for footnotes) and cites more than 30 manuals of style, each of which includes recommendations for citation form. The most widely known standard is probably that embodied in *The Chicago Manual of Style* from the University of Chicago Press. Others include guides from the American Institute of Chemical Engineers, the American Psychological Association, the Modern Language Association and the U.S. Government Printing Office. Most publishers have in-house standards, some of them published as style manuals.

---

*Surround sound didn't completely disappear. Some European classical record companies still produce SQ discs, and recent high fidelity video-cassettes and videodiscs have included the Dolby surround-sound motion picture sound, which is largely compatible with SQ decoding.

The net effect of this multiplicity of styles is that no single standard exists or is likely to arise. Chicago's *Manual of Style* receives wide use, but many associations and publishers use styles that vary to lesser or greater degree. The consistent, clear rules set out in ANSI Z39.29 provide a single style for use in footnotes and bibliographies, a style that is straightforward enough to make computer support for bibliographies more practical. The advantages of Z39.29 have not gained fast or wide acceptance for the standard. While some journals and publishers are moving to use of Z39.29, the standard comes too late to avoid the established multiplicity of citation styles.*

In the case of quadraphonic sound, clear damage resulted from conflicting standards. Damages resulting from conflicting citation styles are subtler, and affect writers more than readers. A reader can usually gather needed information from any style of citation, but a writer who works in more than one field may find it difficult to prepare proper citations for each manuscript.

WELL-TIMED STANDARDS

Where conflicting standards may cause confusion and damage, well-timed standards can help establish new techniques and technologies. Two brief examples follow; once again, the first is from consumer electronics, the second from the library field.

Digital Audio Discs

In the case of digital audio discs or compact discs, an industry-wide consensus standard was adopted prior to commercial introduction. The compact disc (CD), developed by Philips and Sony but established as a multicompany standard, has been recognized as the most successful new consumer product in history, with over one-half million CD players sold during the first eight months of the system's availability in the United States. In this case, a single stan-

---

*My own experience with *MARC for Library Use* suggests that reasonable publishers will agree to use of Z39.29 if an author cites the standard, even when the publisher has a different established style.

dard was adopted prior to commercial battles; as a result, ads focus on comparative advantages of a particular player—but all CD players play all CD records, and consumers don't have to worry about such problems.

Bibliographic Information Interchange

ANSI Z39.2, *American National Standard for Bibliographic Information Interchange* (described in Chapter 10) was approved in 1971. The standard established a structure to carry bibliographic information; the structure is better known as MARC. While the standard was not approved and published until 1971, it was used from the beginning for MARC II. An international equivalent, ISO 2709, was adopted in 1973.

The single structure, adopted early in the history of machine-readable bibliographic information, helped encourage the enormous growth of shared cataloging in the United States and abroad. OCLC, RLG, UTLAS, WLN, LC, Blackwell North America, AMIGOS and other agencies that provide services based on machine readable bibliographic information may all use their own internal formats to store and process that information. All such agencies use a single structural standard to write tapes of bibliographic records, making interchange possible and relatively straightforward.

SUMMARY

Technical standards affect us every day. We're protected by the complex web of standards that support our civilization, and we're sometimes damaged by missing or conflicting standards. We rely on standards without knowing, or needing to know, the precise nature of those standards; we can have problems when building on a base of standards without accurate knowledge of what those standards are. Systems designed with insufficient standards have difficulties and may fail due to conflicting standards. Standards developed at the right time, and with the right care, can speed technical progress and improve the quality of life. The next chapter discusses the variety and development of these essential standards.

FOOTNOTES

1. Hurt, Peyton. *Bibliography and Footnotes*. Third edition. Berkeley, Los Angeles, London: University of California Press; 1968. p. 2.

3

Varieties of Technical Standards

Technical standards evolve in different ways, taking on different forms. Some of these forms lead to ANSI or ISO standards, while others do not. Some things that are called "standards" fail to satisfy any reasonable definition of a technical standard. This chapter deals with technical standards in the broadest sense, how different varieties of standards arise, and how things come to be considered technical standards.

WEIGHTS AND MEASURES

The most fundamental standards describe the physical universe. Such standards establish units for time, distance, area and volume. We take weights and measures for granted and rarely think of them as technical standards. Yet technical standards for weights and measures underlie most other standards. Weights and measures, or *units*, establish the basic vocabulary for specifications. Without a consistent vocabulary, consistent standards cannot be developed. It does no good to specify that the two current-carrying prongs of a standard 110-volt plug are one-half inch apart, center to center, if "one-half inch" doesn't have a clear, consistent meaning.

In 1215, British barons found it necessary to stress formal standards for weights and measures. Clause 35 of the Magna Carta can be summarized: "There is to be one measure of wine and ale and corn within the realm, namely the London quarter, and one breadth of cloth, and it is to be the same with weights."[1] Five centuries later, the Constitution of the United States provided, in Section 8, that "The Congress shall have Power...To coin Money, regulate the value thereof, and of foreign Coin, and fix the Standard of Weights and Measures."

Weights and measures are now commonly established and maintained by governmental bodies. The National Bureau of Standards (NBS), established in 1901, is the primary U.S. agency for physical measurement standards. The Institute for Basic Standards within the National Bureau of Standards works to provide and improve a complete and consistent system of physical measurements, and it coordinates that system with measurement systems of other nations.

Standards for weights and measures are definitions, like all technical standards. Weights and measures must be far more precise than most other definitions, and must be much more stable than most technical standards. Without appropriate technical standards, a given system may be hindered; without precise standards for weights and measures, most systems would founder.

INTERNAL STANDARDS

If standards for weights and measure are the most basic and formal of all technical standards, internal standards are the least formal and most changeable. When a person produces something, that person has internal standards for the product. To maintain a consistent product over time, the person may set down production guidelines. When that person hires an assistant, production guidelines become internal technical standards.

General Motors and IBM could not maintain production facilities without clear technical standards for each piece, assembly and machine being assembled. Mass production without detailed technical standards is nearly impossible. Internal technical standards are important if more than one person is ever expected to work on a single item.

Every organization develops internal practices, some of which are internal technical standards. Any internal practice that unambiguously defines actions to produce a desired effect may be considered a technical standard. An internal technical standard may be as small and specific as a rule by a cataloging department to add a terminal "0" to the Cutter number for LC-like call numbers on all original cataloging and non-LC copy cataloging, to avoid any possibility of conflict with call numbers assigned by the Library of Congress. Such a rule is an effective technical standard, achieving a desired end in a clear and unambiguous manner.*

Limitations of Internal Technical Standards

Internal technical standards fill gaps in external standards. Standards within a single organization should be recognized as limited to that organization. Unless an organization moves to establish its internal standards as industry standards, it may change or abandon its standards unilaterally and without notice.

Incautious competitors and entrepreneurs wishing to build on the work of an organization will happily seize on internal technical standards as a basis for development. Such developers may build substantial systems based on "standards" that were never intended for external use. At some point, the organization may change its internal standards to improve quality, to lower costs or simply because an earlier standard is no longer appropriate. Systems developed by external agencies no longer function properly, and the external agencies have no recourse.

An organization may make an internal document available to others without asserting that the contents of that document are eternal and unchanging. Systems built on the basis of another agency's internal technical standards should be approached with the greatest caution. Internal technical standards can easily become *pseudo-standards*.

PSEUDOSTANDARDS

Pseudostandards are constructs improperly treated or referred to as "industry standards." Pseudostandards can be:

- Misapplied internal standards, definitions used outside an agency without any promise of stability;

---

*The rule only works because of an assumed standard that Cutter numbers assigned by the Library of Congress will never end in an irrelevant terminal "0". Assumed standards can be dangerous.

• Apparent standards for practice, which actually represent temporary or special situations;

• Single names for multiple definitions, where a named "standard" actually has many versions, some of them incompatible.

Misapplied Internal Standards

When an internal standard moves beyond the originating agency, the internal standard may become an industry standard or a formal consensus standard—if the originating agency intends that the standard be useful by others, and does not unilaterally change the standard. Technical standards, other than those internal to a single agency, *must not be subject to unilateral change.* If a company disseminates its standards with proper assurances of stability, a community standard may properly evolve.

Many of us disseminate information without any such intention. LC, OCLC and RLIN have all made their internal EBCDIC* character sets available to interested parties,[2] but none of these agencies considers its EBCDIC set to be anything other than an internal standard, subject to change as needs require. Each agency takes pains to explain this whenever the internal set is provided to an outsider. Even so, a manufacturer could design a CRT terminal that would display diacritics based on EBCDIC character strings, and claim that it was following "established standards for extended EBCDIC." The manufacturer would be mistaken; whether it was using OCLC's set of a certain date or LC's set, it would be using a pseudostandard, one subject to sudden change by the agency.†

---

*EBCDIC, Extended Binary Coded Decimal Interchange Code, is IBM's standard coding for machine representation of characters, and represents the major alternative to the formal consensus standard ASCII.

†None of these agencies distributes bibliographic records in its internal EBCDIC except by special arrangement; all follow an explicit community standard for extended ASCII—one that is also not a formal consensus standard as of this writing, but a "dominant-agent standard" of a special sort. (See later in this chapter for a discussion of this type of standard.)

Apparent Practice Standards

Technical standards have limited scope. Informal and unwritten "standards" may be more limited than they appear. If your experience is within a single region, or with a single type of organization, you may find that certain practices are uniform, and may conclude that these practices constitute industry standards. Much of the time you'll be correct, but some of the time you'll be mistaking a set of examples for a rule. When such pseudostandards fail, the usual comment is "but that's the way it's always been done," which is another way of saying, "I've never seen it done another way, and assumed that this way was standard."

Some have argued that an online bibliographic searching system properly uses search keys derived from initial letters of author names and title words, 4,4,3,3, for example, and that such search keys are part of the *definition* of an online catalog. Thus, an online catalog with word searching and phrase searching but no derived-key searching would be nonstandard. At best, derived-key searching was never more that a pseudostandard. In fact, it was never even that, as the earliest word/phrase catalogs are as old (if not as widespread) as the earliest derived-key catalogs.

Single Names for Multiple Definitions

One example of this variety of pseudostandard has troubled microcomputer users for years: the "industry standard" called Microsoft BASIC.* Dozens of new computers have used as a selling point the wide range of software available because "we use Microsoft BASIC." Even IBM used the "industry standard" of Microsoft BASIC.

If you or your library uses BASIC on more than one brand (or even model) of microcomputer, you know the truth about Microsoft BASIC: it is a single name for dozens of different computer languages, all sharing a single syntax and core of commands, but with many different sets of extensions. Microsoft developed a

---

*Microsoft BASIC is a trademark of Microsoft Corp.

BASIC to run on limited microcomputers; since then, it has developed many versions from that small core. The core language is common to all versions of Microsoft BASIC, but lacks the power of most extended versions. Computer manufacturers commission Microsoft to develop versions that will use the special features of a particular computer; naturally, those special features differ from computer to computer.

Microsoft has never claimed that all Microsoft BASIC programs will run on all systems using Microsoft BASIC. To an observer, Microsoft BASIC would appear to be an almost universal standard language. In fact, it is a common name for a family of dialects; a program written in any dialect may be incompatible with other dialects. You can't take a program written for the Commodore 64 Microsoft BASIC, copy it to an IBM PC, and expect it to run properly. You can't take a program written for the IBM PC and expect it to run on a TRS-80 with its Microsoft BASIC.*

The problem isn't unique to BASIC. Microcomputer languages tend to run to pseudostandards. The programming language Pascal has been heavily touted as standard and transportable. It's a nice idea but it isn't so. There is an ANSI standard for Pascal, but standard Pascal lacks good facilities for manipulating character strings (text), and lacks good input/output (file handling) facilities. As a result, almost nobody uses standard Pascal. Most real-world Pascal versions are extended versions, and the extensions don't usually work the same way.

When you say "standard blank catalog card," you're naming something that has a precise definition. If you buy standard catalog cards from OCLC, you can be reasonably certain that they'll fit in the card drawers you bought from Highsmith or Gaylord, and that they'll blend in with the catalog cards you used to buy from Baker & Taylor. But when you say "standard Microsoft BASIC," you're not saying anything useful: if you're offered a program written in

---

* As noted above, this confusion is not due to malice on the part of the Microsoft Corporation. In fact, Microsoft BASICs are a narrow segment of the broad range of languages called "BASIC," some of which bear little resemblance to others. Microsoft has in fact attempted to establish an industry standard advanced BASIC for MS-DOS computers, GW BASIC (which apparently stands for "Gee Whiz BASIC").

Microsoft BASIC—or one written in Pascal—you may have to ask which Microsoft BASIC or which Pascal.

Pseudostandards frequently evolve into actual standards, but they are dangerous until such evolution reaches formal recognition. If all the libraries that a vendor has dealt with do something the same way, the vendor may assume that a standard exists. When the vendor sells services based on that standard to a library that has always followed a different (and equally legitimate) practice, there will certainly be lost time and resources, and such situations can easily develop into lawsuits. It isn't a formal consensus standard unless it's in writing and has an established formal consensus.*

FIRST-AGENT AND DOMINANT-AGENT STANDARDS

Technical standards are frequently based on the first practical example of a new technique or design. If an agent does so well with that design that other agents see no advantage in developing a different design, the first design takes on the appearance of a standard. In some cases, the complete design becomes a standard—either because there is no real competition, because the design is not subject to patent or copyright protection or because the first agency attempts to create a *licensed standard* or *industry standard* (see below). In other cases, certain fundamental aspects of the design are copied by other agents that make complementary or competitive products, and those basic aspects take on the force of an informal, first-agent standard.

If the first agent makes plans available and asserts that the definitions involved will not change arbitrarily, first-agent standards can evolve into industry standards. Such cases are quite common. Unfortunately, other cases are also common in which the first-agent standard is, and remains, a pseudostandard, subject to change by the first agent at any time. If the standard has become sufficiently well established in other agencies, it may well survive as an industry standard, even though the agent that created it no longer follows it.

---

*Even then, there's no guarantee that everybody will follow the standard; however, vendors who base their services on formal consensus standards have better defenses than those who follow pseudostandards.

"First-agent" standards aren't always created by the first company to create a new design. Sometimes, a large or otherwise important company creates a somewhat different design; if that company dominates the market in question, a dominant-agent standard may be created. All the remarks and cautions that apply to first-agent standards also apply to dominant-agent standards.*

Many technical standards begin as first-agent or dominant-agent standards, become licensed or community/industry standards and are eventually adopted as formal consensus standards. The dimensions, hole placement and paper quality for common catalog cards were originally established as a first-agent standard by Melvil Dewey in the nineteenth century, and solidified as a dominant-agency standard by the Library of Congress at the turn of the century; the ANSI standard was not established until 1969.

First-agent and dominant-agent standards are the least formal level of community standard with good prospects for success as standards. For long-term success, any community standard must have some form of explicit consensus; most such standards begin in a single agency. Typically, the second step is to establish a licensed standard or a consensus industry standard.

Two examples from the microcomputer industry may make this distinction clear. The operating system MS-DOS, designed by Microsoft, is a licensed standard: computer companies pay a fee to use the name and the precise definition of the operating system, and they may add their own extensions. The technical details for adding new circuit boards into an IBM PC make up an industry standard, as do those for the Apple II (a different industry standard). Neither Apple nor IBM licenses the details, but both make them available to other companies. Both have become industry standards because a sufficient number of other companies have formally adopted them, both for additional circuit boards and for competing computers. In the case of the IBM PC, it seems likely that the "PC standard" will continue as an industry standard even if IBM stops building the PC and PC/XT in favor of newer designs that do not follow the same standard. A fuller discussion of these types of standards follows.

---

*Frequently, the dominant agent is regarded as the first agent unless the field in question has unusually good current historians.

LICENSED STANDARDS

Licensed standards can establish a new technology quickly and painlessly. These standards are created when a company (or group of companies or agencies) establishes a new design, gains patent or copyright protection for that design, then explicitly sets out to persuade other companies to use the same design. When a company establishes a licensed standard, it is certifying that the standard will not be unilaterally changed. Companies may license a new technology for profit or simply to establish the new technology in a widespread compatible fashion. In either case, the key to licensed standards is that the use of the techniques is protected by law, and that the techniques are clearly described and stable.

Some of the more astonishing successes in licensed standards have come about when companies license in order to spread a technique rather than for direct gain. One of these is the Compact Cassette, now simply known as the audiocassette. Philips of Holland designed the Compact Cassette two decades ago, and gained patent protection on several elements of the design. Philips licensed the cassette design (and critical design elements for cassette players) to all interested parties, at no charge.* Philips took the view that the market for cassettes was potentially very large, and that they were likely to make more money by gaining some portion of a large market than by controlling all of a small market.

Their planning was sound, and cassettes succeeded far beyond Philips' original expectations. Part of the success of audiocassettes has come from the absolute compatibility of all cassettes and players, a compatibility assured by Philips' strict license agreements. Monaural tape players will always play both channels of stereo cassettes; any compact cassette recorded in any recorder will fit and should play back in any other cassette player. (These standards have become formal consensus standards: ANSI/EIA RS-399-A-1975 and ANSI/EIA RS-433-1976.)

---

*According to one history, Philips intended to license the technology at a royalty amounting to two cents per cassette, but was convinced by Sony to make the license royalty-free in order to establish the design as a standard. See Lyons, Nick. *The Sony Vision*. New York: Crown; 1976. p. 105.

Licensed standards are common in many fields, though only indirectly in the library field. The growth of microcomputers has been aided by licensed standards in many cases; Microsoft's MS-DOS, noted above, is one good instance, with Digital Research's CP/M an earlier example. Bell Laboratories began licensing its UNIX operating system many years ago, encouraging its wider use with nearly free licenses to universities, thus serving to broaden exposure among computer scientists.

Licensed standards are particularly useful in areas such as operating systems. Software written following proper CP/M standards runs on any computer supporting CP/M. The early and continuing success of WordStar was based on the widespread use of CP/M. While no CP/M computer ever sold in the millions of units, MicroPro International was able to sell upwards of a million copies of WordStar to run on dozens of different computers running CP/M.

INDUSTRY STANDARDS

The popular term industry standard is frequently used for pseudostandards and common practices subject to change. There are true industry standards, many of which begin as dominant-agent standards and end as formal consensus standards. Proper industry standards* are those that are explicitly defined and formally supported by several agencies, where the explicit definition is not subject to unilateral change. All successful licensed standards are also industry standards, but not all industry standards are licensed standards. An industry standard may not be a licensed standard because:

• The standard in question is not subject to copyright or patent, but is in the public domain;

• The developing agency is part of the federal government and as such neither copyrights nor, typically, licenses the development;

---

*Community standard is a better term for this type of standard, but industry standard is a more common term; the two terms are used interchangeably in this book, though the term community standard is also used to refer to any technical standard other than an internal standard.

• The standard was developed by a group of agencies working in concert, and the group chooses not to require licensing.

The extended version of ASCII (American Standard Code for Information Interchange) used for MARC records is a library industry standard, also known as ALA Extended ASCII. The character set was established by the American Library Association (ALA) and the Library of Congress, is published as an appendix to the *MARC Formats for Bibliographic Data* and is formally supported by OCLC, UTLAS, WLN, RLG, Blackwell North America, Baker & Taylor and other agencies that create or process tapes in USMARC or extended USMARC formats. ALA Extended ASCII has no status as a formal consensus standard, at least as of 1984. In the past, ALA Extended ASCII was a proper industry standard, not subject to unilateral change by any single agency. It may regain that status in the future.

The USMARC formats for bibliographic data also constitute an industry technical standard, one that is based on a number of formal consensus standards. If the Library of Congress copyrighted the MARC formats and licensed other agencies to use the name and the formats, USMARC would be a licensed technical standard. USMARC as a standard set of content designation is subject to more frequent revision than a formal consensus standard would be, but such revision is not done unilaterally by the Library of Congress. As it is used within the set of MARC-based agencies in the United States and elsewhere, USMARC functions as a proper industry technical standard.

FORMAL CONSENSUS STANDARDS

Most of this book deals with formal consensus standards, those established by accredited standards-making bodies. The common (though imprecise) term for such standards in the United States is "ANSI standards." As noted above, formal consensus standards may begin as internal standards, first-agent or dominant-agent standards, licensed standards or industry standards. Formal consensus standards may also be developed within accredited standards bodies to meet apparent needs, without originating in some other body.

ANSI and ISO, both defined in Chapter 1, are "voluntary" standards organizations. No one is forced to join ANSI, and ANSI standards do not, in and of themselves, have any legal force. ANSI Z39.29-1977, *American National Standard for Bibliographic References,* establishes a standard for citations and bibliographies which is followed in this book but is still not followed in the majority of publications. No publisher could be enjoined to follow ANSI Z39.29-1977.

While ANSI standards have no legal force *as ANSI standards,* many of them have legal force because they are included in building codes or other legislation. In such a case, use of the standard is required by law, but the law is independent of the standard itself. Any law uses explicit terminology; since ANSI standards (and other technical standards) are definitions, they can be and are used as part of laws.

SUMMARY: STANDARDS ARE FOR SHARING

Technical standards, at whatever level, are established so that people and agencies can share information in a known, consistent manner. Standards evolve in various ways depending on how techniques are created, when information must be shared and who wishes to use the information. In every case, technical standards succeed if they allow shared use of stable definitions for desirable purposes. The need to share techniques is so strong that apparent standards evolve or are assumed to exist even where no coherent technical standards actually exist; such pseudostandards endanger the health of the systems built upon them. This need to share technology is just one of the justifications for producing and enhancing standards. A fuller discussion follows in the next chapter.

FOOTNOTES

1. *Encyclopaedia Brittanica.* Chicago: Encyclopaedia Brittanica Inc.; 1957. v. 14, p. 651.

2. Crawford, Walt. "EBCDIC Bibliographic Character Sets— Sources and Uses: A Brief Report." In *Journal of Library Automation.* 12(4):380-83; 1979 December.

4

Motives for Formal Technical Standards

Formal consensus standards cost more and take longer to develop than other technical standards.* Organizations pay membership fees to support standards organizations and to have a voice and vote on standards. Those same organizations pay time and travel expenses and other forms of support, so that people can serve on committees to develop new standards and maintain existing standards. Even the simplest technical standards require thousands of dollars worth of time and effort to write, distribute, review and establish. Complex technical standards can require years of effort and tens of thousands of dollars. Such effort and expense require economic justification.

Reasons for supporting standards differ from standard to standard, from company to company and from field to field. Most library agencies are nonprofit, and most Z39 standards do not serve to assure assemblyline interchangeability or conformity. This chapter considers some of the reasons that agencies develop and support formal consensus standards. Much of the chapter relates more directly to engineering standards than to those promulgated by NISO (Z39).[1]

---

*This statement is true *for a given standard*. If half a dozen companies develop internal standards for the same function, the cumulative cost may well be greater than that of a single consensus standard.

THE BENEFITS OF STANDARDS

Naming and Symbol Standards

Two people usually need a common language in order to agree on something. Common names and meanings permit successful shared specifications. Some standards establish consistent naming conventions, to improve communications and to make more complex standards possible. Many standards agencies develop "standards for standards." Standard symbols provide an agreed shorthand to improve communication. Good symbols compress verbal information in unambiguous, immediately recognizable form.

Specification Standards

Precise specifications are basic to industrialization. Internal standards are created because of needs for precise specifications, and consensus standards can come about when such needs are generalized across an industry. All standards for simplification and interchangeability are specification standards.

Test, Analysis and Safety Standards

Buyers and sellers alike want assurance that products are safe. Underwriters Laboratories (UL) and the American Society for Testing and Materials (ASTM), two of the most important standards-making groups in the United States, develop standards for testing, analysis and safety.

Producers and consumers both have reason to support the efforts of ASTM, UL and others developing similar standards. Standards for testing and analysis allow producers and consumers to verify claims. Given a proper testing standard, any agency testing a given product should achieve results comparable to those of any other agency.

The Z39 standard for permanent paper and the Z85 standard for catalog card stock both use testing standards developed by other agencies, for bending strength, alkalinity and other aspects of paper and cards. Many specification standards rely on testing and analysis standards, as do most safety standards.

Safety standards range from the UL standard 753B (safety standard for electric hair dryers) stamped on most hair dryers sold in the United States, to ANSI/IEEE standard C2, the National Electrical Safety Code, which specifies hundreds of rules for transmission and handling of electricity. Producers benefit from safety, testing and analysis standards because they can determine that their products meet recognized standards for safety. Consumers benefit because they can choose safe products through standard labeling, rather than relying strictly on known brands. The marketplace is open to new producers which follow standards (and those whose products pass standard tests), and all legitimate elements of the marketplace benefit.

Grading and Classification Standards

Grading and classification standards usually concern natural products or refined natural products: wood, oil and the like. Buyers support grading standards because they permit rational tradeoffs between price and quality. Suppliers support grading standards because they provide a common vocabulary and basis for negotiation. Grading and classification standards rarely extend past material standards; none of the Z39 or X3 standards are primarily grading standards.

Simplification: Competition, Efficiency and Stability

Many standards simplify, by reducing pointless diversity where such diversity raises costs or reduces stability. Simplification standards should meet both criteria: only pointless diversity should be reduced, and diversity should only be reduced if it causes economic harm. Much of the push for standardization in the early twentieth century has been for simplification.

Suppose that neither the American Library Association nor the Library of Congress was involved when libraries became fascinated with card catalogs in the late nineteenth century. Each library would buy card stock and catalog drawers. New York Public Libraries might contract with The Library Company to produce card drawers to hold 4-inch x 6-inch cards with two rods for greater stability; The Library Company would probably also supply the card stock. Harvard might contract with a local furniture builder and paper company to make cards and single-rod drawers, the cards being 5-inch x 8-inch to hold Harvard's elaborate entries. The Chicago Public Library might set out to acquire 2-inch x 4-inch cards, saving considerable space and leaving enough room for nominal entries.

That may seem far-fetched, but that's how automobile companies worked until 1910. Parts—washers, tubing, bolts, sheet steel—were custom manufactured to each car maker's own specifications: there were 300 different lock washer designs, and 1100 varieties of steel tubing. If a supplier went out of business, the car maker might be left without a vital part, and would have to wait for another supplier to alter production lines to produce the same part.

This needless and injurious diversity of automobile parts was remedied when the Society of Automotive Engineers (SAE) began to develop standards—224 of them by 1921. The results: 35 different lock washers, 150 varieties of steel tubing and similar reductions elsewhere. A 1916 estimate was that the SAE had effected a 30% reduction in the cost of ball bearings and 20% in steel costs—in all, savings equivalent to 15% of the retail value of automobiles.[2]

Libraries had little time to establish diverse sizes and styles for library cards. The Library of Congress began selling printed cards at about the same time that card catalogs were becoming popular. Melvil Dewey also started various library supply companies (including The Library Company), and believed in standards. A dominant-agent standard of catalog card stock about 5 inches wide and about 3 inches high, taking a single rod about 1/3 inch from the bottom, became commonplace in the United States long before ANSI Z85.1 was written.

The 75mm x 125mm card standard has had the same effect on libraries that SAE standards had on the automotive industry. Customers could put contracts out for competitive bids in the expectation that more than one supplier would make a particular part. New suppliers could enter the market, since the standards were published and readily available; by offering better prices, better delivery or some other special features, these suppliers could hope to take business away from old suppliers. Without simplification, new suppliers would find it difficult to break into a field. Customers and suppliers would be so tightly involved that the thought of changing suppliers would rarely arise.

Simplification eases entry for new suppliers by specifying what a market will accept. Simplification standards also make existing suppliers more competitive by allowing them to improve production efficiency. Assembly lines have startup costs and retooling costs. A factory that produces one million lock washers in each of five sizes will produce them more cheaply than one which produces fifty thousand lock washers in each of one hundred sizes. Increased plant efficiency was certainly the prime motive for any existing automotive supplier to support SAE standards, and this has continued to be a primary motive for simplification standards.

Simplification standards also promote stability. If one supplier goes out of business, a buyer can go to another supplier that will probably have identical parts available. The need for stability has become such a driving force in some industries that a new product won't be accepted until more than one supplier exists. In the microprocessor field, for example, a new (and protected) CPU design may be licensed by its creator to at least one "second source" company in order to make the CPU more competitive in the market. Computer manufacturers are reluctant to buy a CPU that would become unavailable if its only supplier were backlogged or went bankrupt; the second source provides needed stability.

Simplification was the earliest major success of formal consensus standards in the United States. Simplification standards can be damaging if they reduce valuable diversity; if such diversity is valuable enough that customers are willing to pay for it, the standards will be ignored. Where customers and producers have reasonably equal power, simplification standards are self-regulating: those that work will be followed, those that are too restrictive will fade away.

Interchangeability

Simplification works on a product-by-product basis, reducing the variety within a single product category so that producers can produce more cheaply and buyers can encourage competition among sellers. The catalog card example above also involves interchangeability: catalog card drawers must accept standard catalog card stock.

Interchangeability implies cooperation as well as competition. If the Library of Congress had not been on the scene, producers of library furniture could have gathered together with papermakers to develop standards that would assure that any catalog drawer would work with any catalog card. The primary light bulb makers in the United States are not important in the field of light fixtures, but they can compete among themselves in the knowledge that all standard "normal-size" light bulbs (whether 20 watt, 60 watt, 75 watt, 100 watt or higher wattage) will fit in standard Edison sockets.

Consensus standards require cooperative work among agencies that may be competitors. Work on consensus standards is generally not considered to be anticompetitive and has rarely been attacked by the Justice Department (some additional comments on standards and antitrust appear in Chapter 6). Most consensus standards enhance competition by lowering the barriers to new companies. Further, interchangeability permits new companies to build on the work of old companies, using their products and making new ones based on them.

Long-playing records have involved a series of standards, some of them first-agent, some the result of voluntary consensus effort. Freely available standards for speed and size of long-playing records make it easy for new manufacturers to introduce turntables. They also allow Windham Hill to compete with CBS, which promulgated the 33 1/3 rpm speed standard.

Because the size, speed and primary groove dimensions of records are standard, companies can focus on new developments to enhance the medium. Record manufacturers can work with new materials and new pressing methods; turntable makers can work on lower rumble and more sophisticated features for ease of use; cartridge makers can concentrate on lowering distortion and generally making cartridges do a better job of reproducing sound.

The 12-inch and 33 1/3 rpm standards of the late 1940s began the process; voluntary consensus standards for encoding stereophonic sound, adopted in the late 1950s, allowed stereo to take over within a few years.* More recently, one company (Technics) has

---

*The stereo standard was a reactive rather than an active standard, as discussed below; several other methods of stereo were tried, but none became commercially successful until a number of companies agreed on the 45-45 standard.

promulgated a new "first-agent" standard for cartridge mounting, making it possible for consumers to mount cartridges without studying tracking force, overhang and other high fidelity arcana. This system is another case in which a standard improves interchangeability and makes competition easier and more efficient.

Z39.2, the underlying standard for USMARC, is a standard for interchangeability. As stated in the standard itself, it is intended for interchange rather than for use within a single system. USMARC records have the same logical characteristics whether produced by LC, OCLC, WLN or Blackwell North America. A new company wishing to develop an online catalog can rely on the USMARC structure and can compete with older companies on an equal footing.

If there were no standard for bibliographic interchange, libraries using OCLC would have to specify what sort of system tape they wanted: a Data Phase tape, a CLSI tape, a Science Press tape.* If Carlyle or Dynix wanted to bid to replace a Data Phase system, they would be out of luck: the data would be in a format proprietary to Data Phase. Such a situation would serve neither the new companies nor the old ones. Among other consequences, it would prevent a library from building a bibliographic base prior to selecting a system.†

Interchangeability standards foster innovation because they establish a baseline; they can also hamper innovation because they restrict variety within the baseline. Optimists would say that this channels innovation to more useful areas. Standardized battery sizes allow toymakers and radio companies to build products with battery cavities and terminals of known sizes and placement, assuming that a number of highly competitive producers make batteries to fit those cavities. The battery companies don't spend much time on new sizes or shapes for batteries; instead, they develop new and better varieties of battery within the old sizes and shapes. Today's rechargeable nickel-cadmium cells and long-lasting alkaline cells show the effects of channelled innovation.

---

*This example is totally hypothetical: it isn't at all clear that OCLC would ever have developed or grown without USMARC.

†In practice, each system may well have its own data extensions, but the logical form of the data is common to all MARC-compatible systems.

Mass Production and Standards

Simplification standards and interchangeability standards help make mass production possible. When there are fewer varieties of a product to make, a full-line producer can expect to make more of each variety. When one product is so well defined that other products can be based on that definition, producers of the one product can anticipate larger markets and produce in larger quantities.

Mass production is the economic success story of the industrial revolution. Some futurists have said that mass production doesn't matter in the postindustrial society we appear headed toward, but this overlooks the fundamentals. An information-based society may well favor diversity over uniformity, but can only maintain that diversity because the underlying tools of society are mass-produced. Microcomputers have become cheap and powerful thanks to mass production and competition; while research and development have helped to increase the density of circuits, only mass markets and standard circuit packaging have brought prices down to the point that a powerful CPU chip costs $5 or less.

The economics of production favor comprehensive standards. More standardized products offer opportunities for longer production runs. On the other hand, the economics of innovation favor less comprehensive standards, so that new designs and new products can be based on standardized individual parts. Library standards are rarely influenced by questions of mass production. Most Z39 standards relate to intellectual activity, generally ill suited to assemblyline techniques. Z85.1 is an exception (and, as its number implies, was not created by the Z39 committee): a single fixed standard for size and physical quality of catalog cards has made mass card production feasible.

Guidelines

Most technical standards are explicit specifications. Many Z39 standards, and some standards in other organizations, are guidelines: sets of definitions and rules that will produce better results if applied, but that are not designed to produce mechanical uniformity or interchangeability.

Guidelines are more difficult to quantify in economic terms.

Motives for guidelines tend to be "purer" in that they do not involve direct economic gain for the parent organization. A consistent standard for proofreading makes authors and editors more efficient, but has little direct economic impact. A standard for index preparation should improve scholarly access, but has no clear economic impact.

ACTIVE STANDARDS AND EMERGING TECHNOLOGY

Technical standards can be broadly grouped into active and reactive standards. Reactive standards are formed after a technique or product is in use, when agencies see a need to regularize the technique or product. All early SAE standards, and most American consensus standards in the first half of the century, were reactive standards: standards created to improve an existing situation.

Active standards tend to begin with licensed standards (discussed in Chapter 3) and dominant-agent standards, but can be developed through cooperative effort. Libraries stand to benefit in years to come from the active efforts to develop standards based on the Open Systems Interconnection (OSI) model. If successful, the U.S. and international efforts for OSI will result in flexible, effective methods of communication between computers of different types, from different manufacturers.

Z39.2, the standard for interchange of bibliographic information, is also an active standard. The Library of Congress designed the MARC format, and prepared text for Z39.2. In that sense, Z39.2 is a dominant-agency standard blessed by ANSI. Like many other federal agencies, LC is committed to consensus standards. LC proposed Z39.2 in such a way that it was not a direct reflection of LC MARC, but a generalized standard applicable to any interchange of bibliographic information.

Emerging technologies can grow faster when active standards are available. Local area networks for small computers have been used in the United States since the mid-1970s, when Datapoint installed its first ARC network. While Datapoint has gone on to install several thousand ARC and ARCnet networks, local area networks were hampered until IEEE and ASC X3 began to formulate standards. In the last year or two, new network offerings have been simplified by their ability to cite formal consensus standards; these standards should help to make local networks more stable and efficient.

Reactive Standards

Technologies emerge faster than standards organizations can form or meet, and premature standards can have a stifling effect on a new technology. Reactive standards begin when agents within a field find the field mired in confusion. The standards stories of the early twentieth century provide clear examples; current examples are subtler. David Hemenway begins his book on standards with an account of the Baltimore fire of 1904.

> "So serious did the fire become that help was solicited from surrounding communities. Washington, D.C. fire engines reached the scene within three hours, and additional units arrived from as far afield as Annapolis, Wilmington, Chester, York, Altoona, Harrisburg, Philadelphia, and New York. Unfortunately, most of these units proved of little assistance, for their hoses would not fit Baltimore hydrants. Though there was never a shortage of water many fire fighting units had to stand by, virtually helpless...."[3]

When lives are lost due to such differing standards, the need for reactive standards seems obvious, and cries for government intervention begin. Most reactive standards arise from less obvious losses that are no less real. Safety standards have saved thousands of lives by giving manufacturers and consumers alike a basis for building safe appliances. Interchangeability standards have saved billions of dollars in industries where confusion would otherwise reign.

STANDARDS FOR THE SAKE OF STANDARDS

Not all motives for standards are legitimate ones. Some people write standards because they like to write standards, or because their organization will reward them for such efforts. Such motives aren't unique to standards work. Most of us are aware of the explosion of scholarly and specialist journals, and of the mixed quality of articles within some journals. Some suspect that this profusion of articles relates more to tenure and reputation than to advances in knowledge. "Publish or perish" is a fact of life; beyond that, many people publish because they enjoy it. The same can be true for standards writing.

Such problems don't arise often, and are not likely to last long. Standards are expensive. Each organization with a standards committee member can expect to spend travel funds two to four (or more) times a year so that the committee can work on the standard. People who write standards for their own sake tend to run out of corporate support.

SUMMARY

The basic motive for any consensus standard is economic. Standards are adopted to save money or make money. Economics is not a simple field, and standards flourish for a variety of subtle motives. Most of the motives are justified and reasonable. While standards activity can begin for theoretical elegance or personal aggrandizement, the costs of standardization usually prevent such needless effort.

Library standards have less obvious economic impact. Most standards specific to libraries are guidelines rather than precise specifications. They enhance the literature and improve scholarship, an indirect economic benefit.

FOOTNOTES

1. An extended study of motivations for consensus standards can be found in Hemenway, David. *Industrywide Voluntary Product Standards*. Cambridge, MA: Ballinger; 1975. 141 p.

2. Ibid, p. 14-15.

3. Hemenway, David. *Industrywide Voluntary Product Standards*. Cambridge, Mass.: Ballinger; 1975. p. 3.

5

Implementations, Levels and Families

Every technical standard is a definition: words and figures which, if the standard is a good one, provide an unambiguous specification for the subject of the standard. While every standard is a definition, you should not assume that each standard leads directly to a product or system. Just as standards arise through different methods and come in different varieties, standards work at different levels.

Some standards do specify characteristics of a finished product. Some standards provide nothing more than ways to think about something. Most technical standards for library use and automation fall between these two extremes. Many standards offer choices, such that products following the standard may differ from one another. Most standards are based on other standards, and are themselves used as bases for more complex standards, building toward standard systems.

Some technical standards provide only part of the information needed for an implementation, through oversight or through choice. There are "families" of technical standards, all designed to achieve similar goals but maintained as separate standards. Some of these families are explicitly interrelated, while others are the result of changing needs. One standard may lead to additional standards—and, in some cases, several standards may be combined into a single standard.

STANDARDS AND IMPLEMENTATIONS

All technical standards are definitions, not implementations. There is always some distance between standard and implementation, even if a standard permits only one implementation. Weights and measures have the smallest possible distance between technical standard and implementation. The Standard Kilogram, a metal ingot, is an object that embodies a definition. Even in this case, the technical standard for mass is an abstraction. The definition of "one kilogram" is not the same as the Standard Kilogram, and relates only to one aspect of that ingot: its mass. Uniquely, weights and measures standards can incorporate implementations into the definition of the standard. Other technical standards work at a higher level of abstraction.

Unambiguous Physical Implementation: Catalog Cards

The oldest technical standard for American libraries is also one of the least abstract; it specifies the characteristics of a physical object distinctly and unambiguously. That standard is Z85.1-1980: *Permanent and Durable Library Catalog Cards,* described in Chapter 1. Any proper catalog card is an implementation of Z85.1, but Z85.1 does not constitute a catalog card.

Z85.1 specifies characteristics of a physical object. The standard provides:

• Complete specifications for catalog cards: size, hole, finish, color, weight, acidity, endurance and stock;

• Distinctive specifications such that variations are explicitly noted and any good papermaker could work directly from the standard;

• Explicit tests to determine whether an object is, in fact, an implementation of the standard.

Even this most clear-cut of library technical standards allows for more than one implementation: there are four different possible implementations. Cards may be either white or cream-white, and may be either lightweight or medium-weight. What most librarians would think of as a "standard catalog card" is really a cream-white medium-weight standard catalog card; a lightweight white card would also be a "standard catalog card."

Incomplete Physical Implementation: Permanent Paper

Standard Z39.48-1984: *Permanent Paper for Printed Library Materials,* defines a class of objects. (This and other Z39 standards are described in Chapter 10.) Z39.48 is not a complete specification for a physical object; like most physical technical standards, it describes only a few aspects of an object. It specifies alkalinity, lack of groundwood or unbleached pulp, folding endurance and tear resistance for various weights of paper, but it does not specify weight, thickness, size or color of paper. Such specifications would be unreasonably restrictive; the purpose of Z39.48 is to certify permanence rather than to describe appearance.

This is a testable standard: a laboratory can determine whether a sheet of paper meets Z39.48 specifications. It is *not* possible to say what an implementation of Z39.48 would look like, except that it would be paper and it would be durable. Z39.48 is a narrow standard, unambiguous within its own scope, but insufficient to create distinctive physical implementations. The standard can be applied to papermaking, but it will not yield a direct physical manifestation.

Unique Implementations: Standard Numbering Systems

Standard numbering systems tend to be unambiguous. Given proper labeling and an assignment agency, there can be no question what such numbers should look like and whether a given number is an implementation of the standard. Such standards have only one implementation: there can be but one ISBN and one ISSN. These standards may not specify all of the implementation, but do describe how to complete the implementation. Any standard numbering system requires one or more maintenance agencies but need not identify the agencies.

Standards with Multiple Implementations

A standard numbering system permits only one implementation. Z85.1 permits four classes of implementation, but many specific implementations (there is no limit on the number of paper companies that can produce catalog cards). Still, Z85.1 is effectively a "single-implementation" standard: all implementations are essentially equivalent, differing only in known areas. Other technical standards do not provide such precision; some explicitly provide for a wide range of diverse implementations, while others are insufficiently well defined to narrow the range of implementation.

Z39.2 and Z39.49

Z39.2 is the *American National Standard for Bibliographic Information Interchange.*[1] It specifies a record structure to accommodate bibliographic and related information: a leader and its contents, fields, subfields and indicators. Z39.2 was created together with MARC II, and provides the structural basis for the MARC formats. As interpreted by most librarians, Z39.2 is "the MARC standard." But Z39.2 isn't USMARC, and USMARC isn't Z39.2—and the recent approval of Z39.49: *Computerized Book Ordering,* may help to make this clear.

USMARC is an implementation of Z39.2, as are other MARC formats. Z39.49, in its variable-length version, is also an implementtion of Z39.2—but one which differs greatly from USMARC. Z39.2 allows for an enormous variety of different implementations, each self-defining but with different characteristics.

The record leader defined by Z39.2 is always 24 characters long, and most positions in the leader are defined by Z39.2. Five of those positions contain variables that define any specific implementation of Z39.2. The five variables are as follows:

1. Indicator Count: Number of indicators at the beginning of each variable-length field. USMARC: "2". Z39.49: "0". There are no indicators in Z39.49 (BISAC) fields.

2. Identifier Length: Length of the "subfield code." Both USMARC and Z39.49 use "2", as each subfield is identified by a delimiter and a character. Z39.49 uses capital letters for subfield characters, while USMARC uses lower case letters and numbers.

3. Length of the Length-of-Field Portion: Part of the directory entry map, defining the directory. USMARC:"4". Z39.49:"0". Z39.49 directories do not include length of field; the length must be

determined by scanning the fields themselves. This choice conserves space (the length-of-field in the directory is redundant information) but reduces the error-detection capability of Z39.2.

4. Length of the Starting-Character-Position Portion: Both USMARC and Z39.49 use "5", allowing for long records. It is possible to eliminate this element as well, but doing so requires that records be processed end-to-end, considerably reducing the flexibility inherent in Z39.2.

5. Length of the Implementation-Defined Portion: Both USMARC and Z39.49 use "0"; neither includes an "implementation-defined portion." An implementation-defined portion could be used to add meaning to directory entries (for instance, to store multiple subrecords within a record).

Programs to process MARC records may not work well with BISAC (Z39.49) records. Well-written programs will detect that Z39.49 is a different Z39.2 implementation and reject such records. For most uses, different implementations of Z39.2 are not fully compatible. It is possible to write programs that can break down any Z39.2 record into component parts, and it would be possible to build systems that used such generalized "record parsers" as tools. Most computer programs are designed to work with a specific implementation of Z39.2.

The five variable elements of Z39.2 yield 100,000 different possible implementations, ranging from a minimalist format with no subfields, no indicators and nothing in the directory but tags, up to an extremely complex format with "9"s for all values. To make matters more confusing, choices used for the five elements only define mechanical parameters of an implementation; they do not identify the implementation. Any number of different implementations can use the same element choices as USMARC without being identical to USMARC.

Ambiguity doesn't make Z39.2 a "bad standard," but one that is more distant from its implementations than some other standards. The standard provides enough information so that a computer program based only on the text of Z39.2 could test records to see whether they appeared to be self-consistent Z39.2 implementa-

tions. A generalized record parser would perform such tests as part
of its operations.

RS-232C: "Standard Connections"

Electronics Industry Association standard RS-232C was established many years ago to provide standard connections for data
communications.[2] It defines 25 signal paths, usually implemented as
a two-row 25-pin connector (DB-25 connector). Most terminals,
modems and serial printers use RS-232C; however, cables are not
always interchangeable among different devices.

RS-232C applies to "interconnection of data terminal equipment (DTE) and data communication equipment (DCE) employing
serial binary data interchange." The standard is quite explicit. It
defines electrical characteristics, mechanical characteristics, functional description of circuits and a group of standard subsets for the
25 lines called for in the standard. The 13 "standard subsets" provide for specific applications, and require as few as five or as many
as 20 electrical paths.

The standard includes specific voltage limits and other requirements so that two pieces of equipment connected through RS-
232C will not damage one another and will communicate properly.
Three of the 25 lines are undefined, and two are used for testing.
Lines 2 and 3 are the most important: transmitted data and received
data. There are no ambiguities in RS-232C as written. The standard
does *not* call for the DB-25 connector; it does specify that data terminal equipment should have a female connector and that data
communication equipment should include a cable terminating in a
male connector.

Problems with RS-232C arise for several reasons. 25-wire
cables are expensive and cumbersome, and no devices require all 25
signals. Most RS-232C cables use either five wires or nine wires.
While devices requiring five wires will work with nine-wire cables,
nine-wire devices won't work with five-wire cables. Most RS-232C
cables are sold with male connectors (containing pins) on both
ends—but some devices and computer ports (including one on the
ubiquitous IBM PC) carry male connectors, requiring a female
cable end (containing holes). Finally, a cable that connects pin #2 to
pin #2 and pin #3 to pin #3 works for DTE-to-DCE connections,

but some device pairs are both DCE, requiring that the two pins be reversed at opposite ends of the cable.

In short, "a standard RS-232C cable" is largely mythical; the cable that connects your printer to your computer probably won't work between your computer and your modem, or between your computer and your terminal. "An RS-232C cable for minimal Subset D, female-to-male, DTE-to-DCE, using DB-25 connectors" is a precise specification that can only have one implementation. There are many stories of important demonstrations that couldn't be held for lack of a workable RS-232C cable.

With the proliferation of microcomputers and video display terminals, most using RS-232C in various implementations, the problem has gotten large enough to generate new products as partial solutions. One company makes an "intelligent RS-232C cable" with internal electronics to attempt to configure the correct connections; this cable costs four times as much as a standard cable, but will generally provide universal interconnection—if the microprocessor is able to make the correct deductions. Other companies make other devices so that cables can be reconfigured as needed and devices can be tested for presence of signals on various pins.

The case of RS-232C is a complex one. The standard itself is thorough and precise; problems arise with imprecise use. Some novice microcomputer users have purchased "standard RS-232C cables" from incompetent computer store clerks, then found that their equipment wouldn't function.

Bibliographic References: Z39.29

As a final example of a standard with multiple implementations, consider Z39.29, the standard for bibliographic references. This standard includes tables of mandatory, recommended and optional elements for various types of material, and does specify order of elements and punctuation. At least four elements of ambiguity make it difficult to determine what a citation should "look like," based on the text of Z39.29:

1. The standard allows citations to be title-first or author-first, in cases where authorship is apparent;

2. Brief and comprehensive forms of citation are described, in addition to the variety of optional elements within a comprehensive citation;

3. Use of quotation marks to surround article or chapter titles, and boldface, italic or underscores to indicate monograph or journal titles, is allowed but not prescribed by the standard;

4. Titles may be capitalized according to "library rules" (first work and each proper noun) or according to "bibliography rules" (each significant word).

The citations that follow are all for the same chapter and are all proper Z39.29 citations:

> Online Search Strategies. White Plains, NY: Knowledge Industry Publications; 1982: 175-212.

> Patents. William G. Andrus [et al]. Online Search Strategies. Ryan E. Hoover, ed. White Plains, NY: Knowledge Industry Publications; 1982: 175-212. 345 p. (Professional Librarian Series.)

> Andrus, William G. [and others]. Patents. In: Hoover, Ryan E., ed. Online Search Strategies. White Plains, NY: Knowledge Industry Publications; 1982: 175-212.

> Andrus, William G.; Heyd, William E.; Lustgarten, Ronald K.; Pollack, Norman M. "Patents." *In:* Hoover, Ryan E., ed. *Online Search Strategies.* White Plains, NY: Knowledge Industry Publications; 1982: 175-212. 345 p. (Professional Librarian Series.) ISBN 0-86729-004-8 (pbk.).

Such ambiguity means that an author (or editor) must make a series of decisions in order to create a consistent bibliography using Z39.29. The "author-first/title-first" ambiguity must generally be resolved on a case-by-case basis (as in cataloging). Bibliographies within published NISO standards tend to use the simplest options for Z39.29, including the preferred "single type." Users might prefer a slightly more complex implementation. Without careful observation, it is not always clear that citations or bibliographies are done according to Z39.29.

Application Rather Than Implementation

A number of NISO standards appear not to lead to "implementations" as such. Rather, these standards can be applied in order to improve communication. Guideline standards may be some of the most useful generated by NISO, though their direct impact is nebulous. Ambiguities within guideline standards are common and reasonable. Such standards are intended to provide guidance for intelligent human application; the human mind can resolve ambiguities. "Guidelines" for computer application cannot reasonably permit such ambiguity: computers are not inherently capable of resolving ambiguity.

One result of this distinction is that Z39.29, which permits ambiguous implementation, can be used well for computer-generated *output* but not so well for computer *recognition*. Computer programs exist to generate Z39.29 bibliographies given identified data elements provided in any order.* Developing a computer program to break down a machine-readable bibliography into identifiable data elements would be far more difficult, since the options and rules in Z39.29 do not provide sufficient information to allow complete mechanical parsing.

LEVELS OF STANDARDS

Chapters 3 and 4 mention different levels of standards. Any body of technical standards will include standards at various levels (and generally some that work at more than one level). One observer may establish a different set of levels than another observer, depending on the mindset of the observer and the purpose of the categorization. Standards can be categorized by level of abstraction, by level of application, by level of reliance on other standards or by other methods.

A number of writers have attempted to provide theoretical frameworks for standards. Lal C. Verman devotes a large portion of *Standardization: A New Discipline*[3] to the philosophy of standards and to various frameworks in which to place standards. David

---

*The *Professional Bibliographic System* from Personal Bibliographic Systems is one commercial microcomputer example; there are others.

Hemenway[4] also develops categories of standards, from a considerably different perspective. Paul Evan Peters and the Technical Standards for Library Automation Committee (TESLA) of ALA's Library and Information Technology Association are developing a framework to categorize standards within library and automation fields.

James E. Rush proposes a seven-level model for NISO standards in "A Proposed Model for the Development of an Integrated Set of Standards for Bibliographic and Related Data."[5] His seven levels are as follows:

- Level 0. Message Boundaries: the precise limits of a message —sometimes called "protocol data" in computer applications;

- Level 1. Data Structures: such as chapters, fields, subfields and paragraphs;

- Level 2. Data Element Identifiers: explicit and implicit methods for identifying data elements within a structure;

- Level 3. Data Element Values: permissible values or types of value for a given data element, such as code tables or thesauri;

- Level 4. Display (Representation) Formats: the manner in which messages are presented to users;

- Level 5. Media: the carrier for a message;

- Level 6. Housing of Media: standards for storage.

Rush's is one of the simpler models, and provides one useful way of looking at NISO standards. The model assumes that everything of interest to NISO is either a message or a means of conveying or storing a message. This "message-oriented" model differs from "process-oriented" models that concentrate on activities, "actor-oriented models" that concentrate on users and other possible models and frameworks.

This book will not present a formal model or framework for standards. Every proposed model for standards has some validity and some weakness. Informally, this chapter and others in this book have categorized standards by level of abstraction, but these categories are vague. Most standardization efforts have proceeded without any formal framework for standards. Most users can enjoy the advantages of technical standards without any concern for formal models. Interested readers may wish to consult sources mentioned in this chapter or other sources (see the bibliography at the end of this book) to consider and compare various frameworks.

Standards Based on Standards

Most standards are based on other standards, explicitly or implicitly. Standards that provide for direct implementation may well rely on several levels of standards. Z39.49 (discussed above) is itself an implementation of Z39.2; in turn, Z39.2 relies on ANSC X3 standards for magnetic tape and tape labels.

Some standards exist only for the purpose of creating other standards. Z39.33: *Development of Identification Codes for Use by the Bibliographic Community,* a "standard for standard numbers," is one example. In some standards communities, such underlying standards might precede any implementations; this was not the case within NISO (Z39). "Standards for standards" are not needed to develop higher-level standards, but do help to pull together families of related standards.

FAMILIES OF STANDARDS

Standards don't always fall neatly into any given level, but many standards do fall neatly into families. Like levels, families exist more in the mind of the reader than the text of standards; unlike levels, families need not encompass all standards or be exclusive. A single standard can be part of more than one family. For this book, a family is any group of standards with a recognizable common aspect. Organization into families helps to reduce the apparent complexity of NISO's work, or that of any other standards organization. The assignments used here are those of the author, and reflect no judgments on the part of standards-writing bodies.

Specific NISO and X3 standards are discussed in Chapters 10 and 11. Figure 5.1 shows a few of the possible families of NISO and

Figure 5.1: Families of Standards

```
ROMANIZATION STANDARDS
    Z39.11    Japanese
    Z39.12    Arabic
    Z39.24    Slavic Cyrillic
    Z39.25    Hebrew
    Z39.35    Lao, Khmer, and Pali
    Z39.37    Armenian
    Z39.51    Criteria for Romanization

NUMBERING STANDARDS
    Z39.9     ISSN
    Z39.21    Book Numbering (ISBN)
    Z39.23    STRN
    Z39.33    Identification Codes
    Z39.43    SAN
    ---       SCSN

PROGRAMMING LANGUAGES
    X3.9      FORTRAN
    X3.23     COBOL
    X3.37     APT
    X3.53     PL/I
    X3.60     Minimal BASIC
    X3.74     PL/I, General Purpose Subset
    X3.97     Pascal

OPTICAL CHARACTER RECOGNITION
    X3.17     Character Set for OCR-A
    X3.45     Character Set for Handprinting
    X3.49     Character Set for OCR-B
    X3.62     Paper Used in OCR Systems
    X3.86     OCR Inks
```

X3 standards. There are others; for instance, quite a few X3 standards relate to magnetic tape.

Members of a family don't necessarily work equally well, or in precisely the same way. For instance, some Romanization standards can be applied without knowledge of the original language, while others require that a user know the original language to Romanize effectively. The following section considers one well-known family of technical standards in some detail: the family of standard numbers.

A BRIEF CHRONOLOGY OF STANDARD NUMBERS IN LIBRARIES

The earliest "standard number" in the library field, or at least the oldest one still used, started in 1876. That's when Dewey Decimal (DDC) got its start—and, although it isn't part of the NISO numbers game, Dewey Decimal does have some things in common with numbering standards. The younger cousin of Dewey Decimal, the Library of Congress classification system, also bears some resemblance to a standard number. We won't deal with classification systems here, but you might consider the ways in which DDC and LC call numbers are similar to standard numbers and the ways in which they differ.

Around the turn of the century, the Library of Congress began a numbering system that has most of the characteristics of a standard number: LCCN, the Library of Congress Card Number. The LCCN, though not a NISO standard, has many of the characteristics of a standard number:

• The format of an LCCN is distinctive and does not duplicate other codes;

• A code authority maintains LCCN and provides for unique assignment;

• A code identifier "LCCN" is established for use where needed;

• In machine-readable use, LCCN has a fixed root length;

• A single LCCN uniquely identifies a single item (in this case, a bibliographic record rather than a book or serial);

• LCCN is well established, understood by many parties, and used as a means of identifying material.

The next "standard identifier" was also developed by the Library of Congress, and is also widely used—the library identifier established for the National Union Catalog, and generally called the "NUC Code." NUC codes are also fairly distinctive, have a code authority and have been widely used since they were first established in 1932.

More than 30 years after initial publication of the National Union Catalog, ANSI and Z39 began to adopt formal numbering standards. The Standard Book Number (SBN) began in Britain in 1967. Nine digits long, with three sections, it was adopted in America as ANSI Z39.21. By 1973, a leading digit had been added to create the International Standard Book Number (ISBN). The SBN was followed by an Identification Number for Serial Publications, first defined by ANSI Z39.9 in 1971. ISO adoption of this number came in 1974, creating the International Standard Serial Number (ISSN).

Between 1974 and 1980, three more standards arose. The Standard Technical Report Number (STRN) began in 1975, as Z39.23; in 1980, Z39.43 established the Standard Address Number (SAN). After approving the third standard number, but before the fourth, ANSC Z39 developed a "standard for standards," Z39.33: *Development of Identification Codes for Use by the Bibliographic Community*. As of this writing, that's where it stands: four approved standard numbers, and a fifth standard for designing standard numbers.

Other numbers have been suggested, and two are being designed or evaluated. In 1975, Z39 subcommittee 34 proposed a standard for Code Identification of Serial Articles (SCISA). A SCISA could be stored as 0065-23931969000000089065# and displayed as SCISA*ISSN 0065-2393/19690000/0089/0065. SCISA has not been heard from since.[6]

In 1977, a proposed American Standard Identifier for an Item in a Library Collection was published in the *Journal of Library*

Automation.[7] This draft called for a unique global library item identifier consisting of institution ID, item ID and check digit. It depended on adoption of an American Standard Identifier for a Site. Neither one was adopted, but NISO Subcommittee V began working on a new standard site identifier in late 1984. One other proposed standard number entered the NISO comment process in 1985: the Standard Computer Software Number (SCSN).

THE SCSN AND THE ISBN

Standards are frequently controversial, but most standard numbers haven't been. There have been arguments over when a new ISSN should be issued, and there is confusion over whether a publication should use an ISSN, a series of ISBNs or both. One current standard proposal has caused considerable controversy, however: the Standard Computer Software Number (SCSN).

Thousands of companies produce microcomputer software: two new ones seem to form each time one goes bankrupt. Software companies range from one person copying diskettes as orders come in, all the way up to Micropro, Microsoft, Digital Research, Ashton-Tate, IBM and Lotus—the giants of the microcomputer software industry. These companies produce a bewildering variety of products, and they produce programs for a wide variety of computers and operating systems. Bookstores stock software and book jobbers handle software, and they all need ways to identify software.

No one questions the need to identify computer software, only the need for a new standard. ISBNs started out applying only to books, but soon they were applied to anything handled as though it was a book. R.R. Bowker and the International ISBN Agency supported this trend, and they have specifically welcomed software companies. Bowker has been running full-page color ads in major microcomputer magazines to promote use of ISBN for computer software.

ISBN and the proposed SCSN both have virtues. The SCSN is specific to software. The ISBN is much more concise, whereas the SCSN appears to waste numbers through a fixed-length coding scheme that equates Joe's Garage Software House with IBM. The SCSN carries more meaning than the ISBN, allowing a producer to group different versions of the same program with a single group number. ISBN agencies provide log books; the makeup of SCSN makes such provision unlikely. Any microcomputer software publisher should have a microcomputer, making accurate calculation of check digits automatic. The SCSN clearly allows for a large number of software publishers, each with a large number of products; while the ISBN algorithm was designed to last for centuries, it makes more assumptions about the potential size of a publisher.[8]

The main arguments in favor of ISBN are not its technical superiority, but its established state. ISBN has ISO approval; it is heavily promoted; it has been in use for over a decade; it is supported in ISBD and MARC. Bowker has been aggressive in promoting ISBN for software, so that the major producers are likely to adopt ISBN before SCSN could become a standard. As a result, SCSN will probably not be approved or will become a little-used standard like STRN. That may be unfortunate. ISBN does not, under any circumstances, allow vendors to provide a second level of intelligence to a number. An ISBN identifies a publisher but can't be used to link several versions of an item together; the SCSN could link up to 999 different versions of a single program.

It is easier to use an entrenched standard outside its original scope than to see a new standard through to widespread use. The family of standard numbers is a small family, and unlikely to get much larger. It is an odd family; the STRN is less "standard" than the LCCN, and only it and the ISBN have any independent significance. NUC, the "nonstandard standard," is more widely used in the library field than any standard number except ISBN. The SAN appears to be well suited to the publishing industry but ill suited to libraries; as a result, one "address number" may be joined by another standard number for libraries—which really identifies an address. Such is the way of technical standards; they are developed to meet economic needs, with more regard for immediate requirements than for theoretical consistency. The family of standard numbers is just one case, and not an extreme one, of the curious results of developing standards in the real world.

SUMMARY

All technical standards are abstractions; some are more

abstract than others. A single standard may yield a single implementation, or may allow for a wide variety of implementations. Standards are based on other standards, and may involve several levels of nested standards. Some standards allow ambiguity in implementation, while others allow a deliberate but precisely specified range of choices. Explicit standards with multiple options may be cited improperly, giving the impression that the standards are flawed. Standards may be arranged into various frameworks or models, and they may be grouped into families. Such groupings and arrangements can help make sense of standards, but groupings and arrangements can be arbitrary.

FOOTNOTES

1. For more information, see Chapter 10 of this book and Chapter 3 of Crawford, Walt. *MARC for Library Use: Understanding the USMARC Formats.* White Plains, NY: Knowledge Industry Publications; 1984. 222 p.

2. Electronics Industry Association. *EIA Standard Interface Between Data Terminal Equipment and Data Communication Equipment Employing Serial Binary Data Interchange, EIA RS-232C.* Washington, DC: EIA; 1969 August. 28 p.

3. Verman, Lal C. *Standardization: A New Discipline.* Hamden, CT: Archon; 1973. 461 p.

4. Hemenway, David. *Industrywide Voluntary Product Standards.* Cambridge, MA: Ballinger; 1975. 141 p.

5. Rush, James E. "A Proposed Model for the Development of an Integrated Set of Standards for Bibliographic and Related Data." *Library Trends.* 31(2): 237-249; 1982 Fall.

6. "American National Standard Committee Z39 X/C 34 on Code Identification of Serial Articles, Draft Code Proposal." *Journal of Library Automation.* 8(2): 154-161; 1975 June. NISO standards committee CC is working on an issue and item level identifier to serve the same ends as SCISA.

7. "Second Draft Proposal to ISAD/TESLA." *Journal of Library Automation.* 10(2): 181-183; 1977 June.

8. For more information on this controversy, see Wall, C. Edward. "Microcomputer Software Identification: The Search for Another Numbering Standard." *Library Hi Tech News.* 13: 1,11-19; 1985 February.

6

Problems and Dangers of Standards

Technical standards are fundamental to organized society. That doesn't mean that all standardization is good, or that all technical standards are positive achievements. Like most other instruments of civilization, technical standards can be good or bad.

STANDARDS AND COMPETITION

Technical standards development sometimes looks like collusion. Standards may lower or raise barriers to new competitors by making it easier or more difficult to enter an industry. In both ways, standards influence competition. While the historical record is generally good, there can be cause for concern.

Antitrust

When the major competing companies in an industry meet to decide on pricing or territories, it's called collusion. When employees of those companies meet to determine common specifications for parts used by the industry, it's called standards-making. The government has been known to object to the first type of meeting, but rarely to the second.

In 1964, antitrust questions were raised about an American Society for Testing and Materials (ASTM) standard on asbestos cement; it was suggested that the standard constituted a form of price-fixing. The District Court of Pennsylvania said that "because of the heavy reliance of federal, state and municipal governments upon ASTM for specifications, the Society may be regarded as an essential arm, or branch, of the government, and its acts may be entitled to the immunity from antitrust laws accorded governmental acts."[1]

Standardization organizations have generally been considered immune to antitrust laws. Such immunity is not inevitable, and does not mean that technical standards development never functions in a collusive manner. The processes used by major standardization organizations should work to prevent standards that promote monopoly and oligopoly, but collusive standards are possible. Any standard that limits variety can potentially limit competition.

Competition

Uniformity standards can encourage illegal price-fixing. Technical standards that set minimum quality specifications may also be anticompetitive by raising barriers to new competitors. There are two ways to write minimum quality standards. One method concentrates on performance: to meet the standard, something must pass specified tests under specified conditions. Unfortunately, performance-based standards are not always feasible: technology to make proper measurements may be lacking, or the nature of "performance" may be such that any tests would be prohibitively expensive.

Minimum quality standards avoid such problems by specifying material and method. Such standards are prevalent in building codes and similar regulations. This form of standard can be directly anticompetitive. By barring different techniques and materials, the technical standard directly bars one form of competition. If the techniques or materials specified in a standard are proprietary, the technical standard is directly anticompetitive.

Totally unfettered competitive methods can include product adulteration, that is, cutting prices by reducing the size or quality of the product. Standards for weights and measures specifically work to eliminate the competitive thrust to charge less by selling less (and calling it more). Thousands of technical standards, including most of those developed by ASTM, are anticompetitive in that they work to prevent the sale of inferior materials. Such forms of competition endanger life and health; proper technical standards work to shift competition to more acceptable areas.

STANDARDS AND INNOVATION

Well-written standards encourage innovation allowing creators to focus on new tools, techniques and products. Timely standards for new techniques and products can also encourage widespread adoption, moving innovation into practice. While technical standards have aided innovation, technical standards can also work against innovation.

Premature Standards

When a new technology is developing, different developers may proceed along similar but distinct paths. At some point, one or more of the developers may initiate technical standards for the area. If standardization begins too soon, it can damage innovation in two ways:

1. Draining energy: Technical standards require time and energy. Time spent on standards committees may be time taken away from innovation and development. In some cases, standardization may be a deliberate attempt to slow development by draining the energy of competitors.

2. Establishing uniformity: If a standard is written and adopted, it will establish some level of uniformity. Innovation in those aspects will cease or at least be slowed for some time. The more successful the standard, the more innovation will be slowed.

Consumer videocassette recorders (VCRs) lack a single standard. This lack may have slowed the acceptance of VCRs, but seems to have increased the rate of innovation in VCRs. Beta, for several years the minority format, typically leads VHS in new ideas and techniques. Beta recorders were the first with special effects; more recently, Beta recorders introduced high fidelity sound recording to VCRs. In each case, VHS engineers have followed the innovative lead of Sony (the developer of Beta).[2] While consumers and prerecorded tape producers may suffer from the conflicting formats, consumers have benefitted from competitive innovation and sharply competitive pricing.

Established Standards

Well-established standards also pose barriers to innovation. In some cases, the barrier may be impossible to overcome. The QWERTY typewriter keyboard* was created in the late nineteenth century as a way to keep type bars from jamming. The arrangement puts frequently used letters far enough apart that adjacent type bars are less likely to be in action at the same time. QWERTY was used on the first popular typewriters, and became familiar to the thousands, then tens of millions, of trained typists.

Technology eventually solved the jamming problem, but QWERTY faced no serious competition in the early twentieth century. More recently, electronic typewriters and word processing systems have totally eliminated mechanical jamming as an issue in keyboard design, but most students still learn QWERTY in typing class, and the system continues to maintain near-universal domination.

Some decades ago, the Dvorak keyboard promised to improve typing speeds and reduce typing fatigue. Typewriters with Dvorak keyboards have been available by special order for many years, but the system has never made any dent in QWERTY. Many microcomputers permit reassignment of keys; the Apple IIc has a switch to convert the keyboard to Dvorak arrangement. A few pioneers use the switch or reassignment programs and tout Dvorak's advantages, but no significant move away from QWERTY has happened, or seems likely to.

In the library field, some commentators assert that Z39.2 and the MARC formats are poor standards and should be replaced by more innovative standards. Though MARC is less than two decades old, the speed and extent of its success raise a major barrier against any replacement. (In this case, no replacement with any suggestion

---

*ANSI X4.23-1982: *Keyboard Arrangement for Alphanumeric Machines,* though the ANSI standard came much later than the overall adoption of the "industry standard."

of improvement actually exists; unlike supporters of the Dvorak keyboard, opponents of MARC have nothing better to propose.)

OVER-STANDARDIZATION

Over-standardization damages the cause of standardization and can damage standards users. Over-standardization can occur for many reasons, and can take on several guises.

Overly Rigid Standards

Interchangeability standards enhance competition and reduce costs. Good interchangeability standards specify tolerances sufficient to assure real interchangeability; bad standards specify tolerances in excess of such assurance. A dimensional standard with no specified tolerances is incomplete; a standard with extremely narrow tolerances is anticompetitive or useless. Such a standard is anticompetitive when the tolerances are such that they can be met only by using equipment too expensive for a newcomer to obtain, or by using patented or licensed techniques.

Suppose that Z85.1, *Permanent and Durable Library Cards,* specified tolerances of +0 to −0.005mm for all dimensions. To meet such narrow tolerances under a variety of measurement conditions, the card stock might have to be a specially treated stock requiring patented equipment available only to one papermaker. A tolerance of 0.005mm (0.0002 inch) has no possible bearing on interchangeability of cards with an overall size of 75mm x 125mm; such a standard would be a deliberate attempt to prevent new papermakers from entering the market.

A standard is also useless when the tolerances are so narrow that it costs more to assure compliance than any realistic value for the item. For example, if papermakers were required to spend $1.00 per card to assure that each card met Z85.1 standards, papermakers would not attempt to meet the standards: the resulting products would not be saleable.

Standards of this sort tend to be self-limiting. When a standard appears to have been overstated in order to limit competition, courts may be inclined to ignore the traditional antitrust exemption of standards agencies. When a standard is uneconomically precise, it will be modified or ignored.

Overly Detailed Standards

The standard for ISBNs specifies how the numbers are formed, how they should be displayed and how they are assigned. It does not specify how they are to be stored in MARC records, the typeface that must be used to display them or precisely where on a publication they must be displayed. Such specifications would be overly detailed, reducing the use of the standard by overstating the requirements.

The library and publishing field seems prone to overly detailed standards. The standard for single-title orders, Z39.30, begins with a useful set of information to be included on an order. It then goes on to specify how many characters to allow for each item and exactly where on the form each item should appear. What could be a generally applicable standard, assuring that a certain amount of information is included in orders, becomes a rigid standard that some sensible agencies refuse to implement.

The tendency to excessive detail is quite natural, and one that requires care to avoid. Quite probably, standards committees build in too much detail because they fail to focus on the intent of the standard. For each detail, the committee should ask whether it is *necessary* to carry out that intent, and whether it is *justified* to carry out the intent. Requiring that a publisher's name and address appear on the title leaf is necessary to assure that catalogers have sufficient information; requiring that the publisher's name appear on the recto, no less than 3 and no more than 4 inches from the foot of the page, does little to serve the cataloger but much to restrict the book designer. The first is a necessary detail; the second, excessive detail.*

Standards at the Wrong Level or at Mixed Levels

ANSI Z39.30 is an example of excessive detail, but also of mixed levels. The list of data elements is a valuable checklist. The standard form with its detailed placement of elements may well be a valuable standard for typewritten orders. If these were separate standards,

---

*This example is hypothetical, but Z39.30 is not: to the author's eye, Z39.30 fails through excessive detail.

agencies producing computer-printed orders (or machine-readable orders) could follow the first, while ignoring the second. Examination of standards will reveal many with mixed levels. Inappropriate levels represent another issue, one more difficult to judge. A national standard for the size and threads of light bulb bases seems appropriate; a national standard specifying all physical characteristics of a light bulb would seem inappropriate.

Standards arise at too high a level through the assumption that if some standardization is good, then more is better. For example, the terminal at which these words were written* uses many standards: ASCII, RS-232C, the QWERTY keyboard, a standard 3-prong plug, a standard P31 phosphor, and any number of materials, testing and component standards. All those lower-level standards helped a new company enter into competition with established terminal makers. The terminal also uses several "industry standards," with sets of switches to emulate the operation of several well-established terminals. So far, standards encourage competition.

All the standards referred to above are relatively low-level standards. A high-level standard might specify *all* characteristics of a terminal, creating an "ANSI standard terminal." If such a standard had existed in 1975, it is unlikely that the author's terminal could have so many features for such a low price. In fact, a standard based on this terminal's qualities would have retarded improvements within the last two years. Inappropriately high-level standards slow innovation and discourage competition.

Standards with No Clear Scope of Application

Just as standards work best at a single level of specification, standards should always have a defined scope for application. Standards for the title page of a technical report would be inappropriate for the title page of a novel. Z39.2 is appropriate for bibliographic

---

*This manuscript was written using a Liberty Freedom green-screen (P31) terminal; it was edited using a Morrow/Zenith amber-character ("LA" phosphor) terminal with frosted faceplate, tilt and swivel screen, and a remarkably fine keyboard.

records, but would be inappropriate for full-text storage or transmission.

Standards sometimes lack clear scope definitions. A larger problem is misuse of standards beyond intended or appropriate scope. Well-drawn standards will frequently see use beyond original scope, and such extended use may be appropriate. The line between appropriate extension of scope, and inappropriate use out of scope, is a fuzzy line. Use of a standard outside of scope represents overstandardization in an *ex post facto* sense; while the standard may have been drawn correctly, it is being used incorrectly.

Verification Expense and Difficulty

Standards that are too expensive to verify are poor standards. Users at each level should be able to ascertain that producers at that level have followed appropriate standards. If such verification is unreasonably difficult or costly, adherence won't be verified. In such a situation, no certainty exists that any particular producer is actually following a standard. If an unscrupulous producer recognizes that the standard won't be verified, that producer may gain an unfair economic advantage by taking shortcuts, producing substandard goods.

Subjective Standards

Standards that involve subjective criteria are inherently flawed. If verification is only possible "in the mind of the beholder," the standard should be termed a guideline rather than a standard. Z39.6: *Trade Catalogs,* calls for body type 8 points or larger: an objective, easily verifiable standard. If the standard went on to state as a requirement that the type should be "attractive," the standard would be flawed.

Solutions to Trivial or Nonexistent Problems

Standards-makers can err on the side of overly ambitious standards. Similarly, standards-makers may err in the other direction. A standard should solve some problem; if the problem is trivial, or does not exist, the standard is a waste of time and energy.

Several Z39 and ISO standards appear to fall into this category. Z39.6 supposes that trade catalogs were being produced which failed to include sufficient information. Z39.13 must be based on the assumption that publishers don't know what information is needed in advertisements, and that publishers lacking such knowledge are likely to order and follow an American National Standard. Elements of ISO 8 (see Chapter 12) appear to consider use of different typefaces for different articles in a periodical to be a problem; the nature of the problem is unclear.

The first question to ask when any new standards activity is proposed would appear to be, "What is the problem?" Standards should always be solutions, and should always be solutions to problems that deserve expenditures of time and energy.

DEFECTIVE STANDARDS

Defective standards come about for several reasons in addition to those mentioned above. Some standards are poorly written and misunderstood. Standards committees may lack appropriate expertise. Some standards may be approved despite legitimate objections, and others fail to retain compatibility with earlier versions. Finally, standards may fail to consider privacy issues or other issues affecting individual rights.

Poorly Written and Misunderstood Standards

Standards tend to be drawn by interested parties with specialized experience. When no one on a standards committee has good written English skills, the resulting standard may be poorly written. In extreme cases, poor writing may result in a defective standard, one that does not yield the intended results. Defective materials or safety standards can kill people. Preparing a clear standard requires a mix of skills: an editor without specialized skills may damage the standard in the process of clarifying its text.

Those who work on consensus standards or guidelines may know the difficulty of achieving good finished text. Many who work on such matters feel that committee time should not be spent on matters they regard as "simple editorial questions." Editorial questions frequently appear less important than "substantive matters."

When people have spent enormous amounts of time in meetings to establish a standard, their reluctance to spend more time on "editorial questions" is natural enough. This viewpoint, while common, is unfortunate and shortsighted. Clear text allows standards-users to make the most of good substance. Standards-makers understand the details of their standard better than a later reader will; if those details aren't set down in clear, effective English, the standards-makers are weakening their own efforts.

Insufficient Knowledge

Most standards develop from perceived needs, and standards tend to be developed by the community that perceives a need. That community may not contain sufficient expertise to prepare the best possible standard. ANSI boards coordinate efforts of different agencies, partly to assist in this area. Good standards developers make special efforts to reach out for appropriate knowledge. Thus, Z39.48: *Permanent Paper for Printed Library Materials,* takes advantage of standards developed by ASTM and the Technical Association of the Pulp and Paper Industry, and representatives of paper companies served on the developing committee.

Standards developed without sufficient expertise may not be bad standards, but are unlikely to take advantage of the most current and complete information in special fields. Predictably, many standards will be developed without the best experts in some fields, either because the specialists are not well known or because the developing group is unable to enlist their cooperation.

Consensus Problems

Consensus implies more than simple majority, but is a far cry from unanimity. This distinction is necessary for any standardization effort to take place; otherwise, one determined agency could block all efforts to approve standards. For example, NISO makes a special effort to resolve every negative vote on a standard. ANSI rules do not require unanimous approval; agencies can and do approve standards despite strong objections from members.

Consumer agencies claim that some standards organizations give little weight to consumer votes—while a negative vote from a single large manufacturer would doom a proposed standard, a negative vote from a consumer agency may be overridden. ANSI instituted the Consumer Interest Council to deal with this problem; the question is still a valid one.

NISO includes many consumers and has stiffer requirements for consensus than some other standards developers. Such requirements do not assure that legitimate objections will properly block a standard. Politics plays a major role in NISO as in all organizations; negative votes can be resolved by political means rather than by resolving the technical problems. When standards are approved through political consensus rather than technical consensus, the standards begin weakly, have less chance of success and are less useful.

Compatibility

New versions of standards should encompass prior versions, but such is not always the case. For example, X3.9-1978, the standard for FORTRAN, makes illegitimate a data type permitted in previous versions. As a result, some programs developed following ANSI standards require revision prior to compilation under new X3.9 FORTRAN compilers. The best argument for using ANSI standard languages is portability; lack of upward compatibility limits such portability. According to those objecting to the changes, X3 language committees are imposing current ideas of "good language practice" on older languages, at the expense of compatibility and portability.[3]

Privacy

Standards can damage individual rights. Every few years, somebody suggests development of a national standard identifier for library patrons. After a recent attempt to initiate such a standard (turned down by the committee assigned to work on it), a column appeared in the *LITA Newsletter* which summarizes the problem:

> National standard identifiers of one sort or another are neither uniquely a library idea nor particularly novel. The idea of assigning a number to each new U.S. citizen at birth or

naturalization has been proposed many times. The idea has obvious merits: it would eliminate the maze of numbers with which we all deal, by substituting one simple number assigned at birth. It would be of enormous assistance to those attempting to find missing persons, very useful in tracing tax cheats, and so on.

"And so on..." Thanks to the civil libertarians who remain active, "and so on" has so far been enough to prevent establishment of a single standard identification. What serves the IRS will also serve the police; what serves legitimate police will also serve witch-hunters and those setting up lists of enemies.

The problems with a national standard library patron ID are those of a national standard citizen ID. Libraries are places where people go for information—but not, properly, information about the reading habits of other individual patrons or who has read a particular book. At various times, the FBI and other agencies have attempted to use library circulation records to track down those with whom they have a quarrel. Libraries have been consistent in resisting such efforts, based on common understandings regarding privacy and the role of the library.

A national standard library patron ID implies some form of national registry. National registry ties in neatly with the national complex of computers; searches for borrowers and borrowing could be conducted far more efficiently and without all the bother of sending agents out to individual libraries. Paranoia? Perhaps; I once worked in a library which was the scene of a government attempt to inspect old circulation records, so I believe that such attempts are possible.

I've never seen a convincing economic justification for a national standard patron ID. There doesn't seem to be much need for such a standard on any grounds. Most library patrons don't skip from town to town charging books from different libraries—and most libraries would not blindly permit borrowing by out-of-area residents simply because they had a number. The ability to trace book thieves might be useful, but book thieves are unlikely to check out items using a single standard number. In any case, libraries which support confidentiality of patron records should be consistent in that support.

National standard library patron ID's are unlikely to come about in the next year or two; with luck, such standard numbers will never be established. If such a number [were] ever approved, it could well be part of a government trend toward monitoring of citizen activities, and the logical number would be the Social Security number. We've all heard the refrain that "honest people have nothing to hide"; quite apart from the somewhat extreme definition of "honest" this implies, the proper answer is that it all depends on who's looking or might start looking.[4]

FOOTNOTES

1. *U.S. vs. Johns-Manville, et al.* Finding Fact on Application of ASTM. District Court for Eastern Pennsylvania. 1964 July 20. *Cited in:* Hemenway, *Industrywide Voluntary Product Standards,* p. 10-11.

2. Lyons, Nick. *The Sony Vision.* New York, NY: Crown; 1976:151.

3. Dvorak, John C. "Inside Track." *InfoWorld.* 1984 October 8. p. 88.

4. Crawford, Walt. "Standard Fare." Reprinted by permission of the American Library Association from *LITA Newsletter* No. 19 (Winter 1985), copyright © 1985 by ALA.

7

The Standards Process

As we have seen, a "standard" can be anything from one person's practice to the legally mandated practice of a nation or the world. This chapter and those that follow concern formal consensus standards. When knowledgeable people in the United States refer to "technical standards," they usually mean "formal voluntary consensus standards established by an ANSI-accredited standards organization." An inaccurate shorthand for that phrase is "ANSI standards." This chapter reviews a bit of the history of formal consensus standards in the United States, then goes on to discuss the processes required by ANSI and those normally followed by NISO (Z39).

HISTORICAL NOTES ON STANDARDS ORGANIZATIONS

Standards have been with us for thousands of years. The oldest standards organizations are but a few decades old. The oldest American organization specifically devoted to technical standards is probably Underwriters Laboratories, Inc. (UL), organized in 1894. The National Bureau of Standards began in 1901, marking the start of significant, ongoing government interest in standards. The International Electrotechnical Commission (IEC) started in 1906, and substantive interest in technical standards for industry appears to date from that decade. In 1910, as mentioned earlier, the newly formed Society of Automobile Engineers (SAE) began vigorous development of standards, an effort which has continued to this day.

Key national and international organizations began to form later in the first quarter of this century. The American Society for Testing Materials (ASTM) and four engineering societies organized the American Engineering Standards Committee in 1918.[1] That committee became the American Standards Association (ASA) in 1928. In the mid-1960s, the ASA became the United States of America Standards Institute (USASI), and later the American National Standards Institute (ANSI). The national standards body for the United Kingdom (BSI, the British Standards Institute) also began in 1918. Germany's national standards body (DIN, Deutsche Institute fur Normung) began a year before ANSI, in 1917. In 1919, Belgium, Canada, Switzerland and the Netherlands formed national standards bodies; by 1924, eight more countries had followed suit.[2]

Apart from the IEC, international organizations did not begin until the second quarter of the twentieth century. Fourteen countries worked together to create the first international standards organization outside of a particular discipline: the International Federation of the National Standardizing Associations (ISA), founded in 1926 and largely abandoned because of World War II. The United Nations Standards Coordinating Committee (UNSCC) worked from 1943 to 1947, and led to creation of the International Organization for Standardization (ISO), which continues as the primary international standards organization. The IEC continued to work on electrical and electronics standards, and continues as an independent body; it is also considered the Electrical Division of ISO.[3]

Standards bodies of most interest to libraries and automation are relative newcomers. American National Standards Committee Z39 originated in 1940, and became the National Information Standards Organization in 1984. American National Standards Committee X3 (now Accredited Standards Committee X3) was not formed until 1961, together with the ISO technical committee related to automation, ISO/TC97.[4]

The organizations listed above, and others in the field of technical standards, carry out different functions in a variety of different ways. All, however, work to build, recognize or process formal consensus standards. Two key words make that phrase important, formal and consensus; their definitions follow:

• Formal: the standard must take the form of a document, prepared according to the forms and rules of the standards body. These forms and rules help to ensure that the standard does not conflict with other standards, that it was properly developed and that it can be properly identified for use;

• Consensus: the standard must represent general agreement among interested parties. "General agreement" and "interested parties" are the two key terms; both are vague, with definitions varying from organization to agency.

PRINCIPLES AND PROCESSES

Common principles for national standards appear to include:

• National standards should meet a recognized need.

• Standards should protect producer and consumer interests.

• Standards should reflect national consensus of concerned parties.

• Standards should make economic sense now and for the immediate future.

• Standards should reflect current technology but should also be practical.

• Standards should be studied periodically and revised or abandoned as required by changing times.

The best and most successful standards meet all these principles. Standards don't always meet the full set; standards organizations develop procedures to help assure at least partial conformance. Such procedures make standards development a slow and expensive process: most standards require at least three years from initiation to approval. The standards process generally includes some or all of the steps discussed below.

Project Proposal

Some person or agency asserts that a new standard is needed in a particular area, or that an existing standard should be revised, amended or withdrawn. Anyone can prepare a project proposal, if he or she knows where to send it. Organizations, governmental bodies, special conferences and existing standards committees may all generate new project proposals. Sometimes, the most difficult part of proposing a project is determining what standards body should deal with it; some project proposals result in entirely new standards bodies.

Initial Review

When a standards body receives a proposal, it must determine what, if anything, to do with it. Some of the possible results of that review are as follows:

- Existing standards cover the need; these standards are noted, and the proposal is returned.

- Work on the same area, or a closely related one, is currently taking place; the body making the proposal is notified, and the proposal is forwarded to those doing the work.

- The proposal is inherently unsuitable for standardization; reasons for this finding are noted, and the proposal is returned.

- The proposal has insufficient impact to justify the cost of standards development; again, the proposal is returned with this finding.

- Development in the area of the proposal is not yet at a point calling for standards activity; the proposal is rejected as premature.

- The proposal merits development.

In any case but the last, the process ends at this point. Filtering is a critical and difficult part of the work of a standards body. Some bodies are reluctant to determine that a proposed standard is simply not economically sound; as a result, working groups may be formed and may spend considerable time and money without achieving any useful result.

Approval of Project

If initial review shows that the proposal merits development, the standards body should determine whether and when development should take place. Even meritorious proposals must sometimes be postponed for lack of resources; some proposals have more immediate impact than others.

Assignment

The proposal is sent to an existing subcommittee or working group, or a new subcommittee or working group is formed to deal with the proposal. Standards bodies typically rely on voluntary labor, and a good working group must include representatives with the proper skills and from the proper interest groups to handle the project well. Identifying these representatives and assembling a functioning group can be difficult. Attempts to establish working groups sometimes demonstrate that a particular project is not economically justified, because interested parties are unwilling to participate in the development.

Development

A working group meets to consider the need, assess the state of affairs, determine the proper form of one or more standards and prepare the draft standard(s). This process involves meetings, mail, telephone and other methods of working singly and together to formulate sound standards. The process also involves review and feedback from a larger group of interested parties:

• Questionnaires may be used to gather information on current practice and felt need in the area;

• Research may be required, sometimes involving grant proposals or other sources of special funding;

• Comment drafts may be distributed at several points during development;

• Minutes for more formal development groups may be distributed or published;

• Draft standards may go out for draft voting and comments,

with specific deadlines and with a specific commitment to consider and respond to any comments. Several rounds of draft standard voting and comments may be required.

The development process will typically lead to one of three results:

1. Abandoning the proposal and disbanding the working group. This can come about because further study shows standardization to be unwarranted, because the interested parties are unwilling to come to any sort of consensus, because the length of deliberations has exceeded the useful life of the standard or because the working group is unable or unwilling to build workable standards for voting.

2. Referring the proposal to one or more other working groups, after detailed study has determined that the proposal conflicts or overlaps with the work of such groups.

3. Proposing one or more standards.

Most of the time and money spent on technical standards is spent on development; the process above may involve years of meetings and several rounds of review by interested parties. Ideally, the resulting standards proposals should represent clear thinking, careful economic and technical analysis, and a high degree of consensus prior to balloting.

Voting and Public Review

At this point, the proposed standard(s) should be satisfactory to the members of the working group. The working group should also have solicited and received at least one round of feedback from interested parties in the larger standards body. The next two steps may coincide. One step is publicity on the widest feasible scale, so that any interested parties not represented on the immediate standards body may be heard from. The second step is formal voting within the standards body. Such voting involves specific deadlines and often requires that comments accompany negative votes.

As noted earlier, consensus doesn't necessarily mean unanimity. ANSI states that "substantial agreement is more than a simple majority but not necessarily unanimity."[5] Any specific group will have its own standards for "consensus," which may vary with the issue at hand. In some bodies, certain single agencies can prevent adoption of a standard with a single negative vote; in other cases, standards may be adopted despite negative votes from parties with substantive concerns.

Good practice requires that the working group deal with all negative votes and with all comments received during public review. In many cases, votes and comments will lead to revision of the proposed standard and reballoting. In some cases, typically cases where the development work has been faulty or rushed, votes and comments will result in failure: the standards effort will be abandoned.

Adoption

If the standards body determines that a proposed standard has achieved consensus, it reports the standard as approved. In some cases, this establishes the standard. In others, the standards body must certify that approval to a coordinating agency, which adopts the approved standard; ANSI works in this manner. The adopted standard must be formally published if it is to be of any use; either a specific standards body or a national coordinating agency may serve as the publisher (or, in some cases, may delegate publication to a third party).

Publicity and Implementation

An approved standard is nothing more than words and figures on paper. Once that standard has been published, publicity encourages implementation of the standard. Publicity also encourages use of the standard and expectation that the standard is in use; such expectation serves to mandate further implementation. An unused standard is a waste of time and money; useful standards should save enough time and money to justify the cost of development.

Periodic Review

Technical standards are not eternal. Standards bodies or national coordinating agencies establish time limits for most standards. At the end of a certain period, the standard must be reconsidered; it may be abandoned, revised or reaffirmed. Periodic review helps to keep technical standards contemporary and useful, and to avoid a clutter of outmoded, pointless standards.

For many standards, periodic review requires no more than a simple reaffirming vote: an initial review will show that the standard is widely used and contemporary, and should be retained in its existing form. A well-designed review process minimizes the costs of reaffirming such standards, leaving time and energy for those standards that require substantial revision. Standards are eliminated or combined, though a working technical standard should never be abandoned prematurely. New technologies typically supplement and complement older technologies; it may be many years or decades before an obsolescent technology becomes wholly outmoded or useless.

THE ANSI STANDARDS PROCESS

ANSI and the standards-developing agencies follow processes along the lines of those above. ANSI does not develop standards; it approves and establishes standards developed by other bodies. The organization recognizes three different methods by which bodies can show evidence that a standard has gained consensus; the accredited organization method, the canvass method and the standards committee method.

Accredited Organizations

Any organization that develops standards may seek ANSI accreditation. ANSI will grant accreditation to organizations that use a procedure comparable to the procedures of Accredited Standards Committees; ANSI may conduct audits to ensure compliance. Once an organization is accredited, it develops and approves standards and transmits them to ANSI for approval as American National Standards. The transmittal form requires a summary of the final vote and certification of the following criteria:

• Due process requirements were met;

• The standard is within the fields registered by the organization;

• Significant conflicts with other standards were resolved;

• Other known standards were examined for duplication of content;

• All appeals within the development process were completed;

• All known objections are documented as part of the transmittal;

• No substantive changes have been made since the standard was listed in the ANSI publication *Standards Action.*

NISO is an accredited standards organization, as are the IEEE, UL, ASTM and more than 100 other organizations. Accredited standards organizations may assign their own numbers, which will be retained by ANSI. Any given organization may have some standards that are not ANSI standards, as well as others that are. For example, the Electronics Industry Association (EIA) is an accredited standards organization, and most EIA standards are also ANSI standards; however, EIA RS-232C is not an ANSI standard.

Standards Committees

Organizations that were formerly American National Standards Committees have become independent, either as Accredited Standards Organizations or Accredited Standards Committees. For example, ANSC Z39 became NISO (Z39), an Accredited Standards Organization; ANSC X3 became ASC X3, an Accredited Standards Committee.

An accredited standards committee includes a secretariat, with a set of duties defined by ANSI. The duties of a secretariat are to:

• Organize the standards committee in cooperation with and under the operating procedures of the authorizing organization;

• Submit the list of committee members to the authorizing organization for approval;

• Determine that the representatives on the standards committee participate actively, and that all those having a substantial concern with and competence in standards within the committee's scope have the opportunity to participate;

• Submit proposed revisions of the scope of the standards committee for standards management board approval, when recommended by the standards committee;

• Appoint the officers of the standards committee or arrange for their election by the standards committee;

• Propose programs of work, together with proposed completion dates, and give direction and guidance to the standards committee;

• Assume responsibility for the administrative work, including secretarial services, arrangements for meetings, preparation and distribution of draft standards, letter ballots, minutes of meetings, etc.;

• Assume responsibility for processing letter ballots in accordance with the procedures of the organization;

• Report results of voting according to the procedures of the organization;

• Maintain standards within the scope of the standards committee in an up-to-date condition, and arrange for the publication and distribution of approved standards;

• Keep the appropriate standards management board informed of committee activities by sending information copies of all material distributed to the standards committee;

• Submit status reports of the work in progress to the appropriate standards management board, as required by established policy.[6]

Any standard must be submitted for written ballot with a six-week balloting period; typically, notice of the proposed standard appears in *Standards Action* at the same time. (Chapter 9 includes ordering information for *Standards Action*.) All comments (whether from members of the committee or from other interested parties) must be responded to, and the subcommittee or working group must attempt to resolve objections.

Canvass Method

When any organization has existing or new standards that it wants to turn into American National Standards, it may elect a canvass (mail poll) of all organizations known to be concerned in the field. The proposing organization becomes the sponsor of the standard; the canvass list is reviewed by an ANSI Standards Management Board within the field, and a six-month time limit is established for responses.

When a canvass is taken, the sponsoring organization submits all the results to ANSI, including the list, comments received and responses to negative comments. Approval is based on clear evidence of sound practice and a clear consensus. The canvass method is used relatively rarely; standards of interest to libraries and automation are generated through the Accredited Standards Committee and Accredited Standards Organization methods.

ANSI Review

ANSI reviews applications to see that the proper steps have been taken, and that consensus does appear to be present. ANSI does not review standards for technical correctness or quality, and specifically does not interpret standards. The organization does audit accredited standards organizations from time to time, but its own role is that of publisher, clearinghouse and member of ISO; ANSI itself is not a standards-setting organization.

NISO (Z39)

NISO follows the normal process for an accredited standards organization. A secretariat and elected board of directors coordinate NISO activities. Any voting member or other interested party may recommend a needed standard, and NISO provides a form to encourage such recommendations.

A Program Committee evaluates recommendations, and forwards appropriate ones to the board of directors. If the board finds a recommendation worthwhile, it recommends formation of a new standards committee; the voting membership must approve any such formation. The chair of NISO appoints committee chairs; the committee chair recommends members for the committee, who are then appointed by the NISO chair.

Typically, a standards committee will prepare a draft standard; the executive director will send the draft to NISO voting members for comment. A proposed standard will follow, for formal written ballot (in some cases, the comment round may be omitted). The NISO executive director mails the draft standard and sends out reminders to voting members who fail to return ballots. Comments and negative votes are returned to the committee chair, who attempts to resolve them. If necessary, a revised draft is reballoted; standards with unresolved negative votes are always reballoted at least once. Notification in *Standards Action* normally coincides with the formal ballot.

ANSI policies require that any proposed standard receiving at least two-thirds affirmation from all voting members be submitted to the ANSI Board of Standards Review. NISO has always attempted to resolve all negative votes, though some standards have been sent forward with outstanding negative votes.

The same process is followed for revisions of existing standards. Some existing standards appear sound as written; the board of directors may recommend a direct reaffirmation balloting in such cases, avoiding the time and expense of organizing a standards committee.[7]

NISO differs from some standards committees and organizations in maintaining an ongoing publicity program of its own. *Voice of Z39* (ISSN 0163-626X) is a free newsletter published three times a year, giving background information on NISO and standards, and showing the status of all current efforts within NISO.[8]

SUMMARY

Consensus standards require time and effort, to assure that the standards are properly prepared and that consensus has been achieved. Most standards organizations here and abroad have similar principles and similar processes. Consensus standards organizations date from the beginning of the twentieth century; during that brief history, tens of thousands of standards have been drafted and adopted. The standards process, though apparently cumbersome, serves as a means of maintaining the quality of consensus technical standards. The major standards organizations that produce or sponsor these standards are described in the next chapter.

ANSI standards are voluntary standards; they do not carry the force of law (though some are made part of other laws and regulations). Such standards are preferable to mandatory standards, in that they can be ignored when they become obsolete or burdensome. Voluntary standards must be carefully developed and must serve economic needs and achieve consensus; otherwise, the years and dollars spent on the standards will result in useless paper.

FOOTNOTES

1. Hemenway, David. *Industrywide Voluntary Product Standards.* Cambridge, MA: Ballinger; 1975: 81.

2. Verman, Lal C. *Standardization, A New Discipline.* Hamden, CT: Archon; 1973: 110.

3. *Ibid,* 151-152.

4. Prigge, R.D. [and others]. *The World of EDP Standards.* [Blue Bell, PA]: Sperry-Univac; 1978 November. 165 p.

5. *Guide to Submitting Standards to ANSI for Approval.* New York: ANSI; [1984]. 5 p.

6. Prigge, *op. cit.,* p. 10-11.

7. The description of NISO's process was paraphrased from Frase, Robert W. ''Procedures for Development and Access to Published Standards.'' *Library Trends.* 31(2): 225-236; 1982 Fall, revised for recent changes in NISO.

8. *Voice of Z39* is available from the National Information Standards Organization (Z39), U.S. Department of Commerce, National Bureau of Standards, Library—Room E106, Gaithersburg, MD 20899.

8

Standards Organizations

Several hundred organizations in the United States work to create voluntary technical standards. Some, such as the Electronic Industries Association (EIA) and the Institute of Electrical and Electronic Engineers (IEEE), are trade or professional associations that develop standards as one of several programs. Others, such as the National Information Standards Organization (NISO), exist solely to create and promote standards.

Standards organizations rely on voluntary effort. ASC X3 alone has over 1000 people involved in standards efforts at any given time, and an average of eight ISO technical meetings take place every working day.[1] Good standards require substantial investment in time and expertise; such investment must be spread across many participants in many organizations. This chapter considers several standards organizations, with particular emphasis on NISO (Z39) and ASC X3, the two U.S. organizations most central to libraries and automation.

AMERICAN NATIONAL STANDARDS INSTITUTE (ANSI)

ANSI has grown rapidly in the last two decades as the overall clearinghouse for standards activity in the United States. ANSI coordinates the development of national standards, provides an independent mechanism to approve and promulgate voluntary national standards, and represents the United States in nongovernmental international standardization organizations.

ANSI brings together over 200 standards-producing organizations that meet ANSI accreditation standards and submit some or all of their standards for ANSI approval. In 1983, ANSI approved 431 new standards and made available almost 600 revised standards.

Over 1000 companies, governmental agencies, nonprofit organizations and others belong to ANSI, supporting its work. ANSI is the U.S. member of the International Organization for Standardization (ISO) and the International Electrotechnical Commission (IEC), and it is the secretariat for over 240 ISO technical committees and subcommittees.[2]

There are two major aspects to ANSI's organization: the staff and officers and the committees. As of May 1984, ANSI had a staff of over 100, headed by a president, two vice presidents, and seven directors (handling Publications, Government Liaison, Development, Planning, Operations, Administrative Services, and Sales and Services). The officers include a chair, three vice chairs and a board of directors with over 30 members, representing a variety of interests.

Five councils, four committees and several boards carry out the work of ANSI. They are as follows:

• Appeals Board. The Appeals Board hears complaints of those who feel they have been injured by the actions of ANSI boards or councils.

• Board of Standards Review (BSR). The BSR actually approves ANSI standards, verifying that an organization has followed due process and has achieved consensus. BSR does not consider the technical content of any standard, only the process used to approve it. ANSI states that "Approval by ANSI informs the user that the standard may be applied with confidence because those directly affected have reached agreement on its provisions."[3] This presumes that "those directly affected" are actually members of the organization that developed the standard, a shaky presumption but the best available in a nation of voluntary standards.

• Certification Committee. This committee works on certification, that is, the process of establishing that an organization is qualified to develop American National Standards. The certification committee advises the Board of Directors, which must make the final decision on certification.

• Company Member Council. Each company member of

ANSI has one member. Large companies dominate ANSI's funding and naturally have substantial influence over ANSI's work.

• Consumer Interest Council. For many years, consumerists have complained that technical standards activities are dominated by corporations, who alone have the resources to support such activities. The Consumer Council represents some effort by ANSI to address this complaint. Five persons considered to be experienced in the "consumer field" are joined by representatives from those ANSI members who choose to join the Consumer Council.

• Executive Committee. As in most organizations with large boards of directors, ANSI's executive committee acts for the board between meetings.

• Executive Standards Council. Six organizational representatives, six company representatives, four government representatives, two consumer representatives and three others constitute the Executive Standards Council, which bears responsibility for all standards activity within ANSI *except* approval and withdrawal of American National Standards. ANSI is seeing that its committees reorganize as independent entities, which is changing the role of the Executive Standards Council to one of assisting and encouraging organizations to develop needed standards. Patricia Harris, executive director of NISO (Z39), is a member of the Executive Standards Council.

• Finance Committee. This committee reviews ANSI finances and makes recommendations to the board of directors.

• International Standards Council. ANSI is the American member of ISO; this council advises the board of directors on relations with ISO, IEC and other international standards organizations.

• Organizational Member Council. This council includes one member from each organizational member of ANSI and works with the Executive Standards Council to consider the need for new standards activity.

• Standards Management Boards. Various boards take responsibility for a discipline or area, assisting the Executive Standards Council in coordinating standards development. For example, the Information Systems Standards Board is responsible for NISO (Z39) and ASC X3 work.

• U.S. National Committee of IEC. This committee (and many subcommittees) oversees U.S. participation in the IEC.

ANSI publishes *Standards Action,* which includes notices of all standards proposed for approval, and also publishes many of the American National Standards. It issues catalogs for all American National Standards and ISO standards and is the only American source for ISO standards.

Standards development takes place in over 200 accredited organizations belonging to ANSI. Some organizations create large numbers of technical standards. The American Society for Testing and Materials (ASTM), the Society of Automotive Engineers (SAE), and the Aerospace Industries Association (AIA) are quite active; in 1964, for instance, those three organizations prepared over one-half of all new national technical standards.[4]

Figure 8.1 includes a small sampling of ANSI's organizational members. Figure 8.2 lists a few of the 1000 or more company members of ANSI, ranging in size from AT&T, GM and IBM to some small companies and consortia. The most recent *Progress Report* includes current membership lists.

NATIONAL INFORMATION STANDARDS ORGANIZATION (Z39) (NISO)

In June 1939, the American Association of Law Libraries, Medical Library Association and Special Libraries Association petitioned the American Standards Association to form a committee on library standards. American National Standards Committee Z39 began in March 1940, under the sponsorship of the American Library Association. Z39 started slowly and remained relatively inactive for some years. In 1951, the Council of National Library Associations took over the secretariat from ALA; Z39 continued on a small scale, with inadequate funding, producing a few standards over many years.

Figure 8.1: Some Organizational Members of ANSI

```
Abrasive Grain Association
Acoustical Society of America
Aerospace Industries Association of America
Air-Conditioning & Refrigeration Institute
Air Diffusion Council

American Ladder Institute
American Library Association
American Medical Association
American Mining Congress
American National Metric Council

Can Manufacturers Institute
The Carpet & Rug Institute
Cast Iron Soil Pipe Institute
Cemented Carbide Producers Association
Certified Ballast Manufacturers

Human Factors Society
Hydraulic Institute
Illuminating Engineering Society
Industrial Fasteners Institute
Industrial Safety Equipment Association

Sunglass Association of America
Western Wood Products Association
Wire Rope Technical Board
Wood Machinery Manufacturers of America
```

Beginning in 1961, Z39 was jointly funded by the Council on Library Resources (CLR) and National Science Foundation (NSF). The committee became a vigorous proponent of national and international standards. During the 1970s, Z39 grew to 50-odd members and prepared new standards in a variety of areas. In the early 1980s, Z39 was reorganized; in 1984, it became a separate organization, renamed the National Information Standards Organization (Z39) (NISO), retaining the old committee number in its name and in standards numbers.

Figure 8.2: A Few Corporate Members of ANSI

```
Aetna Life & Casualty
Air World Publications
Akebono Brake Industry Co., Ltd. (Japan)
Alabama Gas Corp
Alcan Aluminum Corp
```

```
General Electric Corp
General Motor Corp
General Public Utilities Corp
General Signal Corp
Genie Industries
```

```
International Business Machines Corp
International Flue Saver, Inc
The International Nickel Co, Inc
International Telephone & Telegraph Corp
International University Booksellers, Inc
```

```
OCLC, Inc
Oak Switch Systems
O'Donnell & Associates, Inc.
Ohio Edison Co
Owens-Corning Fiberglas Corp
```

```
Research Engineers, Inc
The Research Libraries Group, Inc
Research & Trading Corp
Rockwell International Corp
```

Unlike the old Z39, funded primarily by CLR and NSF, NISO is funded by voting members, who pay from $200 to $4000 per year. The move to dues caused a temporary drop in membership in NISO, but by January 1985 NISO had as many dues-paying voting members (54) as ANSC Z39 had members in April 1982. In addition to voting members, NISO has more than 100 informational members who pay $100 per year to receive draft standards as they are issued.

NISO is active and broadly supported within its constituent areas of libraries, publishing and information science, and manages to work effectively with a fairly simple organizational structure. NISO also works on international standards, serving as the Technical Advisory Group (TAG) to ANSI for ISO Technical Committee 46 on Documentation. NISO standards are published by ANSI rather than NISO.

NISO is headed by a chair, vice chair and a board of directors including three directors each from the library community, publishing and information services. Officers serve two-year terms; directors serve three-year terms. NISO's operations are headed by an executive director and are currently based at the National Bureau of Standards. Within ANSI, NISO reports to the Information Systems Standards Board (ISSB).

NISO has standing committees to work on Finance, Future Planning, International Relations, Membership, Program and Publicity. Standards committees, which carry out the development and review of NISO standards, are organized as needed. Typically some two dozen standards committees will be active at any time. NISO standards committees cover a range of topics and have chairs from a range of agencies. Appendix B lists active NISO standards committees and the chairs of those committees as of May 1985.

Standards committees in NISO depend entirely on voluntary effort. Committee chairs typically recruit committee members who have the necessary experience or knowledge. Members must be willing to devote substantive effort over several years, including some travel. Active members of NISO contribute far more than the $200 to $4000 required for voting membership; an agency may well devote over $10,000 per year to travel expenses and employee time required for standards committee work. (In some cases, NISO provides travel expenses.)

Voting NISO members contribute money and time to the standards effort. NISO committee members come primarily from organizations with voting membership, and each voting member is committed to serious review of every proposal. Voting and informational members of NISO (as of May 1985) are listed in Appendix B.

ACCREDITED STANDARDS COMMITTEE X3:
INFORMATION PROCESSING SYSTEMS

During a 1960 ISO meeting, Sweden recommended formation of a new ISO technical committee (TC) on standards for information processing. At the same meeting, the United States was suggested as the secretariat for this new committee. Thus TC 97 was formed; ANSI continues as the secretariat.

An American meeting followed the ISO meeting. Representatives of the Business Equipment Manufacturers Association (BEMA) and heads of some manufacturing companies met and recommended formation of an organization to develop standards in the computing field. In September 1960, ANSC X3 was announced; its organizational meetings began in February 1961.

BEMA, now the Computer Business Equipment Manufacturers Association (CBEMA), has been the secretariat throughout X3's existence. Portions of the original charge were split off into two other committees, X4 and X6. X4 concerned itself with standards for office machines, keyboards and supplies. It was disbanded in the 1980s, with X3 taking on its work. X6 disbanded in 1965, with the Electronic Industries Association assuming its duties.

X3 became an Accredited Standards Committee in 1985. The committee is headed by a chair and vice chair, and it includes 3 standing committees, 5 subcommittees and study groups and 74 technical committees and task groups. Unlike NISO, X3 has no council. In 1984, CBEMA estimated that 2500 people were involved in X3 work.

The International Advisory Committee (IAC) coordinates the work of X3 with activities in ISO, IEC and other bodies; IAC develops policy statements rather than technical positions. The Secretariat Management Committee (SMC) is X3's closest equivalent to a council. The Standards Planning and Requirements Committee (SPARC) evaluates the need for new standards, audits standards development on functional and economic grounds, and checks standards for conformance to objectives. As with NISO, actual technical development and review take place within each subcommittee.

Technical committees in X3 are in some ways similar to (though less complex than) those in ISO. The committees are ongoing and deal with standards within a particular area, unlike

NISO's standards committees which are typically organized to deal with one particular standard. X3 technical committees are organized in a three-level hierarchy. As of November 1978, for instance, there were eight groups of technical committees:

> A — Recognition
>
> B — Media
>
> H and J — Languages
>
> K — Documentation
>
> L — Data Representation
>
> S — Communication
>
> T — Systems Engineering

Each group has technical committees: for instance, group J includes X3J1 for PL/I, X3J2 for BASIC and X3J4 for COBOL (among others). Some committees have subcommittees or task forces: for instance, X3J1 (PL/I) includes X3J13 (PL/I General Purpose Subset) and X3J14 (PL/I Real Time Subset).[5]

X3 is much more complex than NISO and involves more people in its work. The voting membership numbers are similar to those of NISO, but the organizations involved are different and typically larger. In some cases, X3 members can retain employees solely to track and participate in standards activities; few NISO members have the size or wealth required for such a level of support. Appendix B includes a list of voting ASC X3 members.

INTERNATIONAL ORGANIZATION FOR STANDARDIZATION (ISO)

The International Organization for Standardization (ISO) is the primary international agency for standardization in all fields except electrical and electronic engineering. ISO is an active, complex organization involving agencies from 89 countries, working through

more than 2300 organizational units. ISO's structure and requirements are much different from those of ANSI or most American
standards organizations.

ISO has two classes of membership: member bodies and correspondent members. A member body is "the national body most
representative of standardization in its country."[6] No country may
have more than one body as a member of ISO, and no international
organizations belong to ISO. A correspondent member is an organization in a developing country which has yet to develop a national
standards body. Correspondent members observe, but neither vote
nor participate in technical development; typically, such members
change to member bodies after a few years. In January 1984, ISO
had 15 correspondent members, from Barbados, Cameroon, Hong
Kong, Iceland, Jordan, Kuwait, Lebanon, Liberia, Malawi,
Mauritius, Mozambique, Oman, Papua New Guinea, the United
Arab Emirates and Uruguay.

ANSI is a voluntary nongovernmental organization and is an
exception within ISO: more than 70% of ISO's member bodies are
governmental or established by law. ANSI is one of the 25 founding
members of ISO, which began to operate on February 23, 1947. The
full list of founding members is as follows:

> Australia. Standards Association of Australia (SAA).
> Austria. Osterreichisches Normungsinstitut (ON).
> Belgium. Institute belge de normalisation (IBN).
> Brazil. Associacao Brasileira de Normas Tecnicas (ABNT).
> Canada. Standards Council of Canada (SCC).
> Chile. Instituto Nacional de Normalizacion (INN).
> Czechoslovakia. Urad pro normalizaci a mereni (CSN).
> Denmark. Dansk Standardiseringsraad (DS).
> Finland. Suomen Standardisoimislitto r.y. (SFS).
> France. Association francaise de normalisation (AFNOR).
> Hungary. Magyar Szabvanyugyi Hivatal (MSZH).
> India. Indian Standards Institution (ISI).
> Israel. Standards Institution of Israel (SII).
> Italy. Ente Nazionale Italiano di Unificazione (UNI).
> Mexico. Direccion General de Normas (DGN).
> Netherlands. Nederlands Normalisatie-instituut (NNI).
> New Zealand. Standards Association of New Zealand
>   (SANZ).
> Norway. Norges Standardiseringsforbund (NSF).

Poland. Polish Committee for Standardization, Measures and Quality Control (PKNMiJ).
South Africa. South African Bureau of Standards (SABS).
Sweden. SIS—Standardiseringskommissionen i Sverige (SIS).
Switzerland. Association suisse de normalisation (SNV).
United Kingdom. British Standards Institution (BSI).
United States. American National Standards Institute (ANSI).
USSR. USSR State Committee for Standards (GOST).

One of the most active national standards bodies, West Germany's Deutsches Institut fur Normung (DIN), joined ISO in 1951.

Administration

ISO has a president, vice president, treasurer and secretary general (the chief administrative officer). A council consisting of the president and 18 members maintains the technical structure of ISO, and appoints members of administrative committees and chairs of technical committees. The eight administrative committees include:

• Executive Committee (EXCO), which is chaired by ISO's vice president, and acts for the Council between meetings;

• Planning Committee (PLACO), which recommends forming new technical committees and dissolving old ones; monitors the technical work of ISO; and approves titles, scopes and projects for technical committees;

• Committee on Certification (CERTICO), which studies ways to improve international acceptance of standards and possible use of ISO marks to certify standards conformance;

• Committee on Consumer Policy (COPOLCO), which promotes consumer interests in standards;

• Development Committee (DEVCO), which is concerned with standardization needs in developing countries;

• Committee on Information (INFCO), which promotes information exchange;

• Committee on Reference Materials (REMCO), which establishes suitability of references for citation in standards;

• Committee on Standardization Principles (STACO), which provides a forum for discussion on fundamental aspects of standardization.

Technical Committees

ISO establishes technical committees (TC) in areas as needed. Each technical committee has a member body as secretariat, and establishes its own subcommittees and working groups to carry out its own work. Technical committees are numbered chronologically as created, beginning with TC 1 (Screw Threads), established in 1947. As of November 15, 1983, the highest number was TC 186 (Cutlery). Twenty-one technical committees had been dissolved as of that date, leaving 165 committees.

Technical committees vary widely in size, complexity and activity. The simplest are those with no current program and no subcommittees, which exist only to review existing standards in their field. The most complex, such as TC 17 (Steel), TC 20 (Aircraft and Space Vehicles), TC 34 (Agricultural Food Products), TC 61 (Plastics), TC 97 (Information Processing Systems) and TC 147 (Water Quality), have 50 or more subcommittees and working groups. The most extensive set of subgroups is in TC 22 (Road Vehicles), with 24 subcommittees and 88 working groups for a total of over 100 subgroups. A sampling of the technical committees (every eighth TC) appears in Figure 8.3.

The sampling in the figure does not accurately reflect ANSI's role in ISO. ANSI is one of the four bodies that provide the bulk of the secretariats for ISO technical committees, subcommittees (SC) and working groups (WG). AFNOR (France), BSI (UK) and DIN (Germany) hold the most TC secretariats and are the most active overall; ANSI is slightly less involved. These four bodies hold 92 of the 165 TC secretariats and 1452 of the 2301 total leadership roles within TCs, SCs and WGs.

Figure 8.3: Some ISO Technical Committees

TC	Area	Sec.	SC	WG
1	Screw threads	SIS	4	0
10	Technical drawings	DIN	9	25
21	Fire prot./fighting	BSI	4	18
29	Small tools	AFNOR	7	18
37	Terminology (princ.)	ON	2	2
46	Documentation	DIN	6	18
56	Mica	ISI	0	0
65	Manganese/chromium	GOST	0	0
76	Transfusion equipt.	DIN	0	0
85	Nuclear Energy	DIN	4	25
96	Cranes, etc.	SAA	9	0
105	Steel wire ropes	BSI	3	3
113	Liquid flow measures	ISI	7	1
121	Anaesthetic equipment	BSI	6	4
131	Fluid power systems	ANSI	9	39
139	Plywood	DIN	0	7
150	Implants for surgery	DIN	4	15
158	Analysis of gases	AFNOR	2	1
166	Ceramic ware, glassw.	SII	2	2
174	Jewellery	DIN	0	0
182	Geotechnics	NNI	4	0

TC 46 and TC 97

NISO is the American counterpart to ISO TC 46, as ASC X3 is the American counterpart to TC 97. Some NISO standards (for instance, ISSN and ISBN) are based on earlier ISO standards, just as some ISO standards (ISO 2709, for example) are based on earlier Z39 work.

DIN is secretariat for TC 46; the scope of the TC is "standardization of practices relating to libraries, documentation and information centres, indexing and abstracting services, archives, information science and publishing." TC 46 began in 1947 and currently has 27 participating countries and 23 observing countries. Appendix B lists the participating and observing countries in TC 46, and its subcommittees and working groups (and their secretariats) as of November 15, 1983. More recently, NISO became secretariat for TC 46 SC 4 (Automation) and the new SC 6 (Statistics).

ANSI is the secretariat for TC 97 (Information Processing Systems), devoted to "standardization, including technology, in the area of information processing systems including computers and office equipment." Twenty-three members participate in TC 97, and another 20 observe. TC 97 is one of the more complex technical committees, including 16 subcommittees and 66 working groups, ranging from SC 1/WG 7 (Vocabulary: Communications) to SC 19/WG 4 (Mail Processing Machines). The structure of TC 97 is dynamic as new needs arise and old areas fade. Appendix B lists the countries involved in TC 97 and the subcommittees.

FOOTNOTES

1. Prigge, R.D. [and others]. *The World of EDP Standards, op. cit.,* p. 1.

2. American National Standards Institute. *1984 Progress Report.* New York: ANSI; 1984 May. p. 7.

3. American National Standards Institute. *Guide to Submitting Standards to ANSI for Approval.* New York: ANSI; [1983 June]. p. 1.

4. Hemenway, *op. cit.,* p. 81.

5. Most historical information was taken from Prigge [and others]. *The World of EDP Standards, op. cit.,* p. 82-87, 151-152.

6. International Organization for Standardization. *ISO Memento 1984.* Geneva: ISO; 1984. 141 p. All information in this section not explicitly cited is taken from this publication.

9

Resources for Agency Involvement

All standardization efforts rest on the same foundation: the intelligence, effort and awareness of people. From the technical standards set down by a single artisan, through the relatively simple organization of the National Information Standards Organization, to the elaborate structure of the International Organization for Standardization, it all begins and ends with individuals. You can involve yourself in technical standards at several different levels, depending on your own needs and those of your agency. Levels of involvement include:

• Awareness: finding out what standards exist, how they apply to your work and how they can be used;

• Use: acquiring the appropriate standards, using them and supporting their use;

• Professional involvement: helping to investigate the need for new standards through professional associations;

• Informational agency involvement: joining appropriate standards organizations as an informational member, to keep up with developing standards;

• Active agency involvement: joining standards organizations as a voting member, committing membership fees and staff support;

• Active personal involvement: developing ideas for new standards, volunteering to serve on standards committees.

This chapter considers some paths through these levels. You and your agency must choose what level of involvement you can afford and choose to support. Technical standards would cease to exist if no one became involved; standardization efforts would become hopelessly complex if every individual in a profession were passionately involved in the process.

AWARENESS

If you're part of a company, library or other agency, you should look into current standards activity within the agency. If there are others in the agency who are interested in standards, you can combine efforts. You may find that your agency already maintains full or partial sets of NISO or X3 standards, that you receive the ANSI *Catalog of American National Standards, Standards Action* or NISO's *Voice of Z39.* Your agency may even be an informational or voting member of NISO.

If not, you should take steps to stay informed on new developments. The three publications just mentioned should provide a good basic level of awareness:

• *Voice of Z39* (ISSN 0163-626X) is issued three times per year by the National Information Standards Organization (Z39) and sent to all Z39 voting members, informational members, members of standards subcommittees and others on request. Subscriptions are free; requests should go to NISO at the U.S. Department of Commerce, National Bureau of Standards, Library-Room E106, Gaithersburg, MD 20899.

• *Standards Action* appears every other week, and lists every standard being proposed for adoption as an American National Standard. Annual subscriptions are $25 for nonmembers, which includes the biweekly *ANSI Reporter*. Subscriptions may be requested from the American National Standards Institute at 1430 Broadway, New York, NY 10018.

• *Catalog of American National Standards,* issued once each year, lists all current American National Standards by category, giving the price for each; an index lists standards by number. The

Catalog is available from ANSI at the address above, for $10 per copy.

The International Organization for Standardization (ISO) also publishes an annual *Catalog*. This catalog is also available from ANSI, for $25. ISO also publishes standards handbooks consisting of photoreduced sets of standards for a given area. Standards Handbook 1, *Information Transfer,* costs $62; handbooks 8, 9 and 10, on the Hardware, Software and Vocabulary of Data Processing, cost $52, $52, and $44, respectively. Each handbook represents a good source of information at a relatively modest price.

ANSI and ISO standards do not exhaust the field, but they do include the most important national and international technical standards. The remaining chapters of this book cover a narrow area of ANSI and ISO standards, certainly not including all that affect libraries or automation. As you consider listings in these catalogs, you will find many other standards which affect your work directly or indirectly.

USE

Awareness should lead to use, which requires purchasing appropriate standards. If your agency is actively interested in the use of technical standards, as it should be, you should be acquiring those standards that appear to be directly relevant.

While ANSI does not publish all American National Standards, you can purchase all American National Standards from ANSI, at the address above. Both NISO and X3 publish standards through ANSI, so ANSI is the only means of acquiring these standards. ANSI is also the exclusive American distributor for ISO standards.

When an agency moves from implicit reliance on technical standards to active use of technical standards, it should evaluate those standards it chooses to support. For each standard, a study should evaluate the following:

• Currency and validity of the standard. If your agency determines that the standard is out-of-date or invalid for your operations, you should *not* implement it, but should record the reasons for that finding and (for NISO standards) inform NISO of the problem.

    • Changes needed to implement the standard. Most likely, the standard will serve your agency well, but it will differ in some details from your current practice. A careful list of those differences and a plan to resolve them should be prepared.

    • Policy requirements to assure proper use of the standard. In some cases, this may involve some announcement that your agency will follow the standard as of a given date. (For new or less-used standards, this may even be a noteworthy announcement.) Proper use of a standard involves explicit reference to that standard, so that new employees can gain full information.

    Explicit support of American National Standards makes sense for most agencies. Such support does not mean that an agency must adopt every standard without question. Deliberate choices to ignore certain standards are in keeping with the voluntary nature of standards in the United States.

    The cost of using appropriate technical standards is relatively small. A complete set of NISO standards costs $198 (including shipping and a free binder), a discounted price, as of February 1985. The newer the agency, the easier it will be to implement technical standards. Even a well-established agency should have little trouble implementing technical standards in emerging technology. An agency that fails to be aware of current standards and to use those that make sense is cutting itself off from a community of users. Such separation reduces the chance for efficiencies of scale and other advantages gained through sharing a common ground. Agencies should not blindly adopt all technical standards, but should certainly use those that can be beneficial.

    If you're a writer or researcher, or work in a library or publishing house, you might consider purchasing a "starter set" of NISO standards. The "starter sets" suggested below are only examples, and include only NISO standards adopted by the end of 1984. Prices shown are those in the 1985 ANSI catalog (prices do not include a $5.00 shipping charge).

Standards for Writers and Editors

Six NISO standards, described further in Chapter 10, deal with various issues of writing and editing:

Z39.4-1984: *Basic Criteria for Indexes*. 24 pages, $7.00. Good suggestions for anyone compiling an index.

Z39.14-1979: *Writing Abstracts*. 15 pages, $6.00. Most nonfiction articles deserve or require abstracts.

Z39.16-1979: *Preparation of Scientific Papers for Written or Oral Presentation*. 16 pages, $6.00. While specifically intended for scientific papers, this standard is full of good advice for anyone preparing nonfiction papers or speeches.

Z39.22-1981: *Proof Corrections*. 24 pages, $7.00. A clearly written explanation of standard proof corrections, with explicit examples.

Z39.29-1977: *Bibliographic References*. 92 pages, $16.00. Any writer who has trouble establishing and maintaining a standard style for citations and references will find this standard helpful. Note that Z39.29 is not the standard specified by the Chicago *Manual of Style* or by many professional associations, but is a clear, consistent standard with extensive examples and explanations.

Z39.34-1977 (R1983): *Synoptics*. 19 pages, $6.00. Only needed for those writers submitting scientific or technical papers to "dual-publication" journals, where the full paper is available on microform or on request and only the brief "synoptic" appears in print. Most nonfiction writers will not need this standard.

Standards for Libraries

Any medium-sized or larger public, special or academic library should have the six standards listed above, as a service to the library's patrons. Other standards will also serve the library's patrons, and some standards specifically serve technical processing, including a group of standards for romanization. In addition to Z39.4, Z39.14, Z39.16, Z39.22, Z39.29 and Z39.34, libraries may wish to consider some or all of the following (shipping charges are not included):

Z39.2-1979: *Bibliographic Information Interchange.* 12 pages, $5.00. The standard which underlies USMARC.

Z39.5-1984: *Abbreviation of Titles of Periodicals.* 11 pages, $6.00.

Z39.7-1983: *Library Statistics.* 44 pages, $11.00.

Z39.9-1979: *International Standard Serial Numbering.* 8 pages, $5.00. Includes a clear explanation of ISSN check digits and how ISSNs are assigned.

Z39.11-1972 (R1983): *System for the Romanization of Japanese.* 11 pages, $5.00.

Z39.12-1972 (R1984): *System for the Romanization of Arabic.* 8 pages, $5.00.

Z39.21-1980: *Book Numbering.* 8 pages, $5.00. The ISBN standard.

Z39.23-1983: *Standard Technical Report Number (STRN), Format and Creation.* 8 pages, $5.00.

Z39.24-1976: *System for the Romanization of Slavic Cyrillic Characters.* 10 pages, $5.00.

Z39.25-1975: *Romanization of Hebrew.* 15 pages, $6.00.

Z39.30-1982: *Order Form for Single Titles of Library Materials in 3-inch by 5-inch format.* 15 pages, $6.00.

Z39.35-1979: *System for the Romanization of Lao, Khmer, and Pali.* 14 pages, $6.00.

Z39.37-1979: *System for the Romanization of Armenian.* 7 pages, $5.00.

Z39.43-1980: *Identification Code for the Book Industry.* 8 pages, $5.00. The SAN standard.

Z39.45-1983: *Claims for Missing Issues of Serials.* 15 pages, $6.00.

Z39.46-1983: *Identification of Bibliographic Data On and Relating to Patent Documents.* 8 pages, $5.00.

Z39.48-1984: *Permanence of Paper for Printed Library Materials.* 8 pages, $5.00.

Z85.1-1980: *Catalog Cards.* $5.00.

Larger libraries and academic libraries may prefer to obtain a complete set of NISO (Z39) standards; smaller libraries with limited foreign-language collections can probably forgo most of the romanization standards and some of the other more specific standards.

Standards for Publishers

Most publishers should have the six standards mentioned for writers, or at least the first five of those six. Some publishers will find use for specific standards such as those for developing thesauri or those for preparing library directories. Publishers should generally find the following standards useful (again, shipping charges are not included):

Z39.1-1984: *Periodicals: Format and Arrangement.* 11 pages, $6.00.

Z39.6-1983: *Trade Catalogs.* 12 pages, $5.00.

Z39.8-1977 (R1982): *Compiling Book Publishing Statistics.* 11 pages, $5.00.

Z39.9-1979: *International Standard Serial Numbering.* 8 pages, $5.00.

Z39.13-1979: *Describing Books in Advertisements, Catalogs, Promotional Materials, and Book Jackets.* 12 pages, $5.00.

Z39.15-1980: *Title Leaves of a Book.* 8 pages, $5.00.

Z39.18-1974: *Guidelines for Format and Production of Scientific and Technical Reports.* 16 pages, $6.00.

Z39.21-1980: *Book Numbering.* 8 pages, $5.00.

Z39.26-1981: *Advertising of Micropublications.* 8 pages, $5.00.

Z39.43.1980: *Identification Code for the Book Industry.* 8 pages, $5.00.

Z39.48-1984: *Permanence of Paper for Printed Library Materials.* 8 pages, $5.00.

While every agency must determine which standards will serve its own needs, the suggestions above may serve as starting points.

PROFESSIONAL INVOLVEMENT

Your personal interest in technical standards can lead to personal involvement through your professional associations. Professional associations make up over a third of NISO's voting membership, including most of the major national organizations in the library field. If you're a member of one or more of those organizations, you should be able to find the committee that studies technical standards. Some associations will have more than one such committee.

You should be able to contact the association's representative to NISO, or the committee which advises that representative, for more information. For those associations which, like the American Library Association, mandate open meetings as a rule, you can attend committee meetings as an observer. Such meetings should show you the level of activity and interest within the association, and will probably lead you to ways in which you can help with standardization efforts.

American Library Association (ALA)

One national organization represents a broader range of library interests than any other: the American Library Association. If you're a professional librarian or otherwise involved in libraries, you should consider membership in ALA. ALA is a voting member of NISO, and the Library and Information Technology Association (LITA) of ALA is a voting member of ASC X3. ALA also has a number of internal standardization activities, not all of them related to technical standards. (Information on ALA membership is available from the American Library Association, Public Information Office, 50 E. Huron St., Chicago, IL 60611. All divisions are also reached through this address.)

The Standards Committee of ALA develops procedures for ALA standards, which are largely professional and service standards rather than technical standards. This committee does coordinate standards efforts within all ALA divisions and has liaisons to each division with any current standards effort.

Resources and Technical Services Division (RTSD)

The Resources and Technical Services Division of ALA coordinates ALA's review of NISO standards and names ALA's representative to NISO (Z39). The ALA representative to NISO (Z39) reports to the RTSD board; reports on standards activity within NISO appear in the *RTSD Newsletter* from time to time. RTSD does not itself have a standards committee. The Reproduction of Library Materials (RLMS) section of RTSD has a standards committee that considers the needs for standards related to the reproduction of library material. This committee works more through representation to the Association for Information and Image Management than through NISO.

Library and Information Technology Association (LITA)
Technical Standards for Library Automation Committee (TESLA)

ALA LITA TESLA is the ALA committee most directly concerned with ANSI technical standards. The committee's function statement reads:

> To encourage and support the development of standards relating to library automation; serve as a clearinghouse for such standards and information about such standards. In the area of library automation, transmit proposed standards and recommendations to standards development committees through appropriate American Library Association representatives to American National Standards Institute (ANSI) Committees; arrange for appropriate standards publicity; cooperate with the American Library Association Standards Committee; and encourage and support technical comunications between the library community and its suppliers in the business machine and computer industries.

> The LITA representative to the ANSI X3 Committee is an ex officio member of this committee.

TESLA has operated for more than a decade as an active, informal combination of appointed committee members and others who are interested in TESLA's work. TESLA carries out its charge by such activities as:

• Program sessions: Once every two or three years, TESLA organizes a program at ALA's Annual Conference. These programs have covered topics as diverse as bar-code standards, library-computer center relations and the Linked Systems Project.

• "Standard Fare": Most issues of the *LITA Newsletter* feature a column edited by the pseudonymous Pierre Badin LaTes, a name used by a succession of editors from TESLA. Each column features news of TESLA's activities and developments in the standards field, with emphasis on NISO and X3; most columns also feature signed sections by guest columnists.

• Checklists and other articles: TESLA has encouraged members and observers to develop useful articles. Several articles based on TESLA work have appeared in *Journal of Library Automation, Information Technology and Libraries* and *Library Hi-Tech*.

• Information packet: With TESLA's encouragement and help, the LITA Education Committee developed an information packet on library technical standards. That packet is available from the LITA office for $2.50, payable to the American Library Association, sent to ALA/LITA, 50 E. Huron St., Chicago, IL 60611.

• Needed standards: TESLA gathers suggestions for needed standards and attempts to interest other committees and agencies in developing those which appear promising. At the same time, TESLA maintains sufficient continuity and balance to answer many suggestions with information on existing standards, or with comments as to the inadvisability of standards within a particular area.

TESLA has always been open and has always acted on the basis that whoever attends a meeting is a functioning TESLA participant. Past, future and possible members of the committee can be as involved as current members; future members almost always come from the ranks of active "observers." TESLA meetings can be an informative and easy way to get more involved in technical standards. TESLA maintains formal liaison with the LITA representative to X3 and attempts to maintain liaison with NISO as well;

TESLA has had good, informal summaries of recent Z39 and X3 activities at each ALA Conference and Midwinter Meeting during the past few years.

INFORMATIONAL AGENCY INVOLVEMENT

An agency may join NISO (Z39) as a non-voting Informational Member for $100 per year. This fee pays for press releases, *Voice of Z39* and copies of draft standards in the process of development. Informational Members are free to comment on such standards.

Informational membership is a first step toward full membership in a particular standards organization. If your agency is uncertain as to its need for, or commitment to, an active role in standards, $100 per year will allow you to keep up with new standards *before* they are adopted. For many libraries and small organizations, informational membership may be the most active level of organizational involvement.

ACTIVE AGENCY INVOLVEMENT

If your library, company or other agency finds that it has a vital interest in technical standards, the agency should become a full member of the appropriate standards agency or agencies: NISO, X3 or others.

Membership in NISO costs $200 to $4000 per year, depending on your agency's budget for libraries, information services and publishing. Membership involves some responsibilities. A voting member is expected to review each proposed standard carefully and to vote responsibly on each standard. An agency that votes to approve standards without careful review is betraying the standards process. When an agency votes against a standard, it is expected to state reasons; negotiation is used to resolve negative votes.

The NISO representative in an agency may expect to spend considerable time dealing with drafts and ballots. The representative may need to circulate draft standards for review, then collate responses into a single agency response. Many NISO members have representatives and alternates; the alternate shares the load of active membership.

Voting membership in NISO commits an agency to review, respond, and probably devote time and travel in order to carry out the standards process. Membership does not commit an agency to adopt all NISO standards. Some standards will be irrelevant for an agency; others may have been adopted over the objections of the agency, or may simply not meet an agency's needs.

ACTIVE PERSONAL INVOLVEMENT

Your own involvement need not be at the same level as your employer's. Many of the members of NISO standards committees, and some of the chairs, are from agencies that are not currently voting members. Standards organizations look for expertise and availability. For example, members of NISO committees frequently come from university libraries. None of these libraries is a voting member of NISO, though most of the librarians are members of associations that have NISO membership.

You can be personally involved in your professional associations, as noted above. You can also serve more actively, typically in two ways:

• Serving on standards committees in areas where you have expertise. Such service requires travel and available time to work on research and drafts; good standards involve careful and extensive preparation.

• Proposing new technical standards, preferably with sufficient background and detail to simplify the work of the standards committee. Proposing a useful standard may well lead to a request that you chair the standards committee to work on the proposal. If you're serious about a needed technical standard, and have the skills needed to make a careful proposal, you should either be prepared to accept such a request, or have another volunteer in mind.

You may also review and comment on draft standards without other involvement; most draft standards are widely publicized to elicit review and comment.

SUMMARY

Technical standards save money and time, avoid redundant effort and encourage both sharing and competition. People make technical standards; time, effort and knowledge go into useful standards. Your awareness of existing standards may make you and your agency more effective. Your involvement and that of your agency can make technical standards more effective. As stated above, participation begins with awareness of standards most useful to your agency; the next chapter provides concise information on these appropriate standards.

10

Current Standards: NISO (Z39) and Z85

This chapter and the two that follow provide brief summaries of some standards applicable to libraries and publishers. Each summary in these chapters includes some or all of the following:

1. Identification: number and brief title of the standard.

2. Purpose, Use and Scope: what the standard is for, who would use it and its intended scope.

3. Details: some of the details of the standard.

4. Related Standards: notes on other standards related to this one.

5. Notes: subjective comments on the document and on the standard as implemented.

6. Bibliographic Citation: Citation for the standard, following the form specified in ANSI Z39.29-1979: *American National Standard for Bibliographic References*. The citation also serves as a footnote for any quoted material within a summary. Z39 standards are a series carrying ISSN 0276-0762.

Note: Summaries in these chapters should not be used in place of the standards. In every case, the summary is just that: an abstracted idea of what is in the standard. Technical details are generally not included. These summaries are intended purely as a guide to those standards that are useful for your own activities. Once you've located useful standards, you or your organization should purchase those standards from the American National Standards Institute. All NISO standards are published by, and are available from, the American National Standards Institute, 1430 Broadway, New York, NY 10018.

NISO standards are discussed in numeric order. Within text, the shorter form of a number is used except where changes within a standard are being discussed. "Z39.2" always refers to the edition of the standard cited at the end of the summary; any other editions will be specifically identified, e.g., "Z39.2-1971."

Every American National Standard includes some caution notice; the following, taken from Z39.48, is one of the more complete ones. These notes and cautions generally apply to all standards discussed in this chapter and the next.

> Approval of an American National Standard requires verification by ANSI that the requirements for due process, consensus, and other criteria for approval have been met by the standards developer.
>
> Consensus is established when, in the judgment of the ANSI Board of Standards Review, substantial agreement has been reached by directly and materially affected interests. Substantial agreement means much more than a simple majority, but not necessarily unanimity. Consensus requires that all views and objections be considered, and that a concerted effort be made toward their resolution.
>
> The use of American National Standards is completely voluntary; their existence does not in any respect preclude anyone, whether he has approved the standards or not, from manufacturing, marketing, purchasing, or using products, processes, or procedures not conforming to the standard.
>
> The American National Standards Institute does not develop standards and will in no circumstances give an interpretation of any American National Standard. Moreover, no person shall have the right or authority to issue an interpretation of an American National Standard in the name of the American National Standards Institute. Requests for interpretations should be addressed to the secretariat or sponsor whose name appears on the title page of this standard.
>
> *CAUTION NOTICE:* This American National Standard

may be revised or withdrawn at any time. The procedures of the American National Standards Institute require that action be taken to reaffirm, revise, or withdraw this standard no later than five years from the date of approval. Purchasers of American National Standards may receive current information on all standards by calling or writing the American National Standards Institute.[1]

Z39.1-1977
PERIODICALS: FORMAT AND ARRANGEMENT

Z39.1 establishes certain standards for periodicals, such as information on the cover, spine, table of contents and masthead; pagination; issue and volume identification. Publishers can apply this standard to all periodicals and to some monographs.

Details

Several sections give specifications (required and suggested) to be followed in different areas:

1. Pages: each double page should include running heads or footlines including title, volume and issue or date, and page numbers. Pagination should be sequential; the inner margin should be a full inch and not less than three-quarter inch, and the outer margin should be at least one-half inch.

2. Cover and Spine: The cover should include title, subtitle, number of volume and issue, date, ISSN and (optionally) location of the table of contents and name of the publisher and sponsoring body. Presence of an index should be noted; covers should not be paginated; if the cover contains the table of contents, that table should also appear inside; if the title has changed, the previous title should appear for at least one volume. Periodicals with flat spines should show the title, volume and issue number, date and pagination on the spine.

3. Table of Contents and Masthead: The table of contents should contain the title, volume, issue and date. The masthead should include title, ISSN, publisher (and address), sponsoring

body (and address), editor or staff, frequency of issue, complete subscription price schedule, copyright notice, postal notice, procedure for filing change of address and "notice if the paper used... meets the criteria for the American National Standard for Permanent Paper for Printed Library Material Z39.48-1984" (new to the 1984 revision).

4. Volume: a volume should include a special volume title page and full-volume index. "It is undesirable for a volume to contain more matter than can be bound in one part."

5. Other Cases: A periodical should only change size at the beginning of a volume; titles "should not be altered unnecessarily" and should only be changed at the start of a volume. A new title requires a new ISSN. Changes in title, frequency or size should be announced in advance and on the title page of the first three issues published after the change. Interruptions, extra issues and divided issues should be labeled prominently and clearly.

6. Supplements: Supplements should be the same size as the periodical, should have separate volume numbering (unless intended to be bound with the main item) and in some cases should be treated as an independent serial.

Definitions follow to clarify the provisions of the standard.

Notes

The standard is straightforward but not universally followed by any means. Many periodicals that carry contents on the cover do not repeat the information inside. Many periodicals with flat spines do not carry pagination on the spine. Many periodicals, probably including most nonscholarly periodicals and many in the library field, do not print a separate volume title page. Periodical volume sizes have little to do with binding abilities: the suggested 2½-inch limit is already exceeded by any five issues of *PC Magazine* (with 26 issues per volume) or any five issues of *Byte* (with 12 issues per volume).

The only area where periodicals tend to follow the standard is in the masthead; since much of a masthead's contents is required by the U.S. Postal Service if a periodical is to retain special mailing rates, this conformance is less to Z39.1 than to government requirements. Relatively few of those checked had full-inch or even three-quarter-inch binding margins; some, such as *Creative Computing,* have as little as one-quarter inch inner margin. *Information Technology and Libraries* has a half-inch inner margin.

Some indications in the current Z39.1 suggest that it is intended primarily for scholarly periodicals. Its scope is not limited to such periodicals, and the definition of "scholarly" can be hazy. All the periodicals mentioned above have significant reference value and some research value; none meets all the requirements of the standard.

Z39.1-1967, which called for inclusion of abbreviated title and a "bibliographic strip" on the cover, was a standard whose apparent cost of implementation outweighed its apparent benefits, at least to those who would bear the costs. Z39.1 primarily benefits libraries and indexing and abstracting services, and the benefits to these agencies are somewhat nebulous. Except for those scholarly journals that rely on library subscriptions, most periodical publishers do not consider libraries to be a primary market.

The current version of Z39.1 is much less onerous to implement, but it still adds some costs to publishing and reduces flexibility. The added paper cost of wide binding margins represents a cost that may not appear justified (and that may restrain the creativity of magazine designers); at the same time, the specified margins are needed if periodicals are to survive binding without loss of legibility. Repetition of a cover table of contents within the issue would seem a clear waste of space and paper.

For Z39.1 to be widely used, those agencies which would benefit from its provisions would have to make a convincing economic case to publishers. An informal survey of publications from most of the library specialist publishers (ALA, Haworth, Ablex, Pierian, Bowker, etc.) showed that, even within this narrow field, the case clearly hasn't been made.

Bibliographic Citation

American National Standards Institute. *American National*

Standard for Periodicals: Format and Arrangement, ANSI Z39.1-1977. New York: ANSI; 1977. 11 p.

Z39.2-1979
BIBLIOGRAPHIC INFORMATION INTERCHANGE

Z39.2 establishes a structural basis to support machine-readable bibliographic records.[2] USMARC and other MARC formats are based on the record structure defined by Z39.2 and the related ISO 2709. The standard is intended for interchange of records between systems, not for processing within a system, and it should be used by programmers and others building systems for bibliographic records. The standard defines a structure, but does not specify content or content designation (with some exceptions).

Details

Z39.2 specifies a record format beginning with a 24-character leader. Several leader positions are specified: record length, status, type of record, bibliographic level, indicator count, identifier length, base address and entry map. Definitions for indicators, delimiters and other elements work with the leader specifications to define properly the structure of a Z39.2 record.

The standard also specifies the directory, reserves tags for control fields and specifies placement of indicators and data element identifiers within a record. Only alphanumeric characters may be used in a tag, and specific characters are defined to serve as element, field and record delimiters.

Z39.2-1979 has no appendixes, and it is quite short. As noted in the foreword, "the appendixes published with the original version of the standard have been deleted as unnecessary because of the appearance of extensive documentation for various implementations since the standard was first approved." The original version, Z39.2-1971, included several footnotes within the standard and 20 pages of appendixes. The longest appendix gave guidelines for the implementation of Z39.2, including the basic elements of the MARC Books format and a suggested COSATI (Committee on Scientific and Technical Information of the Federal Council for Science and Technology) format.

Related Standards

The standard refers to, and relies on, ANSI standards X3.4-1977, X3.22-1973, X3.39-1973, X3.54-1976 and X3.27-1978: ASCII, three standards for magnetic tape and a standard for tape labels. Z39.2-1979 is directly related to ISO 2709: *Documentation— Format for Bibliographic Information on Magnetic Tape,* discussed in Chapter 12.

Notes

Z39.2 specifies a basic structure, sufficiently explicit that a generalized computer program could read any record format based on Z39.2 and select fields, subfields and indicators. Z39.2 deliberately allows a range of options for such factors as number of indicators per field and length, or presence, of subfield codes (or data element identifiers). As a result, two different Z39.2 implementations can be extremely different in details, and a generalized program might not be able to make sense of the elements extracted.

As implemented in USMARC, OCLC MARC, RLIN MARC and related formats, Z39.2 is widely used; tens of millions of MARC records have been distributed. Non-MARC Z39.2 formats also exist, including a recently developed variable-length format for transmitting book orders, Z39.49. Z39.2 is successful as a standard for bibliographic interchange among libraries, but it is less successful in the abstracting and indexing industry, where most record formats do not follow Z39.2 guidelines.

Z39.2 establishes a sound and flexible structure; the standard provides essential information to agencies using or creating MARC records and should be considered by agencies creating other formats for bibliographic information.

Bibliographic Citation

American National Standards Institute. *American National Standard for Bibliographic Information Interchange, ANSI Z39.2-1979.* New York: ANSI; 1979 February 9. 12 p.

Z39.4-1984
BASIC CRITERIA FOR INDEXES

"This standard provides guidelines and a uniform vocabulary for use in the preparation of indexes." The standard deals with principles of indexing; the nature and variety of indexes; and organization, style and means of preparation. Z39.4 is suited for use by authors, editors and others who plan or prepare indexes, and it covers all forms of material and indexes as narrow as back-of-the-book or as broad as library catalogs.

Details

Terms used in the standard are defined with clearly labeled examples. Then the standard goes on to define the function and nature of an index. Brief discussions of various types of indexes include suggestions for style and arrangement. A discussion of scope sets forth useful guidelines for what should and should not be indexed: for instance, a back-of-the-book index would not normally cover the dedication, bibliographies or table of contents, but should cover forewords, appendixes and illustrations.

The longest portion of Z39.4 discusses factors influencing index structure: what's being indexed, level of indexing, arrangement of entries (alphanumeric, classified or chronological), term coordination, vocabulary control and special problems of indexes in parts. Guidelines for entry structure include comments on choice of terminology, use of singular and plural form, use of inverted terms, specificity, differentiation and precision of locators.

A careful treatment of syndetic structure (cross references and explanatory information) covers all major aspects of this topic and includes notes on qualifying expressions [e.g., to distinguish "Seals (animals)" from "Seals (mechanical)"]. The section advises against "see" references within short indexes, preferring duplicate locators to save time for the user.

The final section of Z39.4 discusses physical format, with useful guidelines on indentation, punctuation, style and separation of alphabetical groups within an index; comments on microform indexes and indexes stored in machine readable form complete the section.

A brief bibliography includes source materials used in compiling the standard; this bibliography is referred to within the standard as a source of textbooks on indexing. The index is exceptionally long, over two pages for a document of 21 pages, as it is "designed to exemplify the application of relevant provisions of this standard. . . . It is the nature of a standard to contain a high density of information, and the index to a standard for indexes should be full; hence, this one is much larger than would be expected, based simply on the page count of the standard."

Related Standards

Z39.4 cites no related standards within the text, but ANSI Z39.19-1980 and ISO 999 are included in the bibliography. The bibliography itself follows ANSI Z39.29-1977, though with some inconsistency in capitalizing monographic titles.

Notes

Z39.4 sets forth criteria and guidelines and presents an exceptionally clear and concise view of good indexing. It should be useful for anyone planning an index of any sort, but it is not the sort of technical standard that is "implemented" as such. Unless a publication explicitly credits Z39.4 as a basis for indexing, there would be no way to determine that the standard was used; such explicit credit is rare. There is certainly an abundance of indexes that do not meet the criteria of Z39.4, and it is fair to assume that most of these were developed in ignorance of the standard's existence.

Z39.4 is readable and lively in spots, and presents a large amount of useful information in a small amount of space. It can't help overcome the most serious problem with indexing (that is, the total lack of one in a work), and the writers of the standard would probably agree that a bad index is better than no index at all.

Bibliographic Citation

American National Standards Institute. *American National Standard for Library and Information Sciences—Basic Criteria for Indexes, ANSI Z39.4-1984.* New York: ANSI; 1984. 24 p.

Z39.5-1984
ABBREVIATION OF TITLES OF PERIODICALS

Z39.5 specifies rules for forming the shortest possible abbreviated form of serial (and some nonserial) titles, in such a way that an abbreviated form never refers to more than one publication. The standard should be used by publishers, abstracting and indexing agencies and others who must abbreviate titles. The specification should result in the same abbreviated form when applied to the same title at different times; that is, consistent application of the specification should yield consistent, unambiguous results. The standard applies to serial publications and other title or corporate author entries in library records. It can be used for nonserial publications, but it is not a method of establishing entries as such.

Details

The standard specifies explicit and generally unambiguous rules for abbreviation. The rules depend on an external list[3] of words and abbreviations. Except for words on the standard list, abbreviations must always be formed by truncating final letters, and no words may be omitted (except for articles, conjunctions and prepositions, which are almost always omitted).

Capitalization and periods may follow any of a limited number of patterns, such that IND. ENG. CHEM., Ind eng chem, and Ind. Eng. Chem. are all equally valid abbreviations for *Industrial and Engineering Chemistry*. Commas have the specific purpose of separating segments of the abbreviated entry, hyphens are always retained and other punctuation may be used or omitted at will. Special characters are always retained.

The foreword, not part of the standard, explicitly states that "it is not possible to set down rules that will in every instance assure unassisted reconstruction of the original title....Authors and editors who make extensive use of title abbreviations in their publications are encouraged and urged to make available to their readers, at frequent intervals, lists of the abbreviated titles they use with corresponding equivalent unabbreviated titles."

Notes

The key to Z39.5 is the word abbreviation list. That list is vital to any use of the standard for abbreviation, and equally vital to those wishing to recreate a title when faced with an abbreviated form. Reference librarians are well aware that researchers frequently arrive with citations in abbreviated form, with no clear memory of the source of the citation and thus no clear list for expansion of the abbreviated form. If the source followed Z39.5, and the library has the word abbreviation list, chances of restoring the original title are considerably improved.

Cases of ambiguous abbreviated forms are legion; some of these may result because Z39.5 is not widely used, while others may result because abbreviated citations are transcribed incorrectly—for instance, *J. Math. & Phys.* might well be transcribed as *J. Math. Phys.*, but the former refers to the *Journal of Mathematics and Physics* and the latter to the *Journal of Mathematical Physics.*

The standard is quite explicit in most specifications, and it appears to be a useful tool for creating abbreviations and deciphering them. In both these operations, the standard is nearly useless without the word abbreviation list. The second use assumes that most abbreviated terms are on the list; the standard allows for truncation of other words as well, requiring only that "the same abbreviation is not to be used for unrelated words" and that "words consisting of a single syllable or of five or fewer letters shall not be abbreviated"—in both cases, except as found on the word abbreviation list.

The problem with the first provision is that it will only apply within a given agency; different authors and agencies with different sets of referenced titles may well use the same abbreviation for different, unrelated words. In sum, while the standard should result in an unequivocal abbreviation for each title *within a single list,* it cannot be expected to result in universally unequivocal abbreviations unless the word abbreviation list is readily available and consistently used.

Bibliographic Citation

American National Standards Institute. *American National*

Standard for the Abbreviation of Titles of Periodicals, Z39.5-1984.
New York: ANSI; 1984. 11 p.

Z39.6-1983
TRADE CATALOGS

This standard specifies size and suggests good practice for trade catalogs, and it is "intended to assist in producing trade catalogs that will contain the maximum amount of necessary information in a form that can be used easily."

Details

After defining methods of printing and binding, the standard specifies what information should be provided on the cover, in the index and in each product listing to make a catalog useful. The standard calls for a narrow range of page sizes (from 7½ x 10½ inches to 8½ x 11 inches), calls for body type 8 points or larger, recommends against gatefolds and calls for consistent and visible page numbers. The standard specifies normal paper weights and lists typical printing methods with notes on their applicability. Binding methods are also discussed with specific advantages and disadvantages listed for each; suggestions for appropriate cover stocks are given also.

Title 37 of the Copyright Code (Section 201.20,37 Code of Federal Regulations, Chapter II), concerning placement of copyright notice, is included as an appendix.

Notes

Z39.6 includes valuable checklists for data that should appear in trade catalogs; it has brief but useful advice on printing and binding methods. Observation suggests that most trade catalogs do use standard letter-size pages and meet many of the other criteria of Z39.6, but that many industrial catalogs use type smaller than 8 points.*

---

*8-point type with 1-point leading will yield 8 lines per inch; many industrial catalogs run 10 to 14 lines per inch, using type as small as 5-point.

\ **Bibliographic Citation**

American National Standards Institute. *American National Standard for Library and Information Sciences and Related Publishing Practices—Trade Catalogs, ANSI Z39.6-1983*. New York: ANSI; 1983. 12 p.

Z39.7-1983
LIBRARY STATISTICS

This standard aims "to provide a pool of defined statistical data items about libraries, from which various surveys and studies may be designed by selecting the information most valuable to collect for their purposes." The standard defines a great many items, "more...than any single survey or study is expected to use nationally in the future," but it sets forth explicit categories so that sets of data will be comparable and can be aggregated. Z39.7 is intended for use by libraries and agencies that survey library statistics; it applies to all types of libraries within the United States.

Details

The standard begins with a set of six general principles: categories should be mutually exclusive; collections should be reported as intellectual and as physical resources; equipment needed to use materials should be reported; all major forms of income (including in-kind and contributed services) should be reported; estimates should be made when exact figures are not known; statistical data should be collected annually and published within a year of collection.

Seven detailed sections follow, stating categories of information and defining those categories and how they can be measured:

1. Identification and description of the reporting library;

2. Personnel resources: 28 statistical categories, including employees by category, employment status, work week and year, salaries and fringe benefits;

3. Collection resources: 53 categories, showing units added, withdrawn and held and titles held, by material format;

4. Facilities and equipment: 15 categories, including "stationary service outlets" (e.g., branches), microcomputers, seats and shelves;

5. Finances: 43 categories of income and expenditure;

6. Services and utilization: 18 (or more) categories, such as public service hours, reference transactions, cultural presentations, interlibrary loans and circulation;

7. Computer use: 32 possible categories, consisting of eight applications as supported by four categories of computer access.

These sections take up 10 pages of the standard; another 16 are used for definitions of words and phrases used in the standard. Six appendixes give additional suggestions and guidelines for gathering, reporting and aggregating library statistics.

Notes

This standard provides an explicit and fully detailed basis for standardized reporting of library statistics. Any library that reports statistics—this includes almost any library in the United States—and any surveying agency should be using this standard if they are not already doing so; it allows for generally clear and unambiguous statistical measures. The standard was developed in cooperation with statistics committees of ALA and other major national library associations in the United States, and draws on reports of recent national library statistical projects. Since the standard is in line with current use, it should see extensive use in the future.

Bibliographic Citation

American National Standards Institute. *American National Standard for Library and Information Sciences and Related Publishing Practices—Library Statistics, ANSI Z39.7-1983.* New York: ANSI; 1983. 44 p.

Z39.8-1977 (R1982)
COMPILING BOOK PUBLISHING STATISTICS

This standard establishes definitions and subject categories for book publishing statistics in the United States, in conformance with UNESCO recommendations for such statistics. The standard is for use by those who provide or collect book publishing statistics, and it applies to printed books and pamphlets, excluding periodicals, advertising publications, timetables, calendars, telephone directories, maps and musical scores.

Details

Definitions clarify what constitutes a book, a reprint, a title and a translation. Title counts (rather than volume counts) are preferred, and the meaning of "title" in this case is defined. Twenty-three subject categories are defined, with Dewey Decimal and UDC numbers for nonfiction categories. Annual tables are called for, and various subcategories that could be counted are mentioned. The *Publisher's Weekly* report on "American Book Title Output—1976-1977" is included as an appendix to show use of the standard.

The standard provides a consistent method for reporting publishing statistics; its use by Bowker assures that such statistics can be compared meaningfully.

Bibliographic Citation

American National Standards Institute. *American National Standard for Compiling Book Publishing Statistics, ANSI Z39.8-1977 (R1982)*. New York: ANSI; 1982. 11 p.

Z39.9-1979
INTERNATIONAL STANDARD SERIAL NUMBERING

This standard defines the International Standard Serial Number, how it is formatted, how the check digit is calculated and how numbers will be assigned and disseminated. ISSNs are applicable to all serial publications, including monographic series; for instance, ANSI Z39 standards now carry an ISSN.

Notes

The original Z39.9, *Identification Number for Serial Publications,* concisely stated a number format and how the number would be assigned. The number was adopted by ISO in 1974 as standard ISO 3297, creating the International Standard Serial Number and establishing the International Serials Data System to administer the number. The ISSN, unlike ISBN, is an "idiot number," with no meaning assigned to any portion of the number except the check digit.

The ISSN is an outstanding success in the publishing field; the standard is terse but adequate. Between 1971 and 1979, the number was adopted as an international standard, Bowker assigned tens of thousands of ISSNs based on its files of serial publications and a network of agencies was created to assign and control ISSNs, including the National Serials Data Program at the Library of Congress. While the meaningless nature of the number limits its extended usefulness, and the decisions of assigning agencies may sometimes be questioned, the ISSN has unquestionably succeeded—both in becoming well established and in making it easier to identify serial publications uniquely.

Bibliographic Reference

American National Standards Institute. *American National Standard for International Standard Serial Numbering (ISSN), ANSI Z39.9-1979 (R1984).* New York: ANSI; 1984. 8 p.

Z39.10-1971 (R1977)
DIRECTORIES OF
LIBRARIES AND INFORMATION CENTERS

This standard sets forth detailed and ambitious specifications for directories of libraries and information centers. The standard is intended to apply to all directories at the national, regional or local level.

Details

The introduction recommends that questionnaires for directories be based on the applicable specifications, clearly and concisely stated, use standard terminology and allow enough space for answers. Five short sections define directories, give content specifications for the cover, title page and foreword, recommend a geographic arrangement for most directories (but a subject arrangement or alphabetic arrangement in certain cases), recommend placement and standards for table of contents and indexes and specify format: no larger than 8¾ x 11½ inches, no thicker than 2½ inches, durable binding, 8-point or larger type, well laid out and on 40- to 80-pound book paper.

The heart of Z39.10 is section 7, "Individual Entries." This section specifies a list of information to be included for each of seven types of library and information center. Each list is explicit and quite extensive. The simplest list, that for regional libraries, cooperative systems and processing centers, contains 12 items such as name and address, telephone, Centrex, TWX, etc., purpose and scope, name and title of the head, number of staff and total annual income. The longest lists, for public libraries and college and university libraries, include over 30 items, including number of volumes, important special collections and details on automated operations actually in use. Z39.10 is currently undergoing revision; the committee doing the work is making it primarily a list of data elements, the most important part of the standard.

Related Standards

ANSI Z39.4: *Basic Criteria for Indexes,* is referred to; ANSI Z39.7, *Compiling Library Statistics,* is essential to this standard and contains definitions for many of the terms used in Z39.10.

Notes

This brief standard is clear and unambiguous, and provides a fine checklist for anyone preparing such a directory. Common American library directories appear to follow the standard in most of its details, though some of the items may be omitted. Certainly, any local or regional agency wishing to build a useful directory would be well advised to purchase and follow Z39.10; by doing so, the agency could assure a complete and useful directory, and one that would be comparable to other directories.

Bibliographic Citation

American National Standards Institute. *American National Standard for Directories of Libraries and Information Centers, ANSI Z39.10-1971 (R1979)*. New York: ANSI; 1979. 12 p.

Z39.14-1979
WRITING ABSTRACTS

This standard provides guidelines for abstracts and includes a variety of examples. The standard can cover any form of nonfiction publication but appears most suited to scholarly journals and scientific and technical publications. The standard is intended for use by authors and editors, and it recommends that authors (rather than editors) prepare abstracts.

Details

After a five-paragraph abstract, which appears to violate the standard itself ("write most abstracts in a single paragraph, except those for long documents"), an unusually long scope and definition statement defines abstracts on their own terms and by distinguishing them from annotations, extracts, summaries and synoptics: an abstract is "an abbreviated, accurate representation of the contents of a document."

A section on purpose and use includes specific recommendations for journals, reports and theses, monographs, patents and access publications: for example, *"Journals.* Include an abstract with every journal article or synoptic, essay, and discussion. Notes, short communications, editorials, and 'letters to the editor' that have substantial technical or scholarly content should also have brief abstracts."

"Treatment of Document Content" gives guidelines for preparing a proper abstract in terms of content; "Presentation and Style" gives stylistic advice ("make the abstract self-contained," "begin the abstract with a topic sentence that is a central statement of the document's major thesis...."). An appendix shows 26 different abstracts broken down into six different categories, such as "typical informative abstracts," "abstracts of monographs and chapters," "order of document-content subject elements."

Related Standards

Z39.14 is directly related to ISO 214-1976: *International Standard on Abstracts for Publications and Documentation,* which was largely based on the 1971 edition of Z39.14. The standard refers users to seven other Z39 standards, all described elsewhere in this chapter: Z39.1, Z39.5, Z39.15, Z39.16, Z39.18, Z39.29 and Z39.34.

Notes

Z39.14 is long, detailed and directly usable by any nonfiction author. Combined with the other Z39 standards referenced (particularly Z39.16, Z39.29 and, if needed, Z39.34), this standard can offer a new author a considerable advantage in producing abstracts that will be accepted and used. The foreword to the 1979 edition indicates a belief that abstracts have improved since 1971, and that Z39.14 is part of the reason for that improvement. Certainly, the standard should help to generate abstracts that are directly useful in secondary publications (abstracting and indexing services); in addition, an author's preparation of a good abstract is likely to prevent abstracting by some less knowledgeable reader.

Bibliographic Citation

American National Standards Institute. *American National Standard for Writing Abstracts, ANSI Z39.14-1979.* New York: ANSI; 1979. 15 p.

Z39.15-1980
TITLE LEAVES OF A BOOK

This standard specifies items that should be included on the title leaves of a book and, in some cases, whether the items should appear on the verso or recto of the full title leaf. The standard is for use by publishers, and it applies to all books.

Details and Notes

The list of essential information is well defined and sensible, with one possible exception: "abstracts of contents, in accordance with

American National Standard for Writing Abstracts, Z39.14-1971.'' Other items are standard, although specifications for placement may not be. In practice, nearly all books meet about half the standard and most contemporary books meet most of the standard.

Common deviations from Z39.15 seem to fall into three categories:

1. Date of publication: According to the standard, this should appear on the recto (front). Publishers appear to be evenly split as to placement of publication date. As you may note from the front of this book, Knowledge Industry Publications, Inc., uses the verso (and does not distinguish publication date from copyright date when they are the same). A small sampling of books showed that Neal-Schuman, Online, Greenwood, Hayden, Knowledge Industry, McGraw-Hill, Addison-Wesley and Prentice-Hall use the verso; ALA, Oryx, Pierian and Scarecrow use the recto.

2. Edition statement: Relatively few publishers among those sampled show ''first edition'' explicitly.

3. Abstract: Z39.15 calls for an abstract to appear ''on the verso of the title page or on the right hand page following it; separate abstracts of chapters should appear on or preceding their first pages.'' This recommendation affects only nonfiction books and monographs, but none of the books sampled included leading abstracts.

The call for abstracts is somewhat unrealistic in books other than textbooks, and it has gone largely unheeded, at least by publishers in the library field. The virtue of consistent placement of year of publication on the front of the title leaf is also unclear, though there is clearly need for inclusion of the date somewhere.

Inclusion of ISBN and LCCN is an enormous aid to librarians trying to find cataloging copy; all books checked in an informal sample, even those without Cataloging in Publication (CIP) Data, did contain both ISBN and LCCN on the verso. In each case where CIP was not included, the LCCN was explicitly labeled; most books containing CIP did not separately label the LCCN.

Bibliographic Citation

American National Standards Institute. *American National Standard for Title Leaves of a Book, ANSI Z39.15-1980.* New York: ANSI; 1980. 8 p.

Z39.16-1979
PREPARATION OF SCIENTIFIC PAPERS FOR WRITTEN OR ORAL PRESENTATION

This standard sets guidelines for scientists: when and how papers should be prepared, and how oral presentations differ from papers. The standard is primarily useful for authors in all fields of pure and applied science, but it includes some special recommendations for editors. The advice in Z39.16 will serve almost any nonfiction writer or speaker.

Details

"The purpose of this standard is to help all scientists in all disciplines to prepare papers that will have a high probability of being accepted for publication and of being noticed, read, and completely understood when they are published." After expanding on that purpose and counseling flexibility in applying the standard, Z39.16 presents a series of general recommendations. Each recommendation is one or more paragraphs; they are summarized below:

- Have something to say.

- Put it in context.

- Don't repeat yourself.

- Say it all at once.

- Know your audience and journal.

- Use an appropriate form.

- Consider secondary readers.

Ten forms of presentation are described briefly but clearly, nine written (including original articles, letters to the editor, tutorial papers and theses) and one oral. Seven sections give detailed recommendations for aspects of written presentation:

- Title, Byline, Abstract: Titles should be descriptive and avoid empty words; an author should use the words that would be used in searching for the article. All who have substantially contributed to the work should be included in the byline. Affiliations should be current for the time the work was done; as published, it should be clear that publication does not represent endorsement by the organization. Manuscripts should always begin with a self-contained abstract suitable for direct use by abstracting and indexing services.

- Body: Two pages discuss organization, description of materials and methods, presentation of results, illustrations, discussion and summary.

- Style: Good technical writing isn't much different from any other good nonfiction writing: active voice, verbs rather than abstract nouns, simple language, concise but not cryptic and so on.

- Terminology: Use standard abbreviations and symbols; explain all nonstandard abbreviations and acronyms (and avoid excessive use); use International System of Units measure (metric), but add conventional (inch-pound) measure in those fields that still use it.

- References: "References" must have been cited; other items belong in a separate bibliography. References should be to published material if possible and should include availability where documents are not readily obtainable.

- Acknowledgments, Footnotes, Appendixes: Keep acknowledgments brief, don't use many textual footnotes (as opposed to references) and use an appendix if necessary.

• Submission: Type everything double-spaced, check the final draft and make everything clear for typesetting. Try to get the draft reviewed locally before submitting it. Follow the rules of the journal: duplicate or triplicate copies, as required. Editors should acknowledge submissions as soon as received and should handle them promptly.

A final section gives guidelines for oral presentations and notes that different methods are required for effectiveness. Simplicity is even more important when speaking, and repetition of the major theme is good for talks but bad for papers. Slides should be simple, clear and kept to a reasonable number; people shouldn't be expected to look at slides all through the talk. The speaker should practice the talk before giving it.

Related Standards

A number of American National Standards, one IEEE-recommended practice document and several style manuals are cited. Z39 standards cited are Z39.14: *Writing Abstracts;* Z39.34: *Synoptics;* Z39.29: *Bibliographic References;* and Z39.5: *Abbreviation of Titles of Periodicals.* Other American National Standards cited define symbols and standard practice, such as Y15.1: *Illustrations for Publication and Projection;* Y10.5: *Letter Symbols for Quantities Used in Electrical Science and Electrical Engineering;* and Y32.14: *Graphic Symbols for Logic Diagrams.*

Notes

The standard is self-contained in matters of style and content, and it provides an excellent concise standard for scientific and technical papers. Its use by writers and editors would seem designed to assure the greatest amount of communication with the least difficulty and fewest superfluous publications. The standard does not apply to library and information ''science'' as such, though some of its recommendations would certainly help to cut the amount of excess and redundant publication in the field. Most likely, the standard is not as well used or well observed as it should be. Certainly, any scientist (or librarian) would do well to consider Z39.16; even if some of its provisions are inapplicable to a field, its general advice is sound, well written and concise.

Bibliographic Citation

American National Standards Institute. *American National Standard for the Presentation of Scientific Papers for Written or Oral Presentation, ANSI Z39.16-1979.* New York: ANSI; 1979. 16 p.

Z39.18-1974
GUIDELINES FOR FORMAT AND PRODUCTION OF SCIENTIFIC AND TECHNICAL REPORTS

Where Z39.16 gives guidelines for content and presentation of reports and articles, Z39.18 gives guidelines for format and applies specifically to technical reports published as such. The standard is for use by those who prepare reports for dissemination, including publishers. Most of its recommendations apply only to reports intended for dissemination, whether in manuscript, reproducible copy, duplicated or printed form or microform.

Details

This standard gives specific guidelines for the order of elements within a technical report. The front cover is specified in detail, with elements and their order specified, from report number through name and address of the sponsoring organization (if different from the performing organization). Z39.18 specifies a standard report documentation page to appear following the front cover; an appendix describes each element of the standard page and includes a blank form intended for reproduction.

Other elements of a proper technical report are described briefly, with additional ANSI standards cited as appropriate (largely the same standards cited in Z39.16). Illustrations receive some special attention: how to substitute for color, where to place labels and how to number illustrations. A series of guidelines for report production include a minimum of 8-point type, with 10-point being preferred; single or line-and-a-half spacing for reproduced typewritten reports;

left justification on all columns; one inch or larger margins on all sides; and standard page size, with both sides of sheets being used "to the maximum extent practicable."

Notes

Since the standard includes and explains a reproducible Report Documentation Page and clearly explains the guidelines given, it requires no other documents (except those standards cited) for direct implementation. Its use appears to improve accessibility to technical reports, and the standard (and standard Report Documentation Page) does seem to be widely used.

Z39.18 is more concerned with form, where Z39.16 is primarily concerned with content. The two standards work together to improve the quality and accessibility of scientific and technical presentations.

Bibliographic Citation

American National Standards Institute. *American National Standard Guidelines for Format and Production of Scientific and Technical Reports, ANSI Z39.18-1974.* New York: ANSI; 1974. 16 p.

Z39.19-1980
GUIDELINES FOR THESAURUS STRUCTURE, CONSTRUCTION, AND USE

Librarians and information specialists design and use controlled vocabularies or "authority lists." This standard presents rules and conventions for building and maintaining such a vocabulary, including needed references and scope notes. The standard can be used to build a thesaurus of terms for any use and in any field.

Details

In common and dictionary use, a thesaurus is specifically a dictionary of synonyms; the first task of Z39.19 is to use the different definition common to library and information science: "a compilation of words and phrases showing synonyms, hierarchical, and other relationships and dependencies, the function of which is to provide a standardized vocabulary for information storage and retrieval.'' The key difference is that a common thesaurus would suggest synonyms, where a thesaurus for vocabulary control specifies which synonyms are used and which are not.

A term should represent a single concept and may use more than one word. Nouns are better than verbs, singular forms should be used except for classes of things (''painting'' is process or method, ''paintings'' are objects). Multiword terms should appear in natural order, with cross-references from the inverted form if appropriate. Punctuation should be minimal. Relationships should be specified as Broader Term, Narrower Term, Use, Used For or Related Term. Scope notes and qualifications should be used as needed. Terms should appear in alphabetic order; hierarchical, network and permuted displays may be added. Alphabetical order can be letter-by-letter or word-by-word, and the choice should be stated.

A lengthy section concerns the process of identifying concepts, selecting terms and determining relationships. This section recommends that a draft thesaurus be used for some period, and recommends a process for maintenance of the thesaurus, including a sample ''Thesaurus Term Review'' form. Appendixes show a sample terminology chart and a thesaurus term review form suitable for reproduction.

Notes

The standard is well constructed and quite explicit, and it provides sufficiently clear guidelines to design a thesaurus. While there are some examples, most users would also want to examine a sampling of existing thesauri before developing a new one. Naturally, librarians and information specialists working in a field should check for availability of a thesaurus before setting out to build a new one.

Even with clear guidelines, building a controlled vocabulary is slow and expensive; it makes sense to use existing sources where practical, and to use an existing thesaurus as a basis for a new one if possible. Z39.19 is also useful in this case; its guidelines for maintaining a thesaurus are clear, and the sample form appears useful.

Bibliographic Citation

American National Standards Institute. *American National Standard Guidelines for Thesaurus Structure, Construction, and Use, ANSI Z39.19-1980.* New York: ANSI; 1980. 20 p.

Z39.20-1983
CRITERIA FOR PRICE INDEXES FOR LIBRARY MATERIALS

Z39.20 provides criteria for developing price indexes for library materials, in order to measure change in average list price over time. The standard applies to seven categories of library material: hardcover and paperback books, periodicals, serials services, newspapers, nonprint media and library-produced microfilm. Trade catalogs, scores, maps, school textbooks, multivolume encyclopedias and some "transitory" materials are specifically excluded.

Details

General specifications include full definition of materials and time covered, country or countries of publication, subject classification (for indexes arranged by subject) and methodology. These specifications also call for all prices to be stated in a single currency.

Specific guidelines follow for each of the seven types of material. For instance, a "book" has at least 49 pages, "periodicals" exclude annuals and a "daily newspaper" must be published "on five consecutive days of each week of the calendar year, except for major religious, local or national holidays that occur on weekdays." (College newspapers are apparently not daily newspapers by this definition.) Methods of determining prices and averages are also stated. Some, but not all, indexes are specified as being broken down by subject.

Notes

The standard is clearly written and suitable for use by any library wishing to maintain its own price indexes, and it would allow a library to make sensible comparisons of its own indexes with nationally published indexes. The standard is being used by those agencies that prepare national price indexes for library materials.

Bibliographic Citation

American National Standards Institute. *American National Standard for Library and Information Sciences and Related Publishing Practices—Library Materials—Criteria for Price Indexes, ANSI Z39.20-1983.* New York: ANSI; 1983. 12 p.

Z39.21-1980
BOOK NUMBERING

This standard specifies construction of an ISBN (International Standard Book Number). The standard is intended for use by all publishers; ISBNs are useful for all who buy, sell, distribute or retrieve books. Its scope is all book publication within the United States.

The standard specifies what an ISBN should represent (one title, from one publisher, in one edition), how ISBNs are formulated and where the ISBN should appear on books. Appendixes include the procedure for calculating the check digit, hyphenation instructions for ISBNs beginning with "0," assignment of the Standard Book Numbering Agency to R. R. Bowker and a statement of functions for that agency. Z39.21 is the American implementation of ISO standard 2108. It is almost universally used for current books, and it is used to some extent for other materials. Bowker regards the ISBN as appropriate for software numbering and has been assigning ISBN prefixes to software publishers, although a separate NISO (Z39) subcommittee is working on a separate software numbering standard.

Bibliographic Citation

American National Standards Institute. *American National Standard for Book Numbering, ANSI Z39.21-1980.* New York: ANSI; 1980. 8 p.

Z39.23-1983
STANDARD TECHNICAL REPORT NUMBER (STRN), FORMAT AND CREATION

This standard establishes the STRN, a standard number for technical reports. All technical reports, including those produced on nonprint media, are included in the scope of the standard.

Details

After defining a technical report, Z39.23 defines the STRN: a two-part code consisting of a report code (from two to 14 characters) and a sequential group (from one to seven characters), separated by a hyphen. Further definitions cover each portion: what characters may be used, what punctuation is allowed, an optional local suffix and how it is marked.

The remaining portions of the standard show how STRNs are formatted and used, specify uniqueness and specify that a maintenance agency shall monitor the system and coordinate assignment of report codes (not sequential groups). A brief appendix establishes the National Technical Information Service (NTIS) as the maintenance agency.

Related Standards

Z39.23 specifies placement of the STRN in terms of the format called for in ANSI Z39.18-1974: *Guidelines for Format and Production of Scientific and Technical Reports.*

Notes

Like ISBN (and unlike ISSN), the STRN carries significance within its structure; because it is alphanumeric, an STRN can be partly mnemonic. Unlike most other standard numbers, the STRN varies in length (from four to 22 characters). The STRN was devised "in an attempt to bring order and consistency into a heretofore uncontrolled and chaotic bibliographical field." With good publicity from NTIS and good support by other agencies, the standard can help achieve that goal.

Two key steps in implementing STRN were the establishment of the maintenance agency and provision of a USMARC field to store the STRN in bibliographic records. When the USMARC Books format was extended to cover technical reports, Field 024 was defined for Standard Technical Report Numbers. Subfield ‡‡u in Field 773 (Host Item Entry) and in some other linking entries allows storage of an STRN.

Bibliographic Citation

American National Standards Institute. *American National Standard for Library and Information Sciences and Related Publishing Practices—Standard Technical Report Number (STRN)— Format and Creation, ANSI Z39.23-1983.* New York: ANSI; 1983. 8 p.

Z39.24-1976
SYSTEM FOR THE ROMANIZATION OF SLAVIC CYRILLIC CHARACTERS

Z39.24 provides for standardized romanization of Cyrillic letters used in Russian, Ukrainian, Byelorussian, Serbian, Macedonian and Bulgarian. The standard consists of a romanization table for the modern Russian alphabet followed by a romanization table for Slavic Cyrillic alphabets, with a small number of deviations depending on the source language. Footnotes provide further variations "when it is desirable to respect particular characteristics of Ukrainian, Byelorussian, and Bulgarian."

Related Standards

This standard is based on *ISO Recommendation R-9 1968, International System for the Transliteration of Slavic Cyrillic Characters,* incorporating variations pertinent to the United States.

Notes

Transliteration of Russian names has been a problem for many years, because traditional transliterations vary and tend not to match standard transliterations. This scheme is straightforward and as easy to apply as any other scheme. It uses a minimum of diacritical marks, and it appears to be usable by a nonspeaker, though precise use requires that the user at least know what language a work is in. Whether the romanization is fully reversible is a bit unclear.

Bibliographic Citation

American National Standards Institute. *American National Standard System for the Romanization of Slavic Cyrillic Characters, ANSI Z39.24-1976.* New York: ANSI; 1976. 10 p.

Z39.27-1984
STRUCTURE FOR THE REPRESENTATION OF NAMES OF COUNTRIES, DEPENDENCIES, AND AREAS OF SPECIAL SOVEREIGNTY FOR INFORMATION INTERCHANGE

This standard "provides a structure for the representation of names of the basic geopolitical entities of the world for purposes of general information interchange."

Details

Z39.27 specifies two standard codes: a two-character alphabetic code "recommended for purposes of international information interchange" and a three-character alphabetic code "that is derived from the entity name and serves the requirements for visual and mnemonic value." Two-letter and three-letter codes beginning AA, XA-XZ and ZZ, are reserved for private use and provisional codes. The standard provides that a list of current names and codes will be maintained by the National Bureau of Standards.

Related Standards

This standard is based on ISO 3166-1981: *Code for the Representation of Names of Countries,* though the NBS list adds additional codes.

Notes

The standard is essentially useless by itself, depending entirely on the list maintained by the National Bureau of Standards. Notably, the USMARC codes for Place of Publication or Production do not conform to Z39.27, at least in the majority of MARC records: for the United States, Great Britain, the USSR and Canada, three-character codes are used in which the first two characters represent a political subdivision (state, province or republic), and the third character represents the larger body. Thus, for the largest single use of information interchange within the library community, Z39.27 is not in use and is not likely to be used.

Bibliographic Citation

American National Standards Institute. *American National Standard for Library and Information Sciences and Related Publishing Practices—Structure for the Representation of Names of Countries, Dependencies, and Areas of Special Sovereignty for Information Interchange, ANSI Z39.27-1984.* New York: ANSI; 1984. 8 p.

Z39.29-1977
BIBLIOGRAPHIC REFERENCES

This standard provides guidelines for preparing bibliographic references: citations, entries in bibliographies and references in abstracting and indexing publications. It should be used by writers, editors and publishers. The scope is limited to bibliographies, citations and the like: catalogs, union lists, etc., are not covered. The scope of materials covered in the rules for citation include anything "in some finite form recoverable by the reader"—including all media, but not including unrecorded interviews or speeches for which neither recordings nor manuscripts exist.

Details

An extensive 17-page glossary defines all terms relevant to the standard, including each bibliographic element considered suitable for citations. Following the glossary, six pages of principles and guidelines provide rules and rationale for the standard. The standard provides for hierarchical levels (article within journal, chapter within book within series); for distinctions among essential, recommended and optional elements for citations; and for citations in author-first or title-first form.

Guidelines include recommended sources of bibliographic elements, methods for showing missing information, methods for handling nonprint media and the sequence of bibliographic elements within a reference. Rationales are stated for the order of elements. A limited and unambiguous set of punctuation is defined. The standard as stated recommends that "bibliographic references be presented in a single typeface for the sake of simplicity and convenience," but it leaves the choice of typeface and the use of underscores or italics to the publisher or user. Capitalization may follow either of two standard rules: capitalize each significant word in a title, or capitalize only the first word and proper nouns. Quotation marks for articles or chapters within larger works are optional, not required.

The guidelines of Z39.29 are somewhat dense for everyday use. Appendix A, *Applications of the Standard,* makes the standard easier to implement. The appendix is 50 pages long, a superb piece of work with fine organization and many carefully annotated examples. Dozens of simple and complex situations are analyzed, using real examples that clarify the application of the rules.

Related Standards

Z39.29 refers to a number of other standards: ANSI Z39.1, Z39.5, Z39.9, Z39.16, Z39.23 and X3.30-1971; ISO R30-1956(E), R690-1968(E), 832-1968, 833-1974, 2108-1972(E), 2145-1972 and others. All the Z39 and X3 standards are discussed in this chapter and Chapter 11; some of the ISO standards are discussed in Chapter 12.

Notes

Z39.29 is a clear and admirable standard. Implementation requires only that authors, editors, publishers or some combination of the three agree that the standard is worth supporting. In practice, the standard appears to be easier to use than other guidelines for bibliographic references. For authors wishing to use the standard, the modest cost of the standard is worthwhile, since Appendix A provides a simple way to prepare standard and sufficient bibliographic citations.

Furthermore, Z39.29 is well suited to computer support. The logical order of elements and minimal punctuation make it relatively easy to transform MARC records (whether monographic or analytical) into Z39.29 citations, and at least one microcomputer software package is on the market which will generate Z39.29 references based on direct data entry or downloaded data from bibliographic services or database services.

There are two problems with Z39.29, both of which appear to have slowed its acceptance. First, the default form of standard references is a bit clumsy because it does not use quotation marks or italics. This is a problem only of the default and of ANSI's use of default formats in its publication. The two citations that follow are both legitimate Z39.29 citations; the second is much easier to read than the first:

> Frase, Robert W. Procedures for development and access to published standards. Library Trends. 31(2): 225-236; 1982 Fall.

> Frase, Robert W. "Procedures for development and access to published standards." *Library Trends*. 31(2): 225-236; 1982 Fall.

The second problem is one of history and inertia. Most publications and publishers have long-established house styles for citations, most commonly based on *A Manual of Style* from the University of Chicago Press. Z39.29 has not been widely publicized and promoted. The Fall 1982 issue of *Library Trends*, on Technical Standards for Library and Information Science, carried this foreword:

> In an effort to get this issue to its readership in a timely manner, and because our standard for bibliographic citations has always been *The Chicago Manual of Style* (University of Chicago Press), we have not followed Issue Editor Rush's request to use the newer ANSI standard for citation formats.

> Although individual authors were asked to follow the ANSI standard, they either could not or would not do so, and we therefore chose to follow our past policy and practice. Let the record show that Dr. Rush would have preferred the ANSI standards—one of life's little ironies.[4]

Five years after Z39.29 was published it was still considered "the newer ANSI standard" and largely unused. This situation continues today, to the point where an author may still expect to argue if he or she wishes to use Z39.29 style. However, as mentioned in Chapter 2, citations in this book follow the ANSI standard.

Bibliographic Citation

American National Standards Institute. *American National Standard for Bibliographic References, ANSI Z39.29-1977.* New York: ANSI; 1977. 92 p.

Z39.30-1982
ORDER FORM FOR SINGLE TITLES OF LIBRARY MATERIALS IN 3-INCH BY 5-INCH FORMAT

This standard establishes a standard 3-inch x 5-inch or 3-inch x 10-inch order form suitable for ordering one title. It is designed for use by libraries and those who supply forms to libraries. The standard may be used for serials and monographs, but it is limited to single titles and does not allow for return information.

Details

The standard defines two sets of terms: those used in the standard that do not appear on the order form (purchaser, supplier, library materials) and those that do appear on the order form (title, author, edition, etc.). Definitions for items that do appear include the number of characters available for each element. For instance, the title can run to 87 characters, author to 57 characters, publisher to 27 characters, and series name to 26 characters. Special instructions can run to 78 characters.

After these definitions, the standard states four categories of data elements: item description, conditions of order, local data and instructions to supplier. Dimensions are stated: 3 inches x 5 inches (not 75mm x 125mm), with an optional second 3-inch x 5-inch right-hand portion for custom imprinting. Color and number of copies are explicitly not stated; a sample filled-in form is included, as are three different versions of the blank form, suitable for copying and reproduction: a version suitable for typing, a version for continuous-form stock (suitable for computer printing) and the 3-inch x 10-inch version.

An appendix provides instructions for completing the order form, e.g., *"Title:* Enter the distinguishing name of the material being ordered which forms a separate whole, whether issued in one or several volumes, units, or parts. The title field also includes the number of volumes, units, or parts in a multiunit title. 87 print positions."

Related Standards

Z39.30 refers to Z39.43-1980: *Identification Code for the Book Industry (SAN)* and cites ISBN and ISSN without referring to the actual standards.

Notes

The standard form is typical of those actually in use, and has the virtue of providing a checklist of data elements; for those libraries that prepare orders on a typewriter, and that prepare a separate form for each title, the standard form should be helpful. The biggest drawback for such use is that the form makes no provision whatsoever for vendor reply: there are no specifications for back-of-form response areas, and the standard specifically excludes provision for vendor response.

For computer-produced orders, the form seems to have too many small data areas, and to provide a large number of unnecessary labels that restrict flexibility. When RLG was designing an order form, it seemed clear that a computer-generated order should be as open as possible, so that space not needed for short or missing elements could be used for other purposes. For research libraries and some public libraries, spaces for descriptive data elements may not be long enough; based on RLIN experience, the space provided for special messages is clearly insufficient. The inflexibility of the form makes the already small 3-inch x 5-inch area even smaller.

When standards such as this are proposed, some statement may be needed of the intended beneficiaries. Libraries who prepare manual orders can certainly benefit from availability of an inexpensive standard form with sufficient specifications to assure that enough information reaches the supplier. A statement of data elements which should be included in orders is also useful; a standard limited to such a list, as the Z39 standards on promotional material are limited to lists of data elements, would serve all libraries and all book suppliers.

A reasonable guess is that the primary economic benefit of Z39.30 comes from the list of data elements, not the form itself. Certainly, orders are more likely to be filled correctly and promptly if the supplier has proper information, as long as that information is unambiguously printed and legible; however, it seems unlikely that a supplier would favor a particular format. By including not only the data list but the form in the standard, Z39.30 narrows the possibilities for compliance. (To use RLG as an example, the 3½-inch x 7⅜-inch orders produced in RLIN do include all the data elements specified in Z39.30, but the form is entirely different; thus, though RLG orders are high quality and follow the pertinent portions of the standard, the orders cannot be called standard.)

Bibliographic Citation

American National Standards Institute. *American National Standard for Order Form for Single Titles of Library Materials, Z39.30-1982.* New York: ANSI; 1982. 15 p.

Z39.31-1976 (R1983)
FORMAT FOR SCIENTIFIC AND
TECHNICAL TRANSLATIONS

This standard provides format requirements for translations of scientific and technical material, so that the translations will be useful for researchers, librarians and others. It is intended for use by translators and those preparing translations for publication; it covers all translations, but does not cover abstracts of material in one language that are prepared in another language.

Details

The body of the standard includes five major sections: general forms of publication, particular forms of publication, presentation, translator's notes, and special features of the original text. Some of the points covered are as follows:

• General forms of publication: Any translation should be properly identified, including type of translation, substantive changes to the original, the translated title, its original context, place and date of publication and name and address of translation publisher or source. The original should be identified by its original title (transliterated if necessary), location in original serial (if an article) with the title of the serial in the original language, name and affiliation of the author and other elements.

• Particular forms: Specifications for identification are stated for books, conference proceedings, dissertations, cover-to-cover translations of periodicals, report literature and patent documents.

• Presentation: Guidelines for typography, arrangement, tables, formulas and illustrations are given, generally stating that the translation should follow the patterns of the original.

• Special features: Specific provisions for footnotes, captions, bibliography, symbols, units and other areas finish out the standard.

Related Standards

Four other standards are cited as applicable in some cases: Z39.15, Z39.16, Z39.18 and Z39.23; these are summarized earlier in this chapter.

Notes

As with several other Z39 standards, Z39.31 provides a useful checklist for those preparing documents; it does not impose excessive overhead, and it is designed to make translations more easily accessible. While it will not in any sense assist the translation process, it should help researchers in locating translations and using them.

Bibliographic Citation

American National Standards Institute. *American National Standard Format for Scientific and Technical Translations, ANSI Z39.31-1976 (R1983)*. New York: ANSI; 1983. 10 p.

Z39.32-1981
INFORMATION ON MICROFICHE HEADINGS

Z39.32 recommends eye-legible headings for microfiche intended for use in libraries and information centers. The standard is limited to standard microfiche and to those headings actually created as part of the microfiche.

Details

The standard specifies positive polarity (dark letters on a clear background), type size at least 1.5mm high (a small type, roughly 4 point), and the content and arrangement recommended. The heading consists of three areas: identification, document description and sequential information. Elements that should be included in the document description area are specified, and some examples are given.

Related Standards

Z39.32 explicitly calls for use of the following ANSI standards where applicable: ANSI/NMA MS5-1975: *Microfiche of Documents;* ANSI Z39.5-1969: *Abbreviation of Titles of Periodi-*

cals; ANSI Z39.29-1977: *Bibliographic References;* the standard number standards Z39.9, Z39.21 and Z39.23; and the Romanization standards Z39.11, Z39.12, Z39.24, Z39.25, Z39.35 and Z39.37.

Bibliographic Citation

American National Standards Institute. *American National Standard for Information on Microfiche Headings, ANSI Z39.32-1981.* New York: ANSI; 1981. 12 p.

Z39.33-1977 (R1982)
DEVELOPMENT OF IDENTIFICATION CODES FOR USE BY THE BIBLIOGRAPHIC COMMUNITY

Z39.33 is a standard for standards: a set of considerations for development of new standard numbers or standard codes. It is intended for use by agencies developing standard numbers or codes. Its scope is limited to the bibliographic community and, naturally, to standard identifiers developed after adoption of the standard.

Details

The standard is concise; it calls for statements of scope and purpose, precise description of the proposed code format and guidance for users. A set of general considerations and comments on composition and characteristics follow: for instance, the format of a code should be distinctive and should not duplicate other codes, codes should use check digits where appropriate, and there should be a code authority for any new code. A code identifier (such as "ISBN," "ISSN," "STRN") should be established for any new code.

Notes

Z39.33 has only a narrow use; it is really only useful when developing new standard identifiers. Within that realm, it is a clear statement, though at least two of its points are arguable and not necessarily in line with existing standards or common desiderata: "4.4. Numeric representation should be used in applications where there is no compelling requirement for alpha or alphanumeric representation, since numerics are widely used and will facilitate the use of new code standards on a national and international scale. . . . 5.1.3. The format of a code, as specified in its applicable standard, should be fixed, not variable." The first statement makes it difficult to develop mnemonic codes, and the second is ambiguous.

One inclusion in Z39.33 appears directly aimed at NUC codes: "4.6. If upper- and lower-case letters are to be used when displaying alphabetic code values, the case of the letters should be derivable by algorithm." The reason for this provision is unclear, but it and the call for fixed-length codes would both seem to rule out NUC codes as feasible standard institutional codes, despite their long history of successful use.

The recommendations for numeric characters or single-case alphabetics seem odd for a standard adopted as late as 1977. By that time, one would expect that all or nearly all machine processes would be equally able to handle alphabetic and numeric characters, and that the great majority of systems would be able to handle lower-case and upper-case alphabetics.

Z39.33 does explicitly allow for mnemonic codes, stating that "any code constructed with mnemonic purposes should be fully explained and illustrated by examples." Still, the standard seems to be overly restrictive in terms of machine capabilities and the success of preexisting standards. Since only one new identification code (SAN: Z39.43) has been adopted since 1977, there is no clear indication of the value of this standard.

Bibliographic Citation

American National Standards Institute. *American National Standard for the Development of Identification Codes for Use by the Bibliographic Community, ANSI Z39.33-1977 (R1982)*. New York: ANSI; 1982. 8 p.

Z39.34-1977 (R1983)
SYNOPTICS

This standard defines a concise form, called a "synoptic," in which the gist of a scientific or technical paper may be published in a primary journal. The "synoptic" (a new term derived from synopsis) must be prepared by the author and must represent a full paper that is available at the same time. The standard is intended for use by authors and journals; its scope is largely limited to scientific and technical papers.

Details

Z39.34 is an extensive standard, including examples of actual synoptics taken from scientific journals. It defines a synoptic carefully: "A concise (usually two-page) first publication...of those key ideas and results...that are judged most important and most directly useful to others." The definition continues to require that a synoptic and the full paper be reviewed and accepted before either is published, that the full paper be available and that the synoptic be no longer than "approximately one-third the length of the average full paper." A synoptic must contain an abstract (and is clearly differentiated from an abstract, letter or note).

Detailed sections on parts of a synoptic, style and clarity, length, requirements for the full papers and citation practices make the form and function of synoptics quite clear. An interesting small section suggests that "if machine-readable systems are developed and employed for scientific papers, it may be possible to code the sections and subsections of a full paper in such a way as to permit the extraction of a synoptic from the full paper."

Related Standards

This standard refers to other Z39 standards for papers, abstracts and references: Z39.14, Z39.16 and Z39.29.

Notes

Z39.34 has fairly narrow application at this point, since relatively few journals have gone to either dual publication (where the "synoptic" appears in hardcopy and the full paper is available in microform or on request) or strict publication of "synoptics." The standard does appear to provide good, detailed guidelines for "synoptics," and it seems straightforward to apply. As noted in the standard, it can save typesetting and printing costs but actually increases the author's—and reviewers'—work. For those required to prepare synoptics, the standard would appear to be an essential tool.

Bibliographic Citation

American National Standards Institute. *American National Standard for Synoptics, ANSI Z39.34-1977 (R1983).* New York: ANSI; 1983. 19 p.

Z39.41-1979
BOOK SPINE FORMATS

This standard specifies information that should appear on the spine of a book and how it should appear. It applies to all books and is to be used by publishers and book designers.

Details

A page of definitions consists primarily of illustrations showing books with descending spine title (type that reads sideways if the book lies flat, cover up), pillar spine title (upright letters appearing one to a line, reading top to bottom), or transverse spine title (type in a line at right angles to the spine), and the 32mm space to be reserved at the bottom of the spine for library use. "Essential information" to appear on a spine includes author(s), title, series and the library identification field (the blank space), which may contain the publisher's colophon or name.

The standard is brief, clear and modest in its requirements; most books appear to meet the standard. The most likely failure to meet the standard would be author or title lines extending into the bottom 32mm of the spine; when this happens, it is probably through ignorance of the standard. (A quick survey of books on hand showed only one work, published by a small library publisher, that put the authors' names within the bottom 32mm.)

Bibliographic Citation

American National Standards Institute. *American National*

Standard for Book Spine Formats, ANSI Z39.41-1979. New York: ANSI; 1979. 8 p.

Z39.43-1980
IDENTIFICATION CODE FOR THE BOOK INDUSTRY

Z39.43 is a short, clear standard providing "a unique numeric identification for each address of each organization, in or served by the book industry, that is engaged in repetitive transactions with other members of this group, in order to facilitate communications among them." The standard establishes the Standard Address Number (SAN), a six-digit number (plus check digit) sufficient to accommodate 1,000,000 addresses.

The standard is designed for use by publishers, jobbers, bookstores, distributors and libraries. In the initial pass, 278,000 numbers were assigned by R. R. Bowker, and 100,000 were reserved for special use; a pool of over 600,000 numbers remains. The standard establishes Bowker as the assignment agency. As with other numbering standards, an appendix specifies calculation of check digit for SAN.

Notes

When adopted, SAN seemed to be the "agency identifier." That was not the case; another NISO committee is now considering standard library identifiers. SAN sees some use, and is supported by a number of agencies, but it did not establish a single standard for addresses in the library community. As with some other NISO standards, Z3.43 raises the question of worth: does the standard cover enough ground and provide enough information to promise savings equal to the cost of writing the standard?

Bibliographic Citation

American National Standards Institute. *American National Standard Identification Code for the Book Industry, ANSI Z39.43-1980.* New York: ANSI; 1980. 8 p.

dp Z39.44
SERIAL HOLDINGS STATEMENTS

This draft standard specifies methods to identify, record and display holdings information for serials, at any of four levels of specificity. The standard only defines holding elements but defines those for all serial publications in all physical formats. The standard supersedes Z39.42: *Serial Holdings Statements at the Summary Level,* since it specifies summary and detailed holdings statements.

Details

This long and detailed draft consists of eight textual sections and three appendixes. The eight sections provide explicit, carefully written details on data elements, their meanings, when the elements are required or recommended and how they work together. Some of the areas are as follows:

• Scope, Principles and Guidelines: Holdings should show what a library has, not what it lacks. Holdings should be linked to bibliographic records unambiguously, using any link desired. The standard is independent of cataloging systems, accommodates manual and automated systems, requires unique locational data but does not specify its construction and does not require or recommend special typographic conventions other than punctuation. Four levels are defined: level 1, serial identification and location; level 2, adding date of recording, physical form, completeness, acquisition and retention policy, and local notes; level 3, adding enumeration or chronology; and level 4, adding more detailed enumeration or chronology.

• Glossary: A detailed glossary covering more than 50 terms used in the standard.

• Punctuation: A minimal and unambiguous set of punctuation carrying meaning: for instance, a comma indicates a break or gap in holdings; a semicolon indicates a break in publication.

• Data Areas and Elements: A table and set of guidelines for data elements, and areas containing those elements, for each of the four levels; for instance, the "status data area" includes date of report, type of holdings, physical form, completeness, acquisition status and retention elements for levels 3 and 4. Each coded element (such as "type of holdings") has a code list; each element has an explanatory section.

• Recording and Display Guidelines, by level: Four sections, one for each level. Level 1 is relatively brief, level 2 even briefer (but incorporating level 1); level 3 quite long and detailed (and incorporating levels 1 and 2), and level 4 as long as the others combined (and incorporating levels 1 and 2).

The first appendix diagrams 11 examples of holdings statements at various levels, to illustrate use of the standard. The second appendix shows possible alternatives for correlating enumeration and chronology clearly, when such correlation is not inherent in the holdings level. The last appendix is a table of physical form designations in coded and text form, such as "hg" or "Microopaque" for microopaque microforms.

Notes

As stated, the standard could be implemented on its own in a manual system, but it represents a fairly complex, if clearly defined, method for manual recording. In practice, implementation of levels 3 and 4 is dependent on good computer-supported systems. As a result, the fate of Z39.44 is closely linked to the MARC Holdings Format.[5] The two were developed in parallel, with significant changes in the Holdings Format being made when the original Z39.42 (Summary) and proposed Z39.44 (Detail) were merged into a single standard.

Levels 3 and 4 do provide clear and explicit forms for recording holdings, even when detailed holdings must be recorded. The standard at these levels does not appear to be easily applied, but it does seem to be about as good as any other method for recording detailed holdings. The complexities of the Holdings Format are directly based on the complexities of Z39.44 (and vice versa). It is much too early to judge the general usefulness or likely use of Z39.44; as with the Holdings Format, it is probably the best general solution available.

Bibliographic Citation

Draft Proposed American National Standard for Serial Holdings Statements, ANSI Z39.44. Draft.

Z39.45-1983
CLAIMS FOR MISSING ISSUES OF SERIALS

This standard specifies data elements to be included in serial claims; an appendix suggests a preprinted form for such claims. The standard is limited to claims for missing issues on serial subscriptions; it excludes claims for monographs, invoices or renewal notices.

Details

The standard itself consists of a series of data elements to be supplied by the claimant (library), such as title, publisher, pieces claimed, ISSN and a supplier response section "to simplify the task of responding to the claim," based on the 16 responses that F. W. Faxon Co. asserts account for 98% of supplier responses to claims.

The two appendixes include a preprinted blank claim form with notes on its design and use, examples of completed claim forms and examples of computer-produced claim forms and video displays. The "video display" is clearly a typed printed form, in no way comparable to a video display; the computer-produced claim form is nearly as busy as the overly busy printed form.

Related Standards

Standards specifically used include ANSI X3.30-1971, Z39.1, Z39.9, Z39.42 and Z39.43; ASTM E250-76 *(Recommended Practice for Use of CODEN)*; and ISO 3297-1975, the international version of ANSI Z39.9 (ISSN).

Notes

The recommended blank form, designed to be a preprint form comparable to the ALA ILL form, is clear enough and could be used by almost any library. It is a classic multipart form with minimal space for a bibliographic description and 21 separate data areas on the top half, 18 on the bottom half. It is difficult to predict how widely this standard will be or should be used; its implementation is certainly limited by the deliberate decision to require separate forms for monographic and invoice claims, and by a design that restricts the amount of information that can be provided by demanding too many explicit slots for information.

As with Z39.30 (the standard order form), Z39.45 suffers from including two different levels within a single standard. The list of data elements is sound and appears applicable to all claims, whether produced manually or by computer. The specified form is useful for manually produced claims as a prompting device, but appears unnecessary for computer-produced claims.

RLG includes all data elements specified in the standard (except CODEN), except that dates of previous claims are not included and dates are given in traditional "mm/dd/yy" form rather than "YYMMDD" form. Notably, the descriptive portion of the standard calls for "YY/MM/DD" form, but the standard on which it relies, and the examples, show the unpunctuated "YYMMDD." (Actually, the standard calls for CCYYMMDD, that is, August 1, 1978 would appear as "19780801.") RLG makes no distinction between serial claims and monographic claims: the material claimed should make that distinction. Having worked with the RLG form (which allows much clearer bibliographic data and much more space for special notes), I believe that the requirement for a separate serials claim form is unnecessary complication. The standard is valuable as a list of elements that should be included in claims; its value as prescribing a claim form is much less clear.

Bibliographic Citation

American National Standards Institute. *American National Standard for Library and Information Sciences and Related Publishing Practices—Serials—Claims for Missing Issues, ANSI Z39.45-1983.* New York: ANSI; 1983. 15 p.

Z39.46-1983
IDENTIFICATION OF BIBLIOGRAPHIC DATA ON AND RELATING TO PATENT DOCUMENTS

This standard specifies the minimum bibliographic data elements for the first page of a patent document and means whereby those elements can be identified without knowledge of the language or patent laws involved. The scope is general to the bibliographic community.

Details

The standard itself consists of about 50 data elements, 18 of them required, and some rules for use of those elements and identifying codes. Each data element is identified by an Internationally Agreed Number for the Identification of Data, or INID code, which is to precede the element in a circle or parentheses.

INID codes are central to the standard, because they explicitly identify each bibliographic element without recourse to punctuation or language. Thanks to the INID codes, the standard need not (and does not) specify any order for data. It does allow for use in official gazettes, where INID codes are displayed "in a representative specimen entry" and omitted from individual entries following the same uniform pattern.

Examples of elements and INID codes: 11, "Number of the document"; 25, "Language in which the published application was originally filed"; 51, "International Patent Classification"; 72, "Name(s) of inventor(s), if known to be such."

Notes

Given the INID codes and their placement, the standard is clear and appears universally applicable. The abstract states, "Users of patent documents and patent gazettes often encounter difficulties in identifying the bibliographic data on or relating to patent documents." Therefore, widespread use of the standard would appear to alleviate those difficulties. Use of the standard appears to impose a minimal overhead on those filing patent documents; the bibliographic elements are clearly stated and should be straightforward to provide. In practice, provision of the standard should also serve as a checklist for those preparing patent documents, to assure that all needed identification elements have been included.

Bibliographic Citation

American National Standards Institute. *American National Standard for Library and Information Sciences and Related Publishing Practices—Patent Documents—Identification of Bibliographic Data, ANSI Z39.46-1983.* New York: ANSI; 1983. 8 p.

Z39.47-1985
EXTENDED LATIN ALPHABET CODED CHARACTER SET FOR BIBLIOGRAPHIC USE

This standard establishes a set of characters defined as proper extensions to the standard ASCII character set. Characters defined are generally those that were defined over a decade ago in "ALA Extended ASCII" and used in USMARC records for many years. Characters that required nonstandard code sequences in ALA Extended ASCII also require special code sequences in Z39.47, but the sequences required follow ANSI standards. Z39.47 is intended for use in USMARC records and similar interchange of bibliographic information.

Z39.47 does establish most of the ALA extensions as standard ANSI extensions, and it adds a few more characters (inverted exclamation, inverted question and degree sign). The first few proposals for this standard also incorporated the limited set of superscript and subscript characters already in ALA Extended ASCII, as well as the three Greek letters alpha, beta and gamma. Those first versions would have made all accepted ALA Extended ASCII characters storable as single characters and would have simplified storage and transmission of bibliographic data.

The final version took a more theoretically sound tack, saying that standard escape sequences should be used for *all* superscripts, *all* subscripts and *all* Greek characters, disregarding the practical situation that printing systems devised to support library needs do not typically support any superscripts, subscripts or Greek letters beyond those in ALA Extended ASCII.

Since, however, the escape sequences needed for those characters are not yet established as standard ISO escape sequences, standard Z39.47 leaves MARC processing agencies in a state of suspension. In any case, records transmitted after adoption of the standard will have values different from those transmitted before adoption. This standard is one case in which consistent definition may well have beneficial long-term effects but will certainly hamper short-term adoption and use.

Bibliographic Citation

American National Standards Institute. *American National Standard for Latin Alphabet Coded Character Set for Bibliographic Use, ANSI Z39.47-1985*. New York: ANSI; 1985.

Z39.48-1984
PERMANENCE OF PAPER
FOR PRINTED LIBRARY MATERIALS

This standard sets criteria for uncoated paper that can be expected to last several hundred years under normal library use and storage conditions. It is intended for use by publishers and paper producers and to serve as a buying tool. Although primarily intended for publications that have some lasting significance, it provides useful information for any publication printed on uncoated paper.

Details

This standard addresses one of the most serious problems facing libraries today: the paper used during most of the nineteenth and twentieth centuries is falling apart. Specifically, acidic paper becomes brittle fairly quickly; as the foreword notes, "This embrittlement has made probable the loss of the original hard copy format of much of the published record from the 19th and 20th centuries." By defining standards for permanent paper and a symbol to identify use of such paper, the standard "seeks to encourage wider use of permanent paper . . . and to promote recognition of its need and acceptance by publishers and librarians."

Definitions of certain key terms are followed by minimum requirements: minimum pH of 7.5 (moderate alkalinity), folding endurance and tear resistance for various weights of paper, alkaline reserve and the requirement that no unbleached pulp or ground-wood be included in the paper stock. All requirements are stated with appropriate standard testing methods.

Adherence to Z39.48 is crucial to the future of printed materials in libraries; the standard carries instructions for showing such adherence. A statement that the standard has been met should appear, as should a special symbol (the symbol for infinity, or "lazy eight," within a circle). The statement and symbol should be on the verso of the title page and may be used elsewhere. The standard also recommends use of the symbol in advertising, and calls for adherence information to be included in Cataloging in Publication Data as part of the ISBN qualifier.

Related Standards

Z39.48 refers to three TAPPI (Technical Association of the Pulp and Paper Industry) standards: T-509: *Hydrogen Ion Concentration (pH of Paper Extracts—Cold Extraction Method);* T-511: *Method for Folding Endurance of Paper (MIT Tester);* and T-414: *Standard for Internal Tearing Resistance of Paper.* The standard also refers to the ASTM/ANSI standard D 3290: *Standard Specification for Bond and Ledger Papers for Permanent Records.*

Notes

The deterioration of books printed in the nineteenth and twentieth centuries is one of the great tragedies of publishing history; a substantial literature is destroying itself. The Library of Congress and other agencies are spending millions of dollars to try to maintain some of the damaged books and to microfilm those beyond hope; this standard can at least help to minimize future problems.

Bibliographic Citation

American National Standards Institute. *American National Standard for Information Sciences—Permanence of Paper for Printed Library Materials, ANSI Z39.48-1984.* New York: ANSI; 1985 January. 8 p.

Z39.49-1985
COMPUTERIZED BOOK ORDERING

This standard establishes two formats for computerized book ordering: a fixed format and a variable-length format. The standard is intended "for anyone who buys or sells books and has access to a computer," but it appears to be better suited to bookstores and distributors than to libraries.

Details

Z39.49 is based on industry standards developed by the Book Industry Systems Advisory Committee (BISAC); the variable format is also based on ANSI Z39.2, but it is *not* a MARC format, since it selects different options from Z39.2.

Each element in the fixed format is accommodated in the variable format, but the reverse is not true. An extensive data dictionary shows details of both formats, from "accompanying material" through "volumes in set."

The fixed format consists of a group of 80-character records, with specific tape density and blocking factor specified. Each record contains a tag and sequence number; a file includes a purchase order header record, several optional purchase order handling records and one or more line item records for books ordered, followed by a purchase order control record providing totals for the order.

The variable format is a proper Z39.2 format, containing a 24-byte leader, directory and tags. Unlike MARC, the directory consists only of tags and starting character positions; the length of a field is determined only by the field terminator. Also unlike MARC, there are no indicators in variable data fields, and subfield codes are upper-case alphabetic characters. The variable format is as detailed as a MARC format and is quite flexible.

The most significant difference between Z39.49 and MARC is that the entire format, including content designation, is offered as an ANSI standard.

Bibliographic Citation

American National Standards Institute. *American National*

Standard for Computerized Book Ordering, Z39.49-1985. New York: ANSI; 1985. 84 p.

Z85. 1-1980
PERMANENT AND DURABLE LIBRARY CATALOG CARDS

Please see the discussion of this standard in Chapter 1.

FOOTNOTES

1. American National Standards Institute. *American National Standard for Information Sciences—Permanence of Paper for Printed Library Materials, ANSI Z39.48-1984.* New York: ANSI; 1985 January. This material is reproduced with permission from American National Standard Z39.48-1984, copyright 1985 by the American National Standards Institute. Copies of this standard may be purchased from the American National Standards Institute at 1430 Broadway, New York, NY 10018.

2. An extensive discussion of Z39.2 will be found in Chapter 3 of Crawford, Walt. *MARC for Library Use: Understanding the USMARC Formats.* White Plains, NY: Knowledge Industry Publications; 1984. 222 p.

3. *International List of Periodical Title Word Abbreviations,* maintained and published by the Centre International d'Enregistrement des Publication en Series (ISDS), 20 Rue Bachaumont, 75002 Paris, France.

4. Davis, Charles. "Foreword." *Library Trends.* 31(2): 189; 1982 Fall.

5. For further details, see Chapter 7 of Crawford, Walt. *MARC for Library Use: Understanding the USMARC Formats.* White Plains, NY: Knowledge Industry Publications; 1984.

11

Current Standards: X3

This chapter provides brief notes on some of the standards developed and maintained by ASC X3, the Accredited Standards Committee on Information Processing Systems. Its scope is "standardization in the areas of computers and information processing and peripheral equipment, devices and media related thereto; standardization of the functional characteristics of office machines, plus accessories for such machines, particularly in those areas that influence the operators of such machines."[1] The Computer and Business Equipment Manufacturers Association (CBEMA) is the secretariat for X3. ASC X3 has issued over 110 standards and a dictionary for information processing. X3 standards have always been used in library automation, from standards for punched cards through those for programming languages.

Comments at the beginning of Chapter 10 apply to this chapter as well. This chapter includes less than one-half the ASC X3 standards. Omitted are the standards for paper tape, physical and magnetic properties of magnetic tape and disks, magnetic ink character recognition and data encryption. Standards for tape and disks go into greater detail than those for punched cards and optical character recognition; the detail tends to be more arcane and to require a more substantial technical background. Some other standards are missing because they deal with such technical areas that no meaningful nontechnical summary appeared possible.

The figures in this chapter are reproduced with permission from American National Standards X3.4-1977: *American National Standard Code for Information Interchange;* X3.32-1973: *American National Standard Graphic Representation of the Control*

Characters of American National Standard Code for Information Interchange; X3.45-1982: *American National Standard for Information Systems—Character Set for Handprinting;* and X3.49-1975: *American National Standard Character Set for Optical Character Recognition (OCR-B),* copyright (respectively) 1977, 1973, 1982 and 1975 by the American National Standards Institute. Copies of these standards may be purchased from the American National Standards Institute at 1430 Broadway, New York, NY 10018.

X3.1-1976
SYNCHRONOUS SIGNALING RATES
FOR DATA TRANSMISSION

This brief standard specifies preferred rates for transmitting data over communication channels: for instance, telecommunications over telephone lines using modems. Preferred rates for serial signaling (most common for dial-up and similar computer communications) are 600, 1200, 2400, 4800, 7200 and 9600 bits per seconds. When 600 bits per second is too fast, 75, 150 and 300 bits per second are available. Preferred rates for parallel signaling (where up to eight bits composing a character are communicated simultaneously) are just one-eighth those for serial signaling: 75, 150, 300, 600, 900 and 1200 characters per second. This standard is critical for makers and users of modems and similar equipment, so that data rates will be those understood by a wide range of equipment.

Bibliographic Citation

American National Standards Institute. *American National Standard Synchronous Signaling Rates for Data Transmission, ANSI X3.1-1976.* New York: ANSI; 1976. 8 p.

X3.4-1977
CODE FOR INFORMATION INTERCHANGE

This is ASCII, the American Standard Code for Information Interchange. It is the most fundamental standard for communication of information among information processing systems.

Details

ASCII itself is a "seven-bit" code: each character is defined by seven binary digits, allowing for a total of 128 defined characters. When carried in an eight-bit environment, the extra bit ("most significant bit") is always 0 (off). An additional 128 characters can be defined with a most significant bit of 1: see standard X3.41. Figure 11.1 shows the standard code.

ASCII explicitly reserves the first 32 characters for control characters. The standard provides definitions for each of these. For example: *"1/7 ETB (End of Transmission Block)*. A communication control character used to indicate the end of a block of data for communication purposes. ETB is used for blocking data where the block structure is not necessarily related to the processing format." Appendixes give background for the design of ASCII, specify collating sequence, consider applications and show criteria for the original X3.4 (1968) and the revision.

Notes

ASCII is used almost universally for communication between computers and other information processing devices, with the exception of communication between IBM computers and terminals (carried out in IBM's EBCDIC). ASCII is almost universal in microcomputers, though some manufacturers use the control characters 01-1F for additional graphic characters. More than any other single standard, ASCII and its international counterpart ISO 646 make it possible to create information on one device and expect that any other device will be able to use that information. This assumption, that text can always be transmitted and read, is basic to telecommunications and most automation of any sort.

Bibliographic Citation

American National Standards Institute. *American National Standard Code for Information Interchange, ANSI X3.4-1977.* New York: ANSI; 1977. 20 p.

Figure 11.1: Standard Code, from X3.4-1977

Bits $b_4 b_3 b_2 b_1$	ROW / COLUMN	0 0 0 0	1 0 0 1	2 0 1 0	3 0 1 1	4 1 0 0	5 1 0 1	6 1 1 0	7 1 1 1
0 0 0 0	0	NUL	DLE	SP	0	@	P	`	p
1 0 0 0	1	SOH	DC1	!	1	A	Q	a	q
0 1 0 0	2	STX	DC2	"	2	B	R	b	r
1 1 0 0	3	ETX	DC3	#	3	C	S	c	s
0 0 1 0	4	EOT	DC4	$	4	D	T	d	t
1 0 1 0	5	ENQ	NAK	%	5	E	U	e	u
0 1 1 0	6	ACK	SYN	&	6	F	V	f	v
1 1 1 0	7	BEL	ETB	'	7	G	W	g	w
0 0 0 1	8	BS	CAN	(	8	H	X	h	x
1 0 0 1	9	HT	EM	)	9	I	Y	i	y
0 1 0 1	10	LF	SUB	*	:	J	Z	j	z
1 1 0 1	11	VT	ESC	+	;	K	[	k	{
0 0 1 1	12	FF	FS	,	<	L	\	l	|
1 0 1 1	13	CR	GS	-	=	M	]	m	}
0 1 1 1	14	SO	RS	.	>	N	^	n	~
1 1 1 1	15	SI	US	/	?	O	_	o	DEL

X3.5-1970
FLOWCHART SYMBOLS AND THEIR USAGE

While flowcharting is now rarely used as a programming tool, flowcharts for overall systems still play a vital role in systems development. Flowcharts require commonly understood symbols and methods for indicating flow of control and information. This standard provides just such commonality: a small set of symbols with clear definitions. The symbols do not have obvious meanings, and they are used for cases in which no "obvious" symbols would appear to be available. X3.5 established a solid basis for flowcharting, and the standard has succeeded. Plastic templates for X3.5 symbols, and flowcharting software using the symbols, are at the base of most flowcharts created in the last 15 years.

Bibliographic Citation

American National Standards Institute. *American National Standard Flowchart Symbols and Their Usage in Information Processing, ANSI X3.5-1970.* New York: ANSI; 1970. 17 p.

X3.9-1978
PROGRAMMING LANGUAGE FORTRAN

This controversial standard (see Chapter 6) provides a comprehensive, detailed definition of ANS FORTRAN. As with most program language standards, X3.9 is rigorous and lengthy, defining each aspect of FORTRAN in great detail. X3.9 is sufficient to specify and test a FORTRAN implementation, but it is neither designed for, nor useful as, an introduction to the language. The controversy with "FORTRAN 77" (the common name for this version of the FORTRAN standard, as opposed to "FORTRAN 66," the previous ANS FORTRAN) rises from questions of compatibility. Is it reasonable for a revised standard to make implementations of the earlier version "nonstandard" on an *ex post facto* basis?

Bibliographic Citation

American National Standards Institute. *American National*

Standard Programming Language Fortran, ANSI X3.9-1978. New York: ANSI; 1978. 207 p.

X3.11-1969
GENERAL PURPOSE PAPER CARDS

Punched cards may be obsolescent, but data processing systems still use them, including some library automation systems. This standard defines the physical properties of the cards. "General purpose paper cards" are what are typically called "punched cards," "tab cards," "IBM cards," "80-column cards," or "Hollerith cards." Only the last two names specifically identify such cards, since other punched-card forms do exist.

X3.11 includes 7 physical requirements, 14 paper requirements and 17 test methods. Cards must be between 3.247 and 3.257 inches high and between 7.370 and 7.380 inches wide, with each edge straight to within an 0.003 inch tolerance.* The required corner cut must meet dimension requirements, but can be at the (preferred) upper left or (alternate) upper right. While the standard considers square-cut corners preferable, it provides dimensional specifications for alternate rounded corners.† A range of paper requirements carries similarly exact specifications: for instance, the paper should have a 99-pound basis weight per ream of 24 x 36 sheets, should be 0.0070 inches thick (with a tolerance of 0.0004 inches), and should have a pH of less than 5.0.

Most of us have taken punched cards for granted. This highly detailed standard, with its many tests and references to "average Sheffield roughness" and other areas of paper technology, reveals the extent to which our casual use rests on a basis of standards.

---

* The definition of this tolerance is typical of the precise language in X3.11: each edge must lie completely between two parallel lines 0.003 inches apart.

† The UC Berkeley Library specified round corner cards for its old circulation system based on simple experience: round corners survived longer under the heavy use required in the circulation system.

Bibliographic Citation

American National Standards Institute. *American National Standard Specification for General Purpose Paper Cards for Information Processing, ANSI X3.11-1969.* New York: ANSI; 1969. 11 p.

X3.15-1976
BIT SEQUENCING OF THE
AMERICAN NATIONAL STANDARD CODE FOR
INFORMATION INTERCHANGE
IN SERIAL-BY-BIT DATA TRANSMISSION

This standard provides the necessary follow-up to X3.4, in order to make it possible to communicate data as a stream of on-and-off pulses ("serial-by-bit"). Given a string of seven or eight bits, how should that string be assembled back into a character? For example, using an eight-bit convention, capital "J" in ASCII is character 4/10 or 4A, and capital "R" is 5/2 or 52. As usually expressed, capital J is the bit string 01001010 and capital R is the bit string 01010010—the mirror image of J. Without a standard for which bit is transmitted first, it would be impossible to communicate—would the string 01010010 be J or R?

In fact, the string 01010010 used in serial-by-bit data transmission is J, not R: X3.15 specifies that the least significant bit be transmitted first. X3.15 includes an appendix giving arguments for and against the decision made. For users, X3.15 is transparent: users almost always deal with characters, not bits.

Since transmission begins with the least significant bit, why does the ASCII table in X3.4—and most written representations of bit strings—show the most significant bit on the left and the least on the right? Because the *logical structure* of ASCII is reflected by the written representation, and would be masked if the order were reversed. A table arranged with the least significant bits as rows and most significant as columns would begin as follows (the first four rows, using seven-bit notation):

NUL	BS	EOT	FF	STX	LF	ACK	SO	SOH	HT	ENQ	CR	ETX	VT	BEL	SI
@	H	D	L	B	J	F	N	A	I	E	M	C	K	G	O
SP	(	$	,	"	*	&	.	!	)	%	-	#	+	'	/
'	h	d	l	b	j	f	n	a	i	e	m	c	k	g	o

The "number row" would be 0 8 4 < 2 : 6 > 1 9 5 = 3 ; 7 ?. In short, a table arranged in transmission sequence would not make sense to humans. Further, the collation sequence is properly reflected in the X3.4 table; as a result, any ASCII-based computer system could be expected to store and process characters most significant bit first: it is, after all, the most significant.

Bibliographic Citation

American National Standards Institute. *American National Standard for Bit Sequencing of the American National Standard Code for Information Interchange in Serial-by-Bit Data Transmission, ANSI X3.15-1976.* New York: ANSI; 1976. 8 p.

X3.16-1978
CHARACTER STRUCTURE AND CHARACTER PARITY SENSE FOR SERIAL-BY-BIT DATA COMMUNICATION IN THE AMERICAN NATIONAL STANDARD CODE FOR INFORMATION INTERCHANGE

This standard specifies parity bits and, where needed, start-and-stop bits for data communication. A "parity bit" is, for this standard, an eighth bit added to each seven-bit ASCII character. The "parity bit" is set so that the number of "1" bits in the eight-bit string is odd, called "odd parity" (for synchronous data communication, where start-and-stop bits are not used) or even, for "even parity" (for asynchronous data communication). Thus, for asynchronous communication, the character J would have bit 1 added, since it has three 1 bits, while K, with four 1 bits, would have bit 0 added. The asynchronous standard calls for one start bit and one stop bit, or a total of 10 bits per character.

This standard is not universally followed in telecommunications; while most asynchronous systems (including the majority of online services) do assume even parity, one start and one stop bit, there are those that follow other rules.

Bibliographic Citation

American National Standards Institute. *American National Standard Character Structure and Character Parity Sense for Serial-by-Bit Data Communication in the American National Standard Code for Information Interchange, ANSI X3.16-1976.* New York: ANSI; 1976. 11 p.

X3.17-1981
CHARACTER SET FOR OPTICAL CHARACTER RECOGNITION (OCR-A)

We've all seen OCR-A printing. Many mass market paper-backs carry the ISBN in OCR-A on the back cover; some circulation systems use OCR-A coding. X3.17 specifies shapes for each charac-ter in an expanded 96-character OCR-A set. Three sizes for charac-ters include one size that contains lower-case letters quite similar to OCR-B in shape. The bulk of the standard consists of large dia-grams for each letter, four diagrams to a page.

Bibliographic Citation

American National Standards Institute. *American National Standard Character Set for Optical Character Recognition (OCR-A), ANSI X3.17-1981.* New York: ANSI; 1981. 51 p.

X3.21-1967
RECTANGULAR HOLES IN TWELVE-ROW PUNCHED CARDS

This standard complements X3.11, specifying the size, shape and placement of holes. Standard holes are 0.124-0.126 inches high and 0.054-0.056 inches wide. The top row is 0.250 inches from the top of the card, and each of twelve rows is 0.250 inches lower. The leftmost column is 0.251 inches from the left edge, with each of 80 columns 0.087 inches to the right. All this combines with X3.11 to make it possible for one manufacturer to build keypunches that can be used with cards produced by another manufacturer, resulting in information that can be fed to machines built by yet another manufacturer. This somewhat obsolescent example is what interchangeability standards are all about.

Bibliographic Citation

American National Standards Institute. *American National Standard Rectangular Holes in Twelve-Row Punched Cards, ANSI X3.21-1967.* New York: ANSI; 1967. 8 p.

X3.23-1974
PROGRAMMING LANGUAGE COBOL

This standard establishes a detailed specification for the form and interpretation of programs expressed in COBOL (COmmon Business Oriented Language). Its purpose is to promote "machine independence," that is, to make it possible for the same COBOL program to run on many different computers.

Details

A standard specification for a programming language must specify precisely what will happen when a particular element of the language is used. For example, if a programmer writes CALL, that is what the programmer can expect the computer to do. Different computers work differently; thus, a programming language standard does not specify the operational details of the computer, but it does specify the functional details. If two different computers have COBOL language compilers that conform to standards, the same program (also written to standard) should yield the same final results on each computer given the same starting conditions, even though the order of events and actual processing on each computer may be different.

X3.23 specifies 12 different aspects of COBOL, with two or three functional levels for each aspect. This allows "standard COBOL" on computers that could not support the most detailed level; for each aspect of the language, the standard specifies what level supports it. There are actually two language levels: Level I (simpler) and Level II (more complicated). Of the 12 aspects of COBOL, only three need be present; the other nine may be omitted in simpler COBOL systems, and eight of the nine may appear at Level I or Level II. The 12 aspects of the language specification are as follows:

- Nucleus: The core of the language, including its syntax, fundamental verbs and general organization. Every COBOL must include either a Level I or Level II nucleus.

- Table Handling: Methods for creating and using internal tables and indexes; every COBOL must include a Level I or Level II section.

- Sequential Input-Output (I/O): The simplest form of communication to and from a COBOL program—reading records one at a time from the beginning of a file to the end, and writing records one at a time. Every COBOL must include a Level I or Level II section for sequential I/O (input-output).

- Relative I/O: Where records are read or written based on known position relative to the beginning of a file. This section may be omitted.

- Indexed I/O: Where records are read or written based on some information about the record. This section may be omitted.

- Sort-Merge: The process of sorting a group of records or merging more than one group into a single group. This section may be omitted; COBOL is one of the few languages with internal sort-merge commands.*

- Report Writer: A group of facilities to make it easy to generate reports. Report Writer has only one defined level, but it can be omitted.

---

*Sorting and merging are usually done by "utility programs," carefully written programs that can sort large numbers of records quickly and easily. Such sorting usually takes place as separate steps in a flow of processing; in practice, most COBOL implementations would handle sort-merge by using such utility programs.

• Segmentation: Facilities to allow a large program to run on a relatively small computer, by "overlaying" portions of the program as needed. A segmented program isn't all in the computer's main memory at once; portions of the program that aren't used all the time can be called into memory when needed, replacing other portions not being used at the time. This section can be omitted.

• Library: Facilities to allow commonly used routines to be included in programs by naming them rather than retyping the routine. For example, any program that reads or modifies MARC records will need a routine to search the MARC directory for a specified field and extract that field; typically, that routine is only written once within an institution, then used as a library routine in each new program. This section can be omitted.

• Debug: Facilities to help a programmer in finding and correcting flaws in a program. This section can be omitted.

• Inter-Program Communication: Facilities to allow information to be passed directly from one COBOL program to another program. This section can be omitted.

• Communication: Facilities to allow information to be provided to the program by the person initiating the program. This section can be omitted.

The standard provides detailed, explicit specification for each element of COBOL including characters used, types of data, words reserved for use by the language and elements of each of the 12 sections above.

Notes

X3.23 is not a tutorial document and was not intended to be; it is useful only as a reference and as a tool for those writing COBOL compilers. "ANS Cobol" has been widely accepted as a standard version of the most popular business programming language. COBOL is a complex language, and the length of the standard reflects that complexity.

Bibliographic Citation

American National Standards Institute. *American National Standard Programming Language COBOL, ANSI X3.23-1974.* New York: ANSI; 1974. [600] p.

X3.24-1968
SIGNAL QUALITY AT INTERFACE BETWEEN DATA PROCESSING TERMINAL EQUIPMENT AND SYNCHRONOUS DATA COMMUNICATION EQUIPMENT FOR SERIAL DATA TRANSMISSION

Synchronous data communication requires timing signals to synchronize the equipment at both ends of the communication— thus, "synchronous." This standard defines relationships between timing signals and data signals and tolerances for distortion and frequency deviation. The standard also specifies test methods. This standard was developed by the Electronic Industries Association (EIA) as its standard EIA RS-334.

Bibliographic Citation

Electronic Industries Association. *EIA Standard Signal Quality at Interface Between Data Processing Terminal Equipment and Synchronous Data Communication Equipment for Serial Data Transmission, RS-334, ANSI X3.24-1968.* Washington: EIA; 1967. 9 p.

X3.26-1980
HOLLERITH PUNCHED CARD CODE

While X3.11 specifies the card and X3.21 specifies the holes, this standard adds meaning: standard interpretations for holes and groups of holes within a column. The 1980 version provides an unusually large repertoire for punched cards: 256 codes in all, defining the entire ASCII character set (control codes and graphic character sets) and providing for an additional 128 codes.

X3.26 builds on existing usage to an unusual degree. IBM, the dominant maker of punched-card equipment, uses EBCDIC rather than ASCII for internal processing. X3.26 assigns ASCII characters to the same hole combinations used for EBCDIC characters. Going even further, X3.26 adopts the same control code punches as used by IBM. Many new hole combinations are added to provide lower-case and extended character capabilities.

The standard includes rare explicit recognition of EBCDIC, even including an EBCDIC punch/data equivalence chart to accompany the ASCII equivalence chart. Although punched cards may be nearing the end of their long useful history, this exceptionally clear standard suggests that some life remained in 1980.

Bibliographic Citation

American National Standards Institute. *American National Standard Hollerith Punched Card Code, ANSI X3.26-1980.* New York: ANSI; 1980. 12 p.

X3.30-1971
REPRESENTATION FOR CALENDAR DATE AND ORDINAL DATE

This standard provides two standard ways to represent the date, with two variations on each. The standard is intended only for interchange of data between data systems, though it does not preclude use of the standard form for input or output.

Calendar date is normally expressed as YYYYMMDD, so that December 15, 1985 appears as 19851215; this can be shortened to 851215 or 51215 in some applications. Ordinal date, sometimes called "Julian date," includes a three-digit day-of-year (from 001 to 365 in most years); in that form, December 15, 1985 becomes 1985349, 85349 or 5349. Many, but not all, standards specifying storage of date use X3.30; some use the familiar American MM/DD/YY or European DD/MM/YY. Standards (such as Z39.29) that specify a written form for date almost never use this form. The standard has two major advantages: it allows direct sorting and comparison of dates, and it is unambiguous—an advantage over the two familiar forms.

Bibliographic Citation

American National Standards Institute. *American National Standard Representation for Calendar Date and Ordinal Date for Information Interchange, ANSI X3.30-1971*. New York: ANSI; 1971. 8 p.

X3.31-1973
STRUCTURE FOR THE IDENTIFICATION OF THE COUNTIES OF THE UNITED STATES

This standard specifies a three-digit structure to store codes for counties and "county equivalents." Initial code assignments leave gaps and are designed so that codes can be used to sort county names alphabetically. X3.31 does not include the list of counties and codes, but refers to *Counties and County Equivalents of the States of the United States,* Federal Information Processing Standards Publication 6-1.

Some data structures used in libraries, particularly in cartographic fields, may use X3.31 and the associated X3.38 (see below). This code is not the same as the Geographic Classification Code used in USMARC.

Bibliographic Citation

American National Standards Institute. *American National Standard Structure for the Identification of the Counties of the United States for Information Interchange, ANSI X3.31-1973*. New York: ANSI; 1973. 1 p.

X3.32-1978
GRAPHIC REPRESENTATION OF THE CONTROL CHARACTERS OF AMERICAN NATIONAL STANDARD CODE FOR INFORMATION INTERCHANGE

Only 94 of the 128 characters in standard ASCII represent numbers, letters and punctuation. The other 34 characters are control and special characters. This standard defines pictorial and two-character representations for each of those characters, so that they can be displayed where such display is needed (for instance, when doing diagnostics).

Details

Figure 11.2 shows the pictorial and two-character representations for some of the control and nonprinting characters. Included here are ways of explicitly showing a space: a triangle for pictorial representation, or SP as a two-character code. Figure 11.3 shows part of an appendix that provides dot-matrix patterns to display the two-character codes within a single character slot on a video-display terminal or dot-matrix printer.

Notes

X3.32 is clear, precise and useful; many well-designed terminals and printers incorporate the dot pattern representations illustrated in Figure 11.3 to allow "transparent" display of data received. The standard is not universally followed, for a variety of reasons. Most library-related documents use a slashed lower-case "b" to represent a space explicitly, rather than using the triangle. Code 1/15, the Unit Separator, is the USMARC subfield delimiter; the ASCII picture (see Figure 11.2) is never used in library applications, where the graphic is usually a double dagger, a slashed equal sign or a dollar sign.

Bibliographic Citation

American National Standards Institute. *American National Standard Graphic Representation of the Control Characters of American National Standard Code for Information Interchange, ANSI X3.32-1973*. New York: ANSI; 1973. 12 p.

X3.38-1972 (R1977)
IDENTIFICATION OF STATES OF THE UNITED STATES

This short standard provides two-digit and two-character codes for the states of the United States and the District of Columbia. The

Figure 11.2: Representations of Control and Nonprinting ASCII Characters

Code Position	Character	Pictorial Representation	Alphanumeric Representation
1/7	ETB	⊣	EB
1/8	CAN	⊠	CN
1/9	EM	⬆	EM
1/10	SUB	⸮	SB
1/11	ESC	⊖	EC
1/12	FS	⊟	FS
1/13	GS	⊟	GS
1/14	RS	⊟	RS
1/15	US	⊔	US
2/0	SP	△	SP
7/15	DEL	⫽	DT

Figure 11.3: Selection of Dot-Matrix Patterns for Displaying Two-Character Codes in a Single Slot, from Appendix to X3.32-1978

Character	7 x 9 Matrix	5 x 7 Matrix	Character	7 x 9 Matrix	5 x 7 Matrix
HT			EM		
LF			SUB		
VT			ESC		
FF			FS		
CR			GS		
SO			RS		
SI			US		
SP			DEL		
NL					

numeric codes provide alphabetic sorting; the alphabetic codes do not. The alphabetic codes are those assigned by the U.S. Postal Service.

Bibliographic Citation

American National Standards Institute. *American National Standard Identification of States of the United States (including the District of Columbia) for Information Interchange, ANSI X3.38-1972 (R1977)*. New York: ANSI; 1977. 2 p.

X3.41-1974
CODE EXTENSION TECHNIQUES FOR USE WITH THE
7-BIT CODED CHARACTER SET OF
AMERICAN NATIONAL STANDARD CODE
FOR INFORMATION INTERCHANGE

Standard ASCII includes 94 graphic characters and 32 control characters. Some applications require more characters: graphic, control or both. For example, USMARC uses about 80 additional graphic characters; the RLIN East Asian Computer Code (REACC) includes tens of thousands of additional graphic characters. This standard establishes techniques that allow additional character sets to be defined and communicated while maintaining compatibility with ASCII. The standard is long, detailed and explicit; while it does not itself define any additional characters, it does provide sufficient techniques for an almost unlimited set of extensions.

Standard X3.41 establishes the naming conventions C0, G0, C1 and G1 for the 7-bit control set, 7-bit graphics set, 8-bit control set (with 1 in the most significant bit), and 8-bit graphics set. These conventions are used in discussing and defining character set extensions. Character set extensions are defined using "escape sequences," which are character sequences beginning with the ESC character (1/11, hex 1B). ALA Extended ASCII includes a defined G1 character set and several escape sequences. The REACC character set is a private multicharacter G0 character set as provided for in X3.41.

Bibliographic Citation

American National Standards Institute. *American National Standard Code Extension Techniques for Use with the 7-Bit Coded Character Set of American National Standard Code for Information Interchange, ANSI X3.41-1974.* New York: ANSI; 1974. 32 p.

X3.42-1975
REPRESENTATION OF NUMERIC VALUES IN CHARACTER STRINGS

How does one program recognize a number produced by another program? This standard specifies standard ways to represent numeric values so that such values can be recognized and interpreted correctly. The standard works in every known programming language, is unambiguous and applies to any representation of numbers for machine processing. The various forms specified are all easily readable, but human readability was not a primary factor in designing the standard.

Details

Three varieties of numeric representation are defined, with each variety given in signed and unsigned form; negative numbers can only be given in signed form. The three varieties of representation are as follows:

• NR1, Implicit Point Representations: "whole numbers." These numbers may include leading blanks or zeroes, but no trailing blanks; zero is always positive, and no punctuation is permitted. The quantity zero may be represented by 0, +0 or more than one zero, but not by −0 or a blank.

• NR2, Explicit Point Unscaled: "decimal numbers." The same rules apply as for NR1, with two additions. An NR2 representation always includes a decimal point (possibly as the last character), and numbers less than 1 should include an explicit 0 before the decimal—that is, 1/4 should be represented as 0.25 or +0.25, not .25.

• NR3, Explicit Point Scaled: "floating point" or "scientific notation." The same rules apply as for NR2, and the scale should always appear as E, a plus or minus, and the power, with no spaces. Thus, 4900 may appear as 49.E + 02 or 4.9E + 3, but not as 49 E + 2 or .49E + 4.

None of the three forms allows for spaces between the sign (if used) and the first digit, and none allows for punctuation other than the single decimal point. The decimal point is the American period. The standard includes a detailed set of definitions and is expressed in a structured metalanguage; it is explicit and unambiguous. Appendixes include a discussion of "the meaning of number"; relation to other standards; history and notes on application of the standard in COBOL, FORTRAN and PL/I; and guidelines for the preparation of numeric data.

Notes

The problem addressed by this standard is one that normally seems trivial: we all know a number when we see one. In practice, the situation is not that simple. The common American use of a comma to delimit three-digit groups conflicts with the European use of a comma as a decimal marker. Some programs have used a blank to represent zero. Some notations use trailing signs or symbols (CR, DB) to represent positive and negative numbers.

This standard addresses these problems by providing a clear, totally unambiguous notation with sufficient flexibility to make it work in all known programming languages (though some languages are not able to handle floating point notation NR3). Adherence to X3.42 does not mean that commas or dollar signs should not be added for printed or displayed output; it does mean that the commas and floating dollar signs should not be stored in data that may be transmitted and used by other systems.

Library applications have had various problems with "numbers," some of which can be avoided by use of this standard. Some of the "numbers" in library use are not numeric quantities, and are not in any way covered by this standard; for instance, ISBN, ISSN, LCCN and call numbers are not intended to be used as numeric quantities.

Bibliographic Citation

American National Standards Institute. *American National Standard for the Representation of Numeric Values in Character Strings for Information Interchange, ANSI X3.42-1975.* New York: ANSI; 1975. 26 p.

X3.43-1977
REPRESENTATIONS OF LOCAL TIME OF DAY

This standard provides a range of uniform time representations, allowing unambiguous representation of local time in any of several forms and to any desired degree of precision.

Details

Six combinations of time elements are allowed, in either of two systems and with either of two notations. The six combinations are: hour; hour and decimal fraction; hour and minute; hour, minute and decimal fraction; hour, minute, second; hour, minute, second and decimal fraction. No more than one decimal point may ever be used, and each "whole" element must be expressed as two digits (e.g., 2 a.m. is 02, not 2), so the length of string and position of decimal point always show which combination is being used. The two systems are 24-hour (recommended) and 12-hour: when 12-hour is used, either A or P (for a.m. or p.m.) must immediately follow the time; the standard explicitly makes midnight 120000A and noon 120000P. Finally, the two notations allow colons between elements if desired.

Typically, the only confusion in local time arises when 12-hour timekeeping is used without the A or P; by eliminating that possibility and by stating that any quantity following a decimal point is a decimal fraction (12.25 would be 12:15, not 12:25), the standard makes it easy to recognize and interpret any time notation. This standard can be used with X3.30 to provide a full chronological notation, as is used in USMARC field 005.

Bibliographic Citation

American National Standards Institute. *American National*

Standard Representations of Local Time of the Day for Information Interchange, ANSI X3.43-1977. New York: ANSI; 1977. 8 p.

X3.44-1974
DETERMINATION OF THE PERFORMANCE OF DATA COMMUNICATION SYSTEMS

This standard provides means for determining the performance of an "information path," the functional combination of a sending device, a receiving device and a communications link. It can be used to measure performance of a given system and to compare different systems; it is designed for use by those developing, maintaining and specifying data communication systems.

Details

Four performance criteria are defined:

• Transfer Rate of Information Bits (TRIB): How fast information flows during the time taken to transmit a message or block; measured in bits per second.

• Transfer Overhead Time (TOT): Time spent doing things other than transmitting messages, including establishing and disestablishing the communication path; expressed in seconds per bit.

• Residual Error Rate (RER): Inaccuracy, that is, the sum of characters that are incorrectly accepted and those that are sent but not accepted, divided by the total information characters. Expressed in error characters per information character.

• Availability (A): Given a period during which the communication path was expected to be functional, the percentage of that time during which it was functional.

Tolerances, methods for measuring and examples of performance measurement are provided. Except for availability, new terms were used for the criteria to avoid ambiguous definitions of existing terms.

Notes

X3.44 provides a basis for evaluating and comparing information paths, but the standard is neither simple nor easy to evaluate. Availability can be expressed as a straightforward percentage and can be measured fairly easily. Residual error rate may well be zero or nearly zero in most systems, particularly in those communications systems using error detection and recovery techniques. As noted in one of the appendixes, transmission errors in an error-recovery environment will result in a lower TRIB but may not change any other figures. TOT depends on the length of each message and the number of messages within a session and could only reasonably be specified with reference to such values.

Communications links are ever more vital to library automation and other forms of information processing; the ability to determine the overall quality of an information path is an essential part of system design and evaluation. X3.44 provides the criteria for such determination, and gives developers and users a valuable tool for specification and comparison.

Bibliographic Citation

American National Standards Institute. *American National Standard Determination of the Performance of Data Communication Systems, ANSI X3.44-1974.* New York: ANSI; 1974. 48 p.

X3.45-1974
CHARACTER SET FOR HANDPRINTING

This unusual standard sets forth a character set to be used for handwritten OCR (optical character recognition) input and for "man-to-man" usage where accuracy is more important than speed and flexibility—as, for example, from a programmer to a keypunch operator. The character set includes capital letters, numbers, some punctuation and a set of international characters; it includes characters not in standard ASCII and excludes much of standard ASCII.

Details

Figure 11.4 shows the character set defined by X3.45. Capital letters are to be 4.5mm high (0.180 inches) with a tolerance of 1mm; the tallest characters (dollar sign, parentheses, brackets) are 8mm (0.32 inches) with a tolerance of 1mm. Handprinting for OCR can be 3 lines per inch (when only the alphameric subset, not including overtall characters, is used) or, when all characters are used, 2 lines per inch.

The standard gives recommendations for preprinted forms to be used in handprinting: this is almost a necessity to achieve the results specified. The standard allows use of the slashed "7" common in libraries, but only for international use; as in Figure 11.4, the slashed "Z" is the standard form.

Notes

This standard has been used for designing forms to be scanned by OCR. The standard has had little effect on writing patterns outside of such limited areas, and was probably not intended to have any such effect. Most of the characters are simple, clear forms; the capital O and capital U are unusual, and the capital S has a flourish unlikely to be found in most use. The committee that designed this standard came to a sensible resolution of the long-time split between those who would slash the O and those who slash the zero; meanwhile, the massive spread of terminals and dot-matrix printers has largely settled the issue: if any character is slashed, it is the zero.

Bibliographic Citation

American National Standards Institute. *American National Standard Character Set for Handprinting, ANSI X3.45-1974.* New York: ANSI; 1974. 28 p.

X3.49-1975
CHARACTER SET FOR OPTICAL CHARACTER RECOGNITION (OCR-B)

Two character sets have been defined for optical character

Figure 11.4: Character Set for Handprinting, from X3.45-1974

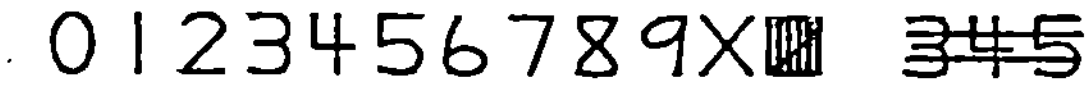

Numeric Subset

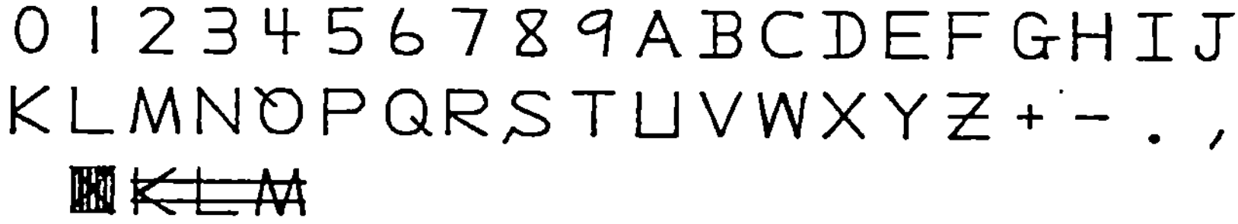

Alphanumeric Subset

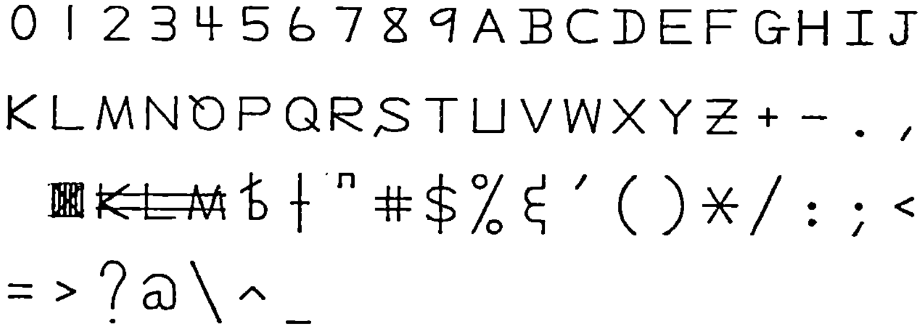

Programming Subset

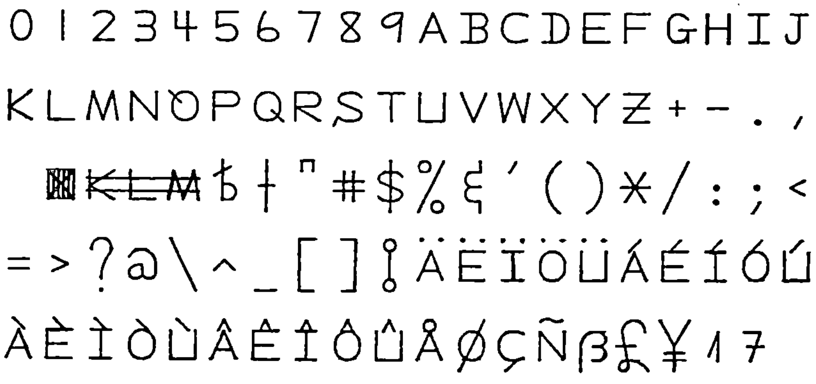

Universal Subset

recognition. X3.17 defines OCR-A, which looks odd but performs well for OCR use even under difficult conditions (degraded print, handheld readers, simple OCR devices). X3.49 defines OCR-B, which is much more conventional and readable, but not as easy to process in OCR use. As shown in Figure 11.5, OCR-B looks much like a simple Gothic font; only the lower-case "l" identifies OCR-B as anything other than a simple sans serif typeface. Both OCR-A and OCR-B are used in data conversion and some other aspects of library automation; OCR-A is also used (to a limited extent) for scanning operations such as circulation.

Figure 11.5: OCR-B Character Sets, from X3.49-1975

```
1234567890
ABCDEFGHIJKLM
NOPQRSTUVWXYZ
abcdefghijklm
nopqrstuvwxyz
*+-=/.,:;"'_
?!()<>[]%#&ə^
¤£$¦\ ¥■ ——
```

Scale 1:1

Bibliographic Citation

American National Standards Institute. *American National Standard Character Set for Optical Character Recognition (OCR-B), ANSI X3.49-1975.* New York: ANSI; 1975. 60 p.

X3.53-1976
PROGRAMMING LANGUAGE PL/I

This standard constitutes an authoritative, explicit definition of PL/I as a language. Like other language standards such as the COBOL standard X3.23, this standard specifies exactly what each element of the language should mean (in functional terms). Unlike X3.23, this standard does not allow for multiple levels of implementation in any structured way; a later standard defines a "general-purpose subset" of the language.

PL/I is a complex language, and the standard is also complex. The standard uses a formal metalanguage to express a full PL/I specification in 400 pages of small print. Without the metalanguage, such a specification would probably take more than 1000 pages (if it were possible at all).

The standard includes, in its introduction, examples of questions about PL/I and how the standard might be used to answer them. The metalanguage is expressed in a way that makes it possible to trace each element of a definition.

X3.53 is careful, explicit and useful; most versions of PL/I released or updated since the standard appeared have followed the standard or provided explicit indication of deviations from the standard. X3.53 is not a tutorial and, like most language standards, would probably frighten a new programmer away from the language.

Bibliographic Citation

American National Standards Institute. *American National Standard Programming Language PL/I, ANSI X3.53-1976.* New York: ANSI; 1976. 403 p.

X3.60-1978
PROGRAMMING LANGUAGE MINIMAL BASIC

Skeptics may regard "standard BASIC" as a contradiction in terms, but X3.60 does specify a limited language that exists as a subset of most existing BASIC implementations. The language specified is indeed minimal, allowing only single-letter and letter-with-$ variable names, a small set of keywords and functions and short string variables. Surprisingly, X3.60 does not specify that variables should be initialized automatically, one feature common to almost all BASICs. Minimal BASIC appears as a textual standard; for each aspect of the language, the standard provides a general description, syntax, examples, semantics, exceptions and remarks. The standard is clear and unambiguous.

Bibliographic Citation

American National Standards Institute. *American National Standard for Minimal BASIC, ANSI X3.60-1978.* New York: ANSI; 1978. 39 p.

X3.61-1978
REPRESENTATION OF GEOGRAPHIC POINT LOCATIONS

Three methods for stating geographic coordinates are widely used here and abroad: Latitude/Longitude, Universal Transverse Mercator (UTM) and State Plane Coordinate Systems. The standard provides methods for recording all three methods using a minimal set of symbols and punctuation. The degree, minute and second signs are not used "because many data processing machines cannot recognize or reproduce them." Instead, the three numbers are given as zero-filled numbers and appear in a continuous string. For example, 40 degrees, 12 minutes, 13 seconds appears as 401213. A worst-case Longitude/Latitude description, accurate down to 0.01 foot, could appear as 401213.1132N,0750015.1214W (an example from the standard).

Bibliographic Citation

American National Standards Institute. *American National Standard Representation of Geographic Point Locations for Information Interchange, ANSI X3.61-1978.* New York: ANSI; 1978. 16 p.

X3.74-1981
PROGRAMMING LANGUAGE PL/I, GENERAL
PURPOSE SUBSET

Friends and foes of PL/I alike may recognize that a subset of PL/I could still be a large, generally useful subset. Standard X3.74 specifies such a subset, referred to as "ANSI subset G" in recent implementations. Most of the standard consists of formal diagrams for the subset; the first few pages specify precisely which elements of PL/I are included, restricted or excluded.

The standards committee makes strong claims for the subset: "small enough to achieve widespread implementation yet large enough to achieve widespread usage," easier to understand, more portable, more economical and less permissive—and thus less error-prone. Clear rationales for decisions made precede the decisions. As a long-time user of full PL/I, this author could find little to criticize in subset G. Some of its restrictions: multiple END statements are not allowed; all variables must be explicitly declared; assignments may not have multiple targets; mixed-type processing is largely eliminated; complex arithmetic is excluded. From a library automation perspective, the only changes that appear significant are elimination of BY NAME and LIKE from declarations; neither elimination is critical.

Implementations of Subset G have spread PL/I to many more computer systems than previously carried PL/I compilers. PL/I is even available on microcomputers.

Bibliographic Citation

American National Standards Institute. *American National Standard Programming Language PL/I General-Purpose Subset, ANSI X3.74-1981.* New York: ANSI; 1981. 36 p.

X3.83-1980
ANSI SPONSORSHIP PROCEDURES FOR ISO REGISTRATION ACCORDING TO ISO 2375

Two pages of text and one diagram state the basic procedure for submitting a new character set for ISO registration. Associations, government agencies and standards committees may submit character sets; individuals and companies may not. Registered character sets are assigned escape sequences for use as specified in X3.41.

Bibliographic Citation

American National Standards Institute. *American National Standard for ANSI Sponsorship Procedures for ISO Registration According to ISO 2375, ANSI X3.83-1980.* New York: ANSI; 1980. 8 p.

X3.88-1981
COMPUTER PROGRAM ABSTRACTS

Standards organizations may overlap in function. This standard could have been written by either Z39 or X3; the proposal was submitted to both agencies for consideration. X3.88 defines the content of an abstract, "a summary of the capabilities, operating environment, and other descriptive information concerning the computer program." The standard is brief and explicit (two pages plus examples), defining 22 categories of information and the sequence in which they should appear. Three examples show use of the standard. The standard uses separate labeled blocks for each category of information. X3.88 provides a clear, useful format for program abstracts; it is widely used and seems appropriate for use by any agencies that feel the need for program abstracts.

Bibliographic Citation

American National Standards Institute. *American National Standard for Computer Program Abstracts, ANSI X3.88-1981*. New York: ANSI; 1981. 11 p.

X3.110-1983
VIDEOTEX/TELETEXT
PRESENTATION LEVEL PROTOCOL SYNTAX
NORTH AMERICAN PLPS

This standard uses standard code extension techniques to define a method for transmitting characters and graphics for videotex and teletext applications (two-way and one-way services to provide "pages" of information on television screens).

Notes

Libraries have been involved in cable television and, in some cases, have hoped to serve as providers of teletext/videotex information. Several different systems of teletext and videotex have begun trial operations in the United States; most have been abandoned, and none has been overly successful. As with other areas of technological innovation, lack of standards has posed problems of acceptance.

This standard allows for fairly high quality color graphics without requiring excessively large amounts of transmitted information. The standard is detailed and builds on other existing standards: the ISO Open Systems Interconnections (OSI) architecture, ANSI X3.41 (described earlier) and others. X3.110 is based on two publications that defined an apparently comprehensive "presentation level protocol syntax" for transmission of text and graphics; these publications came from American Telephone and Telegraph (AT&T) and Canada's Department of Communications.

The resulting standard has been adopted and published jointly by ANSI and CSA, the Canadian Standards Association (as CSA T500-1983). Adoption of such an explicit and encompassing standard comes at a time when teletext and videotex are still fledgling operations in the United States; the standard, typically abbreviated "NAPLPS," should help make such services practical.

Bibliographic Citation

American National Standards Institute; Canadian Standards Association. *Videotex/Teletext Presentation Level Protocol Syntax: North American PLPS, ANSI X3.110-1983, CSA T500-1983.* New York: ANSI; Rexdale, ON: CSA; 1983 December. 158 p.

FOOTNOTES

1. American National Standards Institute. *American National Standard for Information Systems—Text Information Interchange in Page Image Format (PIF), ANSI X3.98-1983.* New York: 1983. p. 5.

12

Current Standards: ISO

The International Organization for Standardization (ISO) has approved thousands of standards, using a single numbering scheme. ISO publishes a series of Standards Handbooks "for easy reference and in order to make the International Standards more easily accessible to a larger public."[1]

These handbooks, available from the American National Standards Institute, contain the full text of all current standards within a specified technical field. The original standards are photographically reduced for the handbooks, and the handbooks omit prefaces.

ISO Standards Handbook 1 includes standards from TC 46 on Documentation and some standards from five other technical committees: TC 6 (Paper, Board and Pulps); TC 37 (Terminology); TC 42 (Photography); TC 154 (Documents and Data Elements in Administration, Commerce and Industry); and TC 171 (Micrographics). ISO Standards Handbook 9, *Data Processing—Software,* includes standards developed by TC 97 (Computers and Information Processing).

This chapter includes brief summaries of 34 of the 57 standards included in the second edition of ISO Standards Handbook 1, excluding standards for photography and micrographics. All information is based on that handbook. Where ISO standards are equivalent to Z39 standards, the summary cites the Z39 standard and notes differences. Anyone interested in international standards relating to libraries and library automation should purchase ISO Standards Handbook 1 and Handbook 9; the two provide complete and economical references.

ISO 4-1972
INTERNATIONAL CODE FOR THE ABBREVIATION
OF TITLES OF PERIODICALS

This standard is the international equivalent to ANSI Z39.5-1984: *Abbreviation of Titles of Periodicals*. No significant differences appear, except that the 1972 ISO standard cites a Z39 source for word abbreviations; the more recent Z39 standard cites a newer international list.

ISO 8-1977
DOCUMENTATION—PRESENTATION OF PERIODICALS

"This International Standard sets out rules intended to enable editors and publishers to present periodicals in a form which will facilitate their use; following these rules should help editors and publishers to bring order and clarity to their own work. These requirements are of varying importance and some may go against certain artistic, technical or advertising considerations." The standard covers title (form and placement), issue size and layout, numbering, volumes, dates, running title, pagination, contents and index.

The NISO equivalent is Z39.1-1984: *Periodicals: Format and Arrangement*. ISO 8 is much more prescriptive and has more in common with the 1967 version of Z39.1. By most American standards, ISO 8 is overly prescriptive. "The title shall be as short and easy to quote as possible." The ISO bibliographic strip (see ISO 30, below) should appear on the cover and contents page. Page numbering is to be continuous within a volume. Contents are either on the front cover, back cover or first page after the front cover. "Typographical uniformity shall be maintained from one article to another within the same publication." The four-page text includes a number of such specific requirements.

ISO R9-1968
INTERNATIONAL SYSTEM FOR THE TRANSLITERATION
OF SLAVIC CYRILLIC CHARACTERS

This recommendation is the basis for Z39.24-1976: *System for the Romanization of Slavic Cyrillic Characters*. The International version differs in some minor variations, and includes a one-page set of "general principles for the conversion of one written language into another." ISO romanization efforts arose because of a proliferation of "mutually incompatible Romanization codes, particularly those for the most important non-Roman script, Cyrillic."[2]

ISO 18-1981
DOCUMENTATION—CONTENTS LIST OF PERIODICALS

This standard provides a more detailed version of the "contents list" section of ISO 8. The standard is brief and clear, and follows typical practice for scholarly journals (but not for popular periodicals). Recommended placement for contents is the first page following the inside front cover, with the recommendation that the contents should also appear on the front or back cover.

ISO R30-1956
BIBLIOGRAPHICAL STRIP

"The bibliographical strip is a concise summary of bibliographical reference data; it is printed at the foot of the front page of the cover of a periodical; it facilitates, on the one hand, the arrangement of periodicals and, on the other, the compilation of citations."

The bibliographical strip, called "biblid" in other ISO standards, consists of abbreviated title, volume, issue, pagination, place of publication and date. The two-page recommendation includes one page of rules and one page of examples. This recommendation is not widely followed in the United States; the "bibliographical strip" called for in the original Z39.1 was different in form and detail, and no longer appears in the standard. To the naive eye, the "biblid" offers no useful assistance for bibliographic citations that would not be available from the masthead.

ISO 214-1975
DOCUMENTATION—ABSTRACTS FOR PUBLICATIONS AND DOCUMENTATION

This international standard is largely based on Z39.14-1971; Z39.14-1978: *Writing Abstracts,* is the American version of ISO

214. Like Z39.14, ISO 214 is careful and detailed, and includes extensive examples of abstracts in different styles.

ISO R215-1961
PRESENTATION OF CONTRIBUTIONS TO PERIODICALS

This two-page set of guidelines for authors and editors has no direct NISO counterpart; Z39.14-1978: *Presentation of Scientific Papers for Written or Oral Presentation,* has some of the same advice (but contains much more extensive guidelines for authors). Recommendations cover the heading (title, author name and author affiliation); synopsis and translation; notes; bibliographical references; tables and illustrations; symbols, abbreviations, and units; installments and series; pagination; classification mark; and date.

The item under "classification mark" would probably not find wide acceptance in the United States: "It is recommended that every article should carry at its head the class mark of some widely recognized system of classification." Otherwise, the guidelines are practical and straightforward.

ISO 216-1975
WRITING PAPER AND CERTAIN CLASSES OF PRINTED
MATTER TRIMMED SIZES—A AND B SERIES

ISO 216 establishes the trim size for writing paper and paper used for printed forms. International paper sizes differ somewhat from typical American sizes. The common "letter size" sheet in the ISO series is size A4, 210mm x 297mm, or roughly 8.27 inches x 11.69 inches, a bit narrower and longer than the standard American 8.5 inch x 11 inch sheet.

ISO sizes are based on a simple set of basic principles. Each size in a series is achieved by dividing the next larger size into two equal parts, halving along the longer dimension. The same principle is followed in common American practice: 8½ x 11 paper is derived from 17 x 11 paper which is, in turn, derived from 17 x 22 paper, the sheet size on which letter-size weights are based (one ream of "20-weight" 17 x 22 sheets weighs 20 pounds). ISO adds one further requirement: the ratio of short side to long side must be the same in each size. The only ratio that will permit this is 1.414 to 1 (1.414 being roughly the square root of 2). The resulting sheets are more slender than common American "letter size" (1.29:1) but wider than common American book size (6 inch x 9 inch, or 1.5:1).

The primary ISO series is based on a sheet with an area of one square meter, yielding an "A0" size of 841mm x 1189mm. Sizes range down to "A10," 26mm x 37mm (or 1.02 inches x 1.45 inches). A secondary "B series" has the same ratios but begins with a sheet 1000mm x 1414mm. ISO paper sizes are well established in much of the world.

ISO R639-1967
SYMBOLS FOR LANGUAGES, COUNTRIES AND AUTHORITIES

This 15-page recommendation provides symbols showing "to which language a term or document belongs, in which country a term is used, and from what authoritative sources a term or definition has been taken." For languages, either letter symbols (one or two letters) or UDC (Universal Decimal Classification) numbers are used. Country symbols are those instituted for motor vehicles, shown between slashes (e.g., /GDN/ or /USA/), or UDC numbers enclosed in parentheses. "Authorities" are mostly national standards agencies, indicated by the symbols determined by the agencies involved.

R639 has no direct NISO equivalent. The standard includes a number of examples of use, such as the following examples from treatises on terminology: "E positron D Positron I positrone F positon S positon" and "EFR ion D Ion SvPl jon." The first gives equivalent terms in English, German (D), Italian, French and Spanish. The second gives one form used in English, French and Russian; another used in German; and a third used in Swedish (Sv) and Polish (Pl). The language list includes only 38 languages and includes optional two-character forms for the 10 languages with single-letter codes. The country list includes only ISO members.

ISO 690-1975
DOCUMENTATION—BIBLIOGRAPHICAL REFERENCES
ESSENTIAL AND SUPPLEMENTARY ELEMENTS

This standard sets out the elements of bibliographical references that are essential for identification, as well as useful supplementary elements. It also states an order for items and gives some recommendations for presentation. ISO 690 is much less detailed than Z39.29-1977: *Bibliographic References,* and does not set forth a consistent standard for punctuation. Z39.29 could be considered a national implementation of ISO 690, but it goes considerably further.

ISO R704-1968
NAMING PRINCIPLES

This recommendation aims "to provide those who are dealing with the terminology in any scientific or technical field with a number of principles designed to help them to unify and standardize concepts and terms or to create new ones." In nine pages of text, the recommendation sets forth principles on concepts, definitions, external form of terms, literal meaning and correspondence between term and concept.

A total of 31 principles appear, some of which conflict. The first principle calls for establishing a higher-priority principle in case of conflict; the most important principles are "language economy" and "established usage." Thus, shorter terms are generally preferred over longer terms, and existing well-established terms are generally preferred over new terms.

ISO 832-1975
DOCUMENTATION—BIBLIOGRAPHICAL REFERENCES
ABBREVIATIONS OF TYPICAL WORDS

This standard sets forth a brief set of rules for forming abbreviations of "typical" words in bibliographic references, and lists more than 1200 words and abbreviations in 16 major languages. The standard is 38 pages long, including a list in word order and one in abbreviation order. Two additional lists include more than 300 Cyrillic words and abbreviations.

ISO R860-1968
INTERNATIONAL UNIFICATION OF CONCEPTS
AND TERMS

In 10 pages of text, recommendation 860 suggests general rules to unify national terminologies (terminology used within one country or language). Discussion and recommendations are divided into concepts and systems, description, external form, internal form and characters. The document is a set of principles, recognized to be somewhat idealistic; a number of examples show problems that arise from different systems of terminology. The discussion is practical; it notes that the use of the same term doesn't help matters if the term doesn't have the same meaning. The value of R860 to existing terminologies is questionable; but the document itself makes interesting reading.

ISO R919-1969
GUIDE FOR THE PREPARATION OF CLASSIFIED VOCABULARIES

Recommendation 919 is directly related to recommendation 860; it provides detailed guidance for authors of standardized technical vocabularies. The recommendation goes through the stages of work required to prepare a vocabulary: limiting the problem, making use of sources of information, preparing the manuscript, compiling alphabetical indexes and publishing. R919 concerns primarily multilingual vocabularies, but many of its suggestions are useful for other glossaries.

The overall organization of the recommendation appears sound; some of the specific recommendations may be a bit odd. For example, point 1.3.3 suggests that "approximately 1000 concepts should be the top limit" for a single-volume vocabulary. Commentary on this point: "the preparation of voluminous vocabularies usually takes so much time that they are either never completed, or are out of date when they do appear. It is found, moreover, that specialists are interested in the terminology of their own particular fields and have little use of extensive and less specialized vocabularies."

ISO 999-1975
DOCUMENTATION—INDEX OF A PUBLICATION

This brief standard defines an index, gives brief guidance and provides guidelines for frequency of publication (for periodical indexes) and layout. The American equivalent, Z39.4-1984: *Basic*

Criteria for Indexes, is several times as long and far more useful. ISO 999 gives almost no assistance to an indexer, while Z39.4 is quite useful to an author who has not previously done indexes. The international standard is almost pointless; the national standard is a sound, useful reference.

ISO 1086-1975
DOCUMENTATION—TITLE LEAVES OF A BOOK

ISO 1086 is a two-page checklist of items to be included on the title-leaves of a book. The American equivalent is Z39.15-1980; in this case, the ISO standard represents a reasonable minimum, where the Z39 version asks for too much. ISO 1086 states the following minimum information: name(s) of author(s), compiler(s) or editor(s); names of others concerned; title of the book; title of the original (for a translation); earlier title (if any); edition number; place of publication, publisher and year of publication; number of volume (in a multivolume work); and series title and number (if part of a series). Date of original edition, date of first printing, and number of present impression and ISBN are considered desirable.

Except that many publishers identify first editions only by the *lack* of an edition statement, few American publications fail to include the minimum and desirable information. ISO 1086 prefers date of publication on the recto, but allows for verso placement; the international standard (unlike Z39.15) makes no mention of an abstract. LCCN, an element in Z39.15, is quite naturally not part of ISO 1086.

ISO R1087-1969
VOCABULARY OF TERMINOLOGY

This 15-page recommendation is a classified dictionary of terms used in other standards and recommendations issued by ISO TC 37 (Terminology). The classified vocabulary, which defines 94 items, is followed by an alphabetical index.

ISO R1149-1969
LAYOUT OF MULTILINGUAL CLASSIFIED
VOCABULARIES

ISO R1149 is a surprisingly lengthy and detailed description of forms of layout for classified multilingual vocabularies. The recommendation covers the vocabulary (printed edition), manuscript and record slips (individual vocabulary items). Samples are included. For those preparing multilingual glossaries or vocabularies, the recommendation includes a useful list of items that should be included in an entry: explanation of the concept; classification (UDC) symbol; terms for the concept, scope and serial number (within the vocabulary). The inclusion of a UDC classification symbol is unusual from an American perspective, but common to ISO terminology recommendations.

Many of the recommendations seem overly precise and somewhat peculiar. Examples of different styles of vocabularies seem excessively structured, and fail to show the virtues of using the ISO R1149 approach. By and large, the recommendation seems to be a case of "overkill."

ISO 1951-1973
LEXICOGRAPHICAL SYMBOLS PARTICULARLY FOR USE IN CLASSIFIED DEFINING VOCABULARIES

ISO 1951 defines a rather astonishing number of symbols to be used in "classified multilingual defining vocabularies." The standard runs to 31 pages and has the interesting aspect that, to be sensible, any vocabulary using the standard would need to reproduce most of the standard.

From a naive perspective, ISO 1951 represents standards-making for the sake of standards. Those who established the standard appear to recognize this; the third paragraph of the standard reads: "The great number of symbols recommended in this International Standard may be surprising at first sight. Indeed, in general dictionaries many of them will not be found. They are all, nevertheless, necessary and no symbol included in this International Standard may be considered superfluous for modern terminological lexicography."

Whatever "modern terminological lexicography" ("technical dictionaries" in English) requires, what can a user make of the differentiation between "bold parentheses" and "light parentheses," the use of a degree sign to mean "bad expression" and so on? The standard itself does not make consistent or coherent sense; many definitions are incomplete or largely useless. One can only speculate on the cost of developing this peculiar standard.

ISO 2014-1976
WRITING OF CALENDAR DATES IN ALL-NUMERIC FORM

ISO 2014 is essentially equivalent to the American standard X3.30-1971: *Representation for Calendar Date and Ordinal Date,* with two differences: X3.30 allows use of ordinal ("Julian") date and allows one-digit years for certain applications; ISO 2014 allows punctuated dates, with the month and day split off by spaces or hyphens. Both call for a normal YYYYMMDD form, e.g., 19840530.

ISO 2015-1976
NUMBERING OF WEEKS

This standard takes up a field that X3 did not choose to cover: numbering weeks within a year. Weeks always start on Monday, and week number one of a year is the week containing the first Thursday of January. Thus, on a year in which January 1 is a Thursday, the last three days of the previous year are considered part of "week one" of the new year. ISO 2015 specifies Monday as the beginning of a week, in contrast to the common placement of Sunday as the beginning of a week.

ISO 2108-1978
DOCUMENTATION—INTERNATIONAL STANDARD BOOK NUMBERING

This two-page standard is the basis for ISBN. ISO 2108 is an extension of the Standard Book Number embodied in the original Z39.21. Z39.21-1980: *Book Numbering,* is the American equivalent to ISO 2108 and establishes ISBN as a standard number for domestic publishers. Despite differences in length and specific texts, the two standards are identical in scope and implications.

ISO 2145-1978
DOCUMENTATION—NUMBERING OF DIVISIONS AND SUBDIVISIONS IN WRITTEN DOCUMENTS

This curious standard establishes a method for numbering divisions and subdivisions of a book, article, standard or other document. The standard specifies arabic numérals with periods dividing levels. Each level is numbered continuously within a single occurrence of the next higher level. While the standard is certainly reasonable, it also seems pointless as a standard. Anyone deciding to number divisions and subdivisions would normally follow this pattern anyway. Most modern outlining programs, and word processing systems that provide numbering, follow the ISO standard as the simplest method. Most likely, none of the program designers has ever considered the ISO standard; again, a reader can only wonder how much money and time was spent preparing it. (Z39 has not seen fit to prepare an American equivalent.)

ISO 2146-1972
DIRECTORIES OF LIBRARIES, INFORMATION AND DOCUMENTATION CENTERS

Z39.10-1971 (R1977): *Directories of Libraries and Information Centers,* predates ISO 2146 and may well be the basis for this much briefer, clearly related standard. ISO 2146 gives fewer detailed recommendations on page size, thickness, paper stock and the like, and it does not go into the details provided in Z39.10. In two pages (one largely empty), ISO 2146 gives a basic set of information that should be included for each library or information center. The "arrangement" section limits itself to seven simple suggestions, including "the table of contents shall be in the front of the volume and the index(es) in the back."

ISO 2384-1977
DOCUMENTATION—PRESENTATION OF TRANSLATIONS

This standard is essentially similar to Z39.31-1976 (R1983): *Format for Scientific and Technical Translations.* The two standards are similarly organized, have similar levels of detail and are both useful guides for those preparing translations.

ISO 2709-1981
DOCUMENTATION—FORMAT FOR BIBLIOGRAPHIC INFORMATION INTERCHANGE ON MAGNETIC TAPE

ISO 2709-1981, the international equivalent of Z39.2-1979:

Bibliographic Information Interchange on Magnetic Tape, establishes the underlying format of USMARC. ISO 2709 is the basis for all MARC formats in use today, and is based on the original Z39.2. The two standards differ mostly in precise terminology: for example, USMARC's "leader" is ISO 2709's "record label" and USMARC's "field terminator" is ISO 2709's "field separator." ISO 2709 explicitly allows for alphameric fields, listing "reserved fields" as "tags 002 to 009 and 00A to 00Z as required" and "bibliographic fields" as "tags 010 to 999 and 0AA to ZZZ as required." (ISO 2709 allows either capital or small letters, but not both, to be used in tags within an implementation.)

ISO 2788-1974
DOCUMENTATION—GUIDELINES FOR THE ESTABLISHMENT AND DEVELOPMENT OF MONOLINGUAL THESAURI

This international standard cites the earlier American equivalent, Z39.19-1974: *Guidelines for Thesaurus Structure, Construction, and Use.* The two standards are closely related though not identical. ISO 2788 uses somewhat more elaborate structure and makes heavier use of symbology. For all practical purposes, Z39.19-1980 is the American implementation of ISO 2788.

ISO 2789-1974
INTERNATIONAL LIBRARY STATISTICS

This standard is the international equivalent to Z39.7-1983: *Library Statistics.* The two standards generally specify similar information in similar ways.

ISO 3166-1981
CODES FOR THE REPRESENTATION OF NAMES OF COUNTRIES

American standard Z39.27-1984: *Structure for the Representation of Names of Countries, Dependencies, and Areas of Special Sovereignty for Information Interchange* is based on ISO 3166 but

adds more codes. ISO 3166 adds a third representation scheme to
the two-letter and three-letter codes used in both standards: a three-
digit numeric code established by the Statistical Office of the United
Nations. ISO 3166 runs to 50 pages, partly because it appears in
English and French, partly because it includes alphabetical lists by
"entity," two-character code, three-character code and numeric
code. Entity (country) lists appear in French and English, and two
more tables provide for algorithmic conversion of two or three
character codes to three-digit codes.

ISO 3297-1975
DOCUMENTATION—INTERNATIONAL STANDARD
SERIAL NUMBERING

As noted in Chapter 10, ISO 3297 is based on the original
Z39.9: *Identification Number for Serial Publications.* ISO adopted
the number and established the International Serials Data System.
The current American standard, Z39.9-1979: *International Standard Serial Numbering,* is the American certification of ISO 3297.
ISSN represents one of the three great international success stories
in bibliographic technical standards, the other two being ISBN and
the Z39.2/ISO 2709 format that underlies MARC.

ISO 3388-1977
PATENT DOCUMENTS—BIBLIOGRAPHIC REFERENCES
ESSENTIAL AND COMPLEMENTARY ELEMENTS

This standard gives rules for presentation of bibliographic
references for patent documents. Closely related to Z39.46-1983:
*Identification of Bibliographic Data On and Relating to Patent
Documents,* ISO 3388 is much simpler, giving only 18 data elements
(basically those required in Z39.46) to Z39.46's 50. The two standards serve identical purposes, differing only in wording and level of
detail. ISO 3388 includes portions of the "ICIREPAT Manual" as
appendixes. ICIREPAT is the Paris Union Committee for International Cooperation in Information Retrieval among Patent Offices,
a body of the World Intellectual Property Organization (WIPO).

ISO 5122-1979
DOCUMENTATION—ABSTRACT SHEETS IN SERIAL PUBLICATIONS

Abstract sheets are pages divided into blocks, each block containing a detailed description of one article sufficient for documentation work. This standard specifies what should head such a sheet, what should be in each block and how the sheet should be presented. Abstract sheets are uncommon in American periodicals; there is no equivalent Z39 standard.

ISO 5127/3a)-1981 — INFORMATION AND DOCUMENTATION—VOCABULARY—SECTION 3a): ACQUISITION, IDENTIFICATION, AND ANALYSIS OF DOCUMENTS AND DATA

This 23-page standard is a vocabulary, in French and English, for selected concepts in information and documentation. The vocabulary is classified and includes 144 different terms: the vocabulary uses terse definitions (italicizing terms defined elsewhere in the vocabulary) and includes many of the common terms of the field. Its status as an ISO standard seems peculiar, but it is a good (if brief and incomplete) vocabulary.

ISO 5426-1980
EXTENSION OF THE LATIN ALPHABET CODED CHARACTER SET FOR BIBLIOGRAPHIC INFORMATION INTERCHANGE

This and the American Z39.47-1984: *Latin Alphabet Coded Character Set for Bibliographic Use* both aim to define a set of graphic characters to accommodate diacritics and special characters. The two sets are not identical. ISO 5426 includes the character set itself, as well as extensive notes on names of symbols, examples of use and languages in which the symbol is used.

OTHER RELATED STANDARDS

Along with ISO R9-1968, the Handbook provides several other

standards covering non-Roman alphabets. They are: ISO R33-1961: *International System for the Transliteration of Arabic Characters;* ISO R259-1962: *Transliteration of Hebrew;* ISO R843-1968: *International System for the Transliteration of Greek Characters into Latin Characters;* and ISO 5428-1980: *Greek Alphabet Coded Character Set for Bibliographic Information Interchange.*

FOOTNOTES

1. International Organization for Standardization. *Information Transfer.* Geneva, Switzerland: ISO; 1982. 522 p. (ISO Standards Handbook 1). ISBN 92-67-10058-0.

2. Wellisch, Hans. *The Conversion of Scripts—Its Nature, History, and Utilization.* New York: Wiley; 1978. p. 246.

Appendix A: Layers of Standards in a Library Catalog

Technical standards work at many levels. A sophisticated product may involve a dozen or more layers of standards, from those for basic materials to those for information. Consider a local integrated library computer system as it might be configured in the late 1980s: specifically, a local system with standard links to a network of other local systems and central data resources.

Such a system might involve literally thousands of technical standards, from those used by parts suppliers, through those used in creating and maintaining information, to those used to maintain linkages. This appendix provides a small sample of some of the standards that might be involved in such a system.

Standards mentioned here come from a number of agencies, including but not limited to former American National Standard Committees. Agency names are abbreviated in the standards. Agencies with standards in this appendix are as follows:

AIChE: American Institute of Chemical Engineers

ANSI: American National Standards Institute

ARI: Air-Conditioning and Refrigeration Institute

ASHRAE: American Society of Heating, Refrigerating, and Air-Conditioning Engineers

ASME: American Society of Mechanical Engineers

ASTM: American Society for Testing and Materials

AWS: American Welding Society

EIA: Electronic Industries Association

IEEE: Institute of Electrical and Electronics Engineers

IPC: The Institute for Interconnecting and Packaging Electronic Circuits

NFPA: National Fire Protection Association

TAPPI: Technical Association of the Pulp and Paper Industry

UL: Underwriters Laboratory Inc.

MATERIALS AND MATERIALS TESTING

The lowest layer of standards, other than standards for weights and measures, includes standards for basic materials and for testing those materials. The computer equipment in an integrated library system might be built from materials made following these standards, among many others of their type.

ANSI H35.2-82: *Dimensional Tolerances for Aluminum Mill Products.*

ASTM A781-81: *Common Requirements for Steel and Alloy Castings for General Industrial Use, Specification for.*

ASTM B209-82: *Aluminum and Aluminum-Alloy Sheet and Plate, Specification for.*

ASTM B373-82: *Aluminum Foil for Capacitors, Specification for.*

ASTM D748-71: *Natural Block Mica and Mica Films Suitable for Use in Fixed Mica Dielectric Capacitors, Specification for.*

ASTM D1730-67: *Preparation of Aluminum and Aluminum-Alloy Surfaces for Painting, Recommended Practices for.*

ASTM D2753-68: *Electrolytic Capacitor Paper, Specification for.*

ASTM F77-69: *Apparent Density of Ceramics for Electron Device and Semiconductor Applications, Test Method for.*

ASTM F80-74: *Crystallographic Perfection of Epitaxial Deposits of Silicon by Etching Techniques, Test Method for.*

ASTM F518-77: *Determining Effective Adhesion of Photo-*

resist to Hard-Surface Photomask Blanks and Semiconductor Wafers During Etching, Recommended Practice for.

ASTM-F569-78: *Filterability Index of Reagent Grade Water and High-Purity Waters for Microelectronic Device Processing, Test Method for.*

IPC 2.3.2.3-70: *Circuit Characteristics (Printed Wiring Design Guide).*

IPC 2.3.14-73: *Print, Etch and Plate Tests.*

IPC L-110A-70: *Preimpregnated B-State Epoxy Glass Cloth for Multilayer Printed Circuit Boards.*

The above list is only a tiny sampling of the fundamental materials standards involved in preparing components of an integrated system. There are standards for solvents, standards for ingredients in paint, standards for cleaning agents. Companies that build components rely on their suppliers to follow materials standards, so that the components created from those materials will work properly.

COMPONENT STANDARDS

The next layer of standards covers components: everything from resistors, capacitors and printed circuits to wall plugs. The three lists below include a few of the component standards that might help to assure that a computer system can be assembled properly.

Electronic Components

Electronic components are the heart of a computer. The following standards include standard definitions, labeling standards and standard specifications for electronic components of various sorts.

ASTM F729-81: *Temperature Coefficient of Resistance of Film Resistors, Test Methods for.*

ASTM F769-82: *Transistor and Diode Leakage Current, Method of Measurement of.*

ASTM F772-82: *Noise Quality of Film-Type Resistors, Test Method for.*

AWS SM Ch 20: *Printed Circuits (Soldering Manual, 1978).*

EIA JEDEC 87-73: *Forward Turn-On Time Measurement in Semiconductor Diodes.*

EIA JEDEC 95-76: *JEDEC Registered and Standard Outlines for Solid State Products.*

EIA JEDEC 100-82: *Terms, Definitions and Letter Symbols for Microcomputers and Memory Integrated Circuits.*

EIA RS-153-B-72: *Molded and Dipped Mica Capacitors (Wire Lead Styles).*

EIA RS-162-56: *Test Standard for Ceramic Board Printed Circuits.*

EIA RS-196-A-70: *Fixed Film Resistors—Precision and Semi-Precision.*

EIA RS-228-B-72: *Fixed Electrolytic Tantalum Capacitors.*

EIA RS-236-B-68: *Color Coding of Semiconductor Devices.*

EIA RS-282-63: *Standards for Silicon Rectifier Diodes and Stacks.*

EIA RS-370-B-82: *Designation Systems for Semi-Conductor Devices.*

IEEE 162-63: *IEEE Standard Definitions of Terms for Electronic Digital Computers.*

IEEE 274-66: *Standard Definitions of Terms for Integrated Electronics.*

IEEE 662-80: *IEEE Standard Terminology for Semiconductor Memory.*

IEEE 696.1: *Standard Specification for S-100 Bus Interface Devices.*

IPC 2.4-81: *Edge Boards Connector Connector Contacts.*

IPC 5-815A-81: *General Requirements for Soldering Electronic Interconnectors.*

IPC DR-570-77: *General Specification for 1/8 Inch Diameter Shank Carbide Drills for Printed Boards.*

IPC H-855-82: *Hybrid Microcircuit Design Guide.*

IPC T-50B-80: *Terms and Definitions for Interconnecting and Packaging Electronic Circuits.*

UL 810-81: *Capacitors.*

Electrical Components

Electronic components are of little use without electricity. Electrical supply systems are based on a complex web of standards, including hundreds of standards for power transmission. The list below includes standards for electrical components directly related to a local system, that is, those that make it possible for the electronic components to draw power from the national power grid.

ANSI C37.16-80: *Preferred Ratings, Related Requirements, and Application Recommendations for Low-Voltage Power Circuit Breakers and AC Power Circuit Breakers.*

ASTM B3-74: *Soft or Annealed Copper Wire, Specification for.*

ASTM B33-81: *Tinned Soft or Annealed Copper Wire for Electrical Conductors, Specification for.*

ASTM B539-80: *Measuring Contact Resistance of Electrical Connections (Static Contacts), Methods for.*

ASTM D1351-78: *Polyethylene Insulated Wire and Cable, Specification for.*

ASTM D2633-82: *Thermoplastic Insulations and Jackets for Wire and Cable, Methods of Testing.*

EIA RS-364-69: *Standard Test Procedures for Low Frequency (Below 3 MHz) Electrical Connectors.*

EIA RS-406-74: *General Document for Connectors, Electric, Printed-Wiring Board (IPC-C-405A).*

IEEE 290-80: *IEEE Standard for Electric Couplings.*

IEEE C37.13-81: *Low-Voltage AC Power Circuit Breakers Used in Enclosures (ANSI/IEEE).*

IEEE S-135-1-62: *Power Cable Ampacities. Volume I—Copper Conductors.*

UL 44-83: *Rubber-Insulated Wires and Cables.*

UL 83-80: *Thermoplastic-Insulated Wires and Cables.*

UL 231-82: *Power Outlets.*

UL 817-80: *Cord Sets and Power-Supply Cords.*

Mechanical Components

Electronic equipment also requires mechanical structures to hold the electronics. There are literally hundreds of standards for mechanical components, including the sampling of standards for connectors listed below.

ANSI B18.8.1-1972(R1983): *Clevis Pins and Cotter Pins.*

ANSI B18.12-1962(R1981): *Mechanical Fasteners, Glossary of Terms for.*

ANSI B18.18.1M-1982: *General Purpose Metric Fasteners, Inspection and Quality Assurance for.*

ANSI B18.21.1-1972(R1983): *Lock Washers.*

ANSI/ASTM F592-80: *Collated and Cohered Fasteners and Their Application Tools, Definition of Terms Relating to.*

ANSI/ASTM F606-79a: *Threaded Fasteners, Washers, and Rivets, Test Method for Conducting Tests to Determine the Mechanical Properties of Externally and Internally.*

ASME B18.2.1-81: *Square and Hex Bolts and Screws Inch Series Including Hex Cap Screws and Lug Screws.*

ASME B18.6.3-72: *Machine Screws and Machine Screw Nuts.*

ASTM F467-81: *Nonferrous Nuts for General Use, Specification for.*

PERIPHERAL EQUIPMENT AND SUPPLIES

A local library system isn't just a computer. For the system to work, it must have peripheral equipment and supplies. Additional layers of standards help to assure that such equipment and supplies will function properly as part of the system.

Video Terminals

Some of the standards used in building a video display terminal appear here, excluding standards that allow the terminal and computer to communicate.

ANSI X4.23-82: *Office Machines and Supplies—Alphanumeric Machines—Keyboard Arrangement.*

EIA RS-256-A-65: *Deflection Yokes for Cathode Ray Tubes.*

EIA TEPAC 92-75: *Cathode Ray Tubes, Glossary of Terms and Practices.*

EIA TEPAC 103-A-81: *Recommended Practice for Measurement of X-Radiation from Raster-Scanned Direct-View Data Display Cathode-Ray Tubes.*

EIA TEPAC 110-80: *Cathode Ray Tube Bulb Criteria.*

EIA TEPAC 116-80: *Optical Characteristics of Cathode Ray Tube Screens.*

Mass Storage

Mass storage supports the database and transactions in a library system, and allows the library to save copies of its files. A few of the standards for mass storage devices are listed below.

ANSI X3.22-1973: *Recorded Magnetic Tape (800 CPI, NRZI).*

ANSI X3.27-1978: *Magnetic Tape Labels and File Structure.*

ANSI X3.39-1973: *Recorded Magnetic Tape (1600 CPI, PE).*

ANSI X3.40-1983: *Unrecorded Magnetic Tape (9-track 800 CPI, NRZI; 1600 CPI, PE; and 6250 CPI, GCR).*

ANSI X3.54-1976: *Recorded Magnetic Tape (6250 CPI, Group Coded Recording).*

ANSI X3.84-1981: *Unformatted Twelve-Disk Pack (200 Megabytes) General, Physical, and Magnetic Requirements.*

ANSI X3.101-1984: *Interfaces Between Rigid Disk Drive(s) and Host(s).*

ANSI X3.112-1984: *14-inch (356-mm) Diameter and Low Surface Friction Magnetic Storage Disk.*

ANSI X3.115-1984: *Unformatted 80 Megabyte Trident Pack for Use at 370 TPI and 6000 BPI—Physical, Mechanical and Magnetic Characteristics.*

EIA RS-352-68: *One Half-Inch (12.7-mm) Magnetic Tape Reel for Computer Use (Requirements for Interchange).*

Communications

The computer and terminals must send data back and forth; the computer may also send data through other paths to other computers. The list below samples a few technical standards that apply to some forms of communication but does not include standards for local area networks or for linked systems.

ANSI X3.1-1976: *Synchronous Signaling Rates for Data Transmission.*

ANSI X3.15-1976: *Bit Sequencing of the American National Standard Code for Information Interchange in Serial-by-Bit Data Transmission.*

ANSI X3.16-1978: *Character Structure and Character Parity Sense for Serial-by-Bit Data Communication in the American National Standard Code for Information Interchange.*

ANSI X3.24-1968: *Signal Quality at Interface Between Data Processing Terminal Equipment and Synchronous Data Communication Equipment for Serial Data Transmission.*

ANSI X3.25-1976: *Character Structure and Character Parity Sense for Parallel-by-Bit Data Communication in the American National Standard Code for Information Interchange.*

ANSI X3.28-1976: *Procedures for the Use of the Communications Control Characters of [ASCII] in Specified Data Communication Links.*

ANSI X3.44-1974: *Determination of the Performance of Data Communication Systems.*

EIA RS-232-C-69: *Interface Between Data Terminal Equipment and Data Communication Equipment Employing Serial Binary Data Interchange.*

EIA RS-269-B-76: *Synchronous Signaling Rates for Data Transmission.*

EIA RS-334-A-81: *Signal Quality at Interface Between Data Terminal Equipment and Synchronous Data Circuit Terminating Equipment for Serial Data Transmission.*

Optical Fibers

Academic library systems will increasingly be connected to networks covering the entire campus and providing communications for various computer uses. Such networks are likely to use optical fiber technology. The Electronics Industry Association (EIA) has mounted a major program in the last few years to establish necessary standards for fiber optics. The *1985 Catalog of American National Standards* lists 49 such standards, all adopted since 1977 and most adopted in 1983 or 1984, including the sampling below.

ANSI/EIA RS-455-21-1984: *Mating Durability.*

ANSI/EIA RS-455-22-1983: *Ambient Light Susceptibility.*

ANSI/EIA RS-455-45-1984: *Fiber Geometry of Optical Waveguide Fibers, Microscopic Method for Measuring.*

ANSI/EIA RS-455-50-1983: *Light Launch Conditions for Long Length Graded-Index Optical Fiber Spectral Attenuation Measurements.*

ANSI/EIA RS-455-56-1983: *Evaluating Fungus Resistance of Optical Waveguide Fibers.*

ANSI/EIA RS-455-66-1983: *Measuring Relative Abrasion Resistance of Optical Waveguide Coatings and Buffers.*

ANSI/EIA RS-455-58-1984: *Core Diameter Measurement of Graded Index Optical Fibers.*

ANSI/EIA RS-455-83-1983: *Cable to Interconnecting Device Axial Compressive Loading.*

ANSI/EIA RS-455-87-1983: *Knot Test for Fiber Optic Cable.*

Bar Code and OCR Readers and Equipment

Typical library systems use either bar codes or OCR fonts for circulation and borrower labels. Several technical standards cover OCR. Several competing industrial bar code standards exist, but are not reflected in ANSI standards. Some of the standards related to codes and readers are as follows:

ANSI X3.17-1981: *Character Set for Optical Character Recognition (OCR-A).*

ANSI X3.49-1975: *Character Set for Optical Character Recognition (OCR-B).*

ANSI X3.62-1979: *Paper Used in Optical Character Recognition (OCR) Systems.*

ANSI X3.86-1980: *Optical Character Recognition (OCR) Inks.*

ANSI Z136.1-80: *Safe Use of Lasers.*

ASTM F149-76: *Optical Character Recognition, Definition of Terms Relating to.*

TAPPI T537 PM-81: *Dirt Count for Paper and Paperboard (Optical Character Recognition—OCR).*

TAPPI TI 399-4-70: *TAPPI OCR Glossary.*

Paper and Supplies

If an integrated library system produces overdue notices, orders and other printed products, the system needs supplies. Many technical standards cover such supplies. A few appear below.

ANSI X4.4-1955(R1972): *Bond Papers and Index Bristols, Basic Sheet Sizes and Standard Stock Sizes for.*

ANSI X4.19-1979: *Printing Ribbons, Minimum Markings to Appear on Containers for.*

ANSI X4.20-1977: *Office Machines and Printing Machines Used for Information Processing—Widths of Fabric Ribbons on Spools from 0.1875 inch (4.8 mm) to 0.750 inch (19.0 mm).*

ANSI/TAPPI T411-os-76: *Thickness (Caliper) of Paper and Paperboard.*

ANSI/TAPPI T414-om-82: *Internal Tearing Resistance of Paper.*

ANSI/TAPPI T425-os-75: *Opacity of Paper.*

ANSI/TAPPI T494-om-81: *Tensile Breaking Properties of Paper and Paperboard (Using Constant Rate of Elongation Apparatus).*

ASTM F153-78: *Wear Resistance of Inked Computer Ribbons, Test Method for.*

ASTM F549-78: *Carbonless Copy Products, Definition of Terms Relating to (Revision A).*

ASTM F598-78: *Determining the Resistance of Carbonless Papers to Capsular Damage, Practice for.*

ASTM F634-79: *Measurement of the Coating Transfer Resistance of Mechanical Carbonless Cb Paper, Practice for.*

ENVIRONMENT

Computer systems don't work in a vacuum. All systems require space; larger systems require air conditioning and may require filtering. A number of organizations create technical standards that deal with the necessary environment for a library system.

AIChE A16-72: *Efficiency Testing of Air-Cleaning Systems Containing Devices for Removal of Particles (ANSI N101.1).*

ARI 110-80: *Air-Conditioning and Refrigerating Equipment Nameplate Voltages, Standard for.*

ARI 130-82: *Graphic Electrical Symbols for Air-Conditioning and Refrigerating Equipment, Standard for.*

ARI 220-67: *Load Calculation for Commercial Buildings Using Unitary Equipment, Standard for.*

ARI 260-75: *Application, Installation, and Servicing of Unitary Equipment, Standard for.*

ARI 390-78: *Computer Room Unitary Air-Conditioning Equipment, Standard for.*

ASHRAE 52-76: *Method of Testing Air-Cleaning Devices Used in General Ventilation for Removing Particulate Matter.*

ASHRAE Ch 1-80 : *Principles for Evaluation of Air-Conditioning Systems.*

ASHRAE Ch 17-82: *Data Processing System Areas.*

ASHRAE Ch 35-80: *Sound and Vibration Control.*

NFPA Sec 11-1: *Electronic Computer/Data Processing Equipment.*

UL 867-80: *Electrostatic Air Cleaning.*

UL 943-72: *Ground-Fault Circuit Interruptors.*

UL 1077-81: *Supplementary Protectors for Use in Electrical Equipment.*

SOFTWARE

No computer is useful without software. Technical standards for software involve another set of layers: languages, structures, techniques and content designation.

Languages, Techniques and Character Sets

Standards for character sets and for languages likely to be used in library systems, and for good use of those languages, include the following:

ANSI X3.4-1977: *Code for Information Interchange.*

ANSI X3.9-1978: *Programming Language FORTRAN.*

ANSI X3.23-1974: *Programming Language COBOL.*

ANSI X3.41-1974: *Code Extension Techniques for Use with the 7-Bit Coded Character Set of American National Standard Code for Information Interchange.*

ANSI X3.53-1976: *Programming Language PL/I.*

ANSI/IEEE770/X3.97-1983: *Programming Language Pascal.*

ASTM E919-83: *Software Documentation for a Computerized System, Specification for.*

IEEE 730-81: *IEEE Standard for Software Quality Assurance Plans.*

IEEE 829-83: *IEEE Standard for Software Test Documentation.*

Standards specifically required for library software include:

ANSI Z39.2-1977: *Bibliographic Information Interchange on Magnetic Tape.*

ANSI Z39.47-1984: *Latin Alphabet Coded Character Set for Bibliographic Use.*

A family of standards for computer-to-computer linkages is emerging, with work going on in Europe and the U.S. This work builds on ISO's Open Systems Interconnect model. The best-known example in the United States is the Linked Systems Project involving the Library of Congress, Research Libraries Group, Washington Library Network, OCLC and others.

Content Designation and Printed Products

High-level standards include ways of specifying information and full specifications for printed products. A few of the technical standards for identifying and arranging content:

ANSI X3.38-1972 (R1977): *Identification of States of the United States.*

ANSI Z39.9-1979: *International Standard Serial Numbering.*

ANSI Z39.21-1980: *Book Numbering.*

ANSI Z39.23-1983: *Standard Technical Report Number (STRN), Format and Creation.*

ANSI Z39.27-1984: *Structure for the Representation of Names of Countries, Dependencies, and Areas of Special Sovereignty for Information Interchange.*

ANSI Z39.29-1977: *Bibliographic References.*

ANSI Z39.43-1980: *Identification Code for the Book Industry.*

NISO (Z39) has developed two standard forms for printed products, mixing careful specifications for content with specifications for form which make the standards restrictive and lessen their usefulness in automated systems:

ANSI Z39.30-1982: *Order Form for Single Titles of Library Materials in 3-inch by 5-inch Format.*

ANSI Z39.45-1983: *Claims for Missing Issues of Serials.*

SUMMARY

Any complex product, such as an integrated library system, relies on hundreds or thousands of standards. Standards help define basic materials. Components are built using standards and rely on material standards. Systems emerge from standard components and use standard peripherals. Further standards provide sound environments for systems, and they help define the data to make systems useful.

Producers at any system level are consumers of items at lower levels. Consumers may concern themselves with technical standards for items they purchase, but they tend not to be concerned with the layers of standards underlying those purchases. Through choice and necessity, we all trust that standards have been followed at every level.

Appendix B:
Members and Subcommittees:
NISO, ASC X3, ISO TC 46 and TC 97

Information in this appendix is taken from publications of standards agencies. Standards agencies are dynamic, with changing membership and shifting structures.

NATIONAL INFORMATION STANDARDS
ORGANIZATION (Z39)
VOTING MEMBERS AS OF MAY 1985

Academic Press
American Association of Law Libraries
American Chemical Society
American Library Association
American Psychological Association
American Society for Information Science
American Society of Indexers
American Theological Library Association
Aspen Systems Corporation
Association of American Publishers (AAP)
Association of American University Presses (AAUP)
Association of Information and Dissemination Centers (ASIDIC)
Association of Jewish Libraries
Association of Research Libraries

Book Manufacturers' Institute
R.R. Bowker Company, Inc.

CAPCON Library Network
Colorado Alliance of Research Libraries (CARL)
Cooperative College Library Center (CCLC)
Council of Biology Editors
Council of National Library and Information Associations

EBSCONET

F.W. Faxon Company, Inc.

Indiana Cooperative Library Services Authority (INCOLSA)
Information Handling Services
Information Industry Association

Library Binding Institute
The Library Corporation
Library of Congress

Medical Library Association
Music Library Association

National Agricultural Library
National Archives and Records Administration
National Bureau of Standards, Information Resources and
    Services Division
National Commission on Libraries and Information Science
    (NCLIS)
National Federation of Abstracting and Information Services
    (NFAIS)
National Library of Medicine
National Technical Information Service

OCLC, Inc.
OHIONET

PALINET
Pittsburgh Regional Library Center (PRLC)

Reference Technology, Inc.
The Research Libraries Group, Inc.

Society for Scholarly Publishing
Society for Technical Communication
Special Libraries Association
SUNY/OCLC Network

Technique Learning Corporation

U.S. Department of Commerce Printing and Publishing Division
U.S. Department of Defense
U.S. Department of Energy, Office of Scientific and
  Technical Information

Waldenbooks
H.W. Wilson

NATIONAL INFORMATION STANDARDS ORGANIZATION (Z39) INFORMATIONAL MEMBERS AS OF MAY 1985

United States
American Mathematical Society
Association for Library and Information Science Education
  (ALISE)

Baker & Taylor Co., Inc.
Battelle Memorial Institute
Bibliographical Center for Research (BCR)
Blackwell Library Systems, Inc.
Brigham Young University
BroDart, Inc.
Brown University Library

California State University
CBS Records Center
Clemson University
CL Systems, Inc.
Colorado State University
Columbia University
Cornell University

Duke University

Emory University

Ferris State College
Folger Shakespeare Library
Follett Corporation
Fort Lewis College Library

Georgetown University Law Library
Greenwood Press

Illinois State University
Indiana University
International Standard Information Systems
Iowa State University

Johns Hopkins University

Kansas State University
Kent State University

Linda Hall Library

Macmillan Publishing Company
Mars Hill College
Massachusetts Institute of Technology
Michigan State University

Nebraska Library Commission
Nelinet, Inc.
New York Public Library
New York State Library
New York University
Northern Illinois University
North Texas State University

Ohio State University
Oklahoma State University

Pennsylvania State University
Philadelphia College of Pharmacy & Science
Public Affairs Information Service, Inc.

RILA—International Repertory of the Literature of Art
Rutgers University

Smithsonian Institution
South Carolina State Library
Southeastern Library Network (SOLINET)
State of Delaware, Delaware Division of Libraries
SUNY at Albany
SUNY at Buffalo

Texas A & M University
Tufts University

University of Alabama
University of Arizona
University of California—Los Angeles
University of California—San Diego
University of Chicago
University of Cincinnati
University of Colorado
University of Florida
University of Georgia
University of Hawaii
University of Houston
University of Maryland
University of Miami
University of Michigan
University of Missouri
University of New Hampshire
University of Notre Dame
University of North Carolina
University of Pennsylvania
University of Pittsburgh
University of Rochester
University of South Carolina

University of Southern California
University of Tennessee
University of Texas—Austin
University of Tulsa
University of Virginia
University of Washington
University of Wisconsin
University of Wyoming

VPI & State University

Washington University
Wilson-Cambridge, Inc.

Canadian and Foreign
McMaster University
National Library of Canada
Queen's University
University of Alberta
University of British Columbia
University of Waterloo
University of Western Ontario
UTLAS
Maruzen Co., Ltd.
University of Antwerp

NISO STANDARDS COMMITTEES AS OF MAY 1985

SC 4: Bibliographic References. Reviewing Z39.29 for revision or reaffirmation. Chair: Bob Tannehill, Chemical Abstracts Service.

SC 5: Romanization of Hebrew and Yiddish. Chair: Herbert C. Zafren, Hebrew Union College.

SC C: Language Codes. Preparing a first draft for comment or vote in 1985. Chair: John Byrum, Library of Congress.

SC D: Computer-to-Computer Protocol. Reviewing negative votes on Z39.50, and will prepare a revised standard in 1985. Chair: Ray Denenberg, LC.

SC E: Serial Holdings Statements. Revised proposed Z39.44, has forwarded the standard to ANSI for review and publication. Chair: Susan Brynteson, University of Delaware Libraries.

SC G: Common Command Language. Committee met in October 1984, and in February 1985, and has defined its focus: "specifying the vocabulary, syntax, and semantics of a common command language to facilitate the use of interactive information." Chair: Charles Hildreth, OCLC.

SC H: Patent Information Standards. Will circulate a first draft for comment in 1985. Chair: Philip Pollick, Chemical Abstracts Service.

SC J: Bibliographic Data Source File Identification. A draft standard was circulated for comment in September 1984. The committee is reviewing the comments. Chair: Ted Brandhorst, ERIC Processing and Reference Facility.

SC L: Romanization. Draft standard Z39.51 was submitted for vote in September 1984, and received two negative votes. The votes and extensive comments are being evaluated. Chair: Charles Husbands, Harvard University Library.

SC N: Coded Character Sets for Bibliographic Information Interchange. Chair: Charles Payne, Chicago.

SC P: Guidelines for Format & Production of Scientific and Technical Reports. The committee, including thirteen people in all, met in April 1984 to begin a major rewrite and revision of Z39.18. Chair: Tom Pinelli, NASA Langley Research Center.

SC Q: Periodicals: Format and Arrangement. This committee has been working on a revised Z39.1 since 1983, and will circulate a new revision for vote in 1985. Chair: Ed Barnas, John Wiley & Sons.

SC R: Environmental Conditions for Storage of Paper-Based Library Materials. A first draft will be circulated for comment or vote in 1985. Chair: Paul Banks, Columbia University School of Library Service.

SC S: Permanence of Paper for Printed Library Materials. Standard Z39.48-1984 was approved by the ANSI Board of Standards Review and will be published in January 1985; the committee dissolved after a successful four-year effort. Chair: Gay Walker, Yale University Library.

SC T: Standard Order Form for the Purchase of Multiple Titles. A draft standard will be circulated for voting in 1985. Chair: Peter Jacobs, Professional Media Service Corporation.

SC U: Format for Computerized Book Ordering. Standard Z39.49 will be published in 1985. Chair: Ernest Muro, Baker & Taylor.

SC V: Identifier for Information Organization. The committee is gathering information on library identifiers now in use. Chair: Marjorie Bloss, IIT Library.

SC W: Non-Serials Holdings Statement. A first draft will be circulated for comment in 1985. Chair: Stephen Paul Davis, Library of Congress.

SC X: Directories of Libraries and Information Centers. The committee is revising Z39.10 to apply to directories of all types of organizations, and will circulate a comment draft in 1985. Chair: Scott Bruntjen, PRLC.

SC Z: Eye-Legible Information on Microfilm Leaders, etc. A first draft will be circulated in 1985. Chair: Louis C. Willard, Speer Library, Princeton Theological Seminary.

SC AA: Interlibrary Loan Form. A draft standard form is being field tested in ALANET. Chair: Olive James, Library of Congress.

SC BB: Standard Computer Software Number. A draft standard was circulated for comment, with the comment period closing in February 1985. Chair: David Cohen, Technique Learning Corporation.

SC CC: Serial Item Identifier. A draft standard will be circulated for comment in 1985. Chair: Wendy Riedel, Library of Congress.[1]

ASC X3
VOTING MEMBERS AS OF JANUARY 1985

Producers
AMP Incorporated
AT&T Information Systems

Burroughs Corporation

Control Data Corporation

Data General Corporation
Digital Equipment Corporation (DEC)

Harris Corporation
Hewlett-Packard
Honeywell Information Systems

IBM Corporation

Moore Business Forms

NCR Corporation

Perkin-Elmer Corporation
Prime Computer, Inc.

Sperry Corp.

Texas Instruments
3M Company

Wang Laboratories, Inc.

Xerox Corporation

Consumers
Association of American Railroads

CUBE

DECUS

General Electric Company
General Services Administration
GUIDE International

Lawrence Berkeley Laboratory
Life Office Management Association

National Communications System

Recognition Technology Users Assn.

SHARE, Inc.

Travelers Insurance Companies

U.S. Department of Defense

VIM Incorporated

General Interests
American Library Association
American Nuclear Society
Association for Computing Machinery
Association of the Institute for Certification of Computer
   Professionals
AT&T Communications

Data Processing Management Association

IEEE

National Bureau of Standards

ASC X3: COMMITTEES AS OF JANUARY 1985

Standing Committees
Secretariat Management Committee
International Advisory Committee (X3/IAC)
Standards Planning and Requirements Committee (X3/SPARC)

Technical Committees
A—Recognition
  X3A1—OCR and MICR
    X3A1.1—Font Design
    X3A1.2—OCR Supplies and Forms
    X3A1.3—Image Definition and Measurement

B—Media
  X3B2—Perforated Media (Inactive)
  X3B3—Punched Cards (Inactive)
  X3B5—Digital Magnetic Tape
  X3B6—Instrumentation Tape
  X3B7—Magnetic Disks
  X3B8—Flexible Disks
    X3B8.1—Track Formats for Flexible Disk Cartridges
  X3B9—Paper Forms/Layouts
  X3B10—Credit/ID Cards
    X3B10.1—Integrated Circuit Cards
    X3B10.2—Revision of X4.18
    X3B10.3—Min. Physical Requirements of Savingsbooks
    X3B10.4—Optically Encoded Card Media
  X3B11—Optical Digital Data Disk

H and J—Languages
  X3H2—Database
  X3H3—Computer Graphics
    X3H3.1—Core Graphics System
    X3H3.2—Reference Models
    X3H3.3—Virtual Device Interface

X3H3.4—Conformance & Binding
X3H3.5—Min. Interface to Graphics
X3H4—Information Resource and Dictionary System
X3J1—PL/I
X3J1.3—General Purpose Subset
X3J1.4—Real-Time Subset
X3J2—BASIC
X3J3—FORTRAN
X3J4—COBOL
X3J4.3—COBOL DML
X3J5—COMPACT/ACTION/SPLIT
X3J7—APT
X3J7.1—Processor Language
X3J7.2—Postprocessor Language
X3J7.3—Lathe Language
X3J7.4—Robotics Language
X3J9—Pascal
X3J9.1—Pascal Extensions
X3J10—APL
X3J11—C Language
X3J12—DIBOL

K—Documentation
X3K1—Project Documentation
X3K2—Flowchart Symbols (Inactive)
X3K5—Vocabulary
X3K7—Program Abstracts (Inactive)

L—Data Representation
X3L2—Codes & Character Sets
X3L2.1—Videotex/Teletext
X3L2.2—Additional Control Functions for X3.64
X3L2.3—Two-Byte Graphic Character Set
X3L5—Labels and File Structure
X3L8—Data Representation
X3L8.4—Geographical Units

S—Communication
X3S3—Data Communication
X3S3.1—Data Communication Planning

X3S3.2—Data Communication Vocabulary
X3S3.4—Data Link Layer
X3S3.5—Quality of Service
X3S3.7—Public Digital Network Access

T and V—Systems Technology
  X3T1—Data Encryption
  X3T5—Open Systems Interconnection (Inactive)
    X3T5.1—OSI Architecture
    X3T5.4—OSI Management Protocols
    X3T5.5—Application and Presentation Layers
  X3T9—I/O Interface
    X3T9.2—Lower Level Interface
    X3T9.3—Device Level Interface
    X3T9.5—Loc. Dis. Data Interface
    X3T9.6—Cartridge Tape Drives
  X3V1—Office Systems
    X3V1.1—User Requirements
    X3V1.2—Symbols and Terminology
    X3V1.3—Text Structure
    X3V1.4—Text Interchange
    X3V1.5—Text Preparation and Presentation
    X3V1.6—Technology Integration in Office Systems

ISO TC 46: DOCUMENTATION

Participating Countries
Austria (SAA)

Belgium (IBN)
Brazil (ABNT)

Canada (SCC)
China, People's Republic of (CAS)
Cuba (NC)
Czechoslovakia (CSN)

Denmark (DS)

Egypt, Arab Republic of (EOS)

Finland (SFS)
France (AFNOR)

Germany, Federal Republic (DIN—*Secretariat*)

Hungary (MSZH)

India (ISI)
Indonesia (YDNI)
Italy (UNI)

Japan (JISC)

Netherlands (NNI)

Poland (PKNMiJ)
Portugal (DGQ)

Romania (IRS)

South Africa, Republic of (SABS)
Spain (IRANOR)
Sweden (SIS)
Switzerland (SNV)

United Kingdom (BSI)
United States (ANSI)
USSR (GOST)

Observing Countries
Australia (SAA)

Chile (INN)
Colombia (CONTEC)

Ethiopia (ESI)

Ghana (GSB)
Greece (ELOT)

Hong Kong (correspondent)

Iran (ISIRI)
Ireland (IIRS)
Israel (SII)

Jamaica (JBS)

Korea, Republic of (KBS)

Malaysia (SIRIM)
Mexico (DGN)

Norway (NSF)

Pakistan (PSI)

Saudi Arabia (SASO)
Singapore (SISIR)
Syria (SASMO)

Tanzania (TBS)
Thailand (TISI)
Turkey (TSE)

Venezuela (COVENIN)

Yugoslavia (SZS)

Subcommittees and Working Groups
Secretariat names follow working group/subcommittee names.

WG 2/DIN: Coding of country names and related entities.
WG 8/DS: Price indexes for library materials.
WG 9: International library statistics.
SC 2/AFNOR: Conversion of written languages.
  WG 1/AFNOR: Transliteration of Slavic-Cyrillic.
  WG 2/AFNOR: Transliteration of Arabic.
  WG 3/AFNOR: Transliteration of Hebrew.

WG 4/UNI: Transliteration of Korean.
WG 5/DIN: Transliteration of Greek.
WG 6/AFNOR: Romanization of Chinese.
WG 7/JISC (Japan): Romanization of Japanese.
WG 8: Joint SC2/SC4 working group: Relations between transliteration and machine representations of characters.
SC 3/DIN: Terminology of documentation.
SC 4/SIS: Automation in documentation.
WG 1/ANSI: Character sets for documentation and bibliographic use.
WG 3/DIN: Bibliographic filing principles.
WG 4/SIS: Format structure for bibliographic information interchange in machine readable form.
WG 5/UNI: Application level protocols.
SC 5/DIN: Monolingual and multilingual thesauri and related indexing practices.
SC 6/SCC: Bibliographic data elements in manual and machine processing.
WG 1/SCC: Documentary data elements.
WG 3/BSI: Revision of ISO 3388—Patent documents.
SC 7/AFNOR: Presentation of publications.
WG 1/DIN: Biblid.

ISO TC 97: INFORMATION PROCESSING SYSTEMS

Participating Countries
Austria (ON)

Belgium (IBN)

Canada (SCC)
China, People's Republic of (CAS)
Czechoslovakia (CSN)

Finland (SFS)
France (AFNOR)

Germany, Federal Republic (DIN)

Hungary (MSZH)

Ireland (IIRS)
Italy (UNBI)

Japan (JISC)

Netherlands (NNI)
Norway (NSF)

Poland (PKNMiJ)

Romania (IRS)

Spain (IRANOR)
Sweden (SIS)
Switzerland (SNV)

United Kingdom (BSI)
United States (ANSI—*Secretariat*)
USSR (GOST)

Observing Countries
Australia (SAA)

Brazil (ABNT)
Bulgaria (BDS)

Chile (INN)
Colombia (ICONTEC)
Cuba (NC)

Denmark (DS)

Greece (ELOT)

Hong Kong (correspondent)

India (ISI)

Iran (ISIRI)
Israel (SII)

Korea, Republic of (KBS)

Pakistan (PSI)
Portugal (DGQ)

Saudi Arabia (SASO)
South Africa, Republic of (SABS)

Thailand (TISI)
Trinidad and Tobago (TTBS)
Turkey (TSE)

Venezuela (COVENIN)

Yugoslavia (SZS)

Subcommittees and Secretariats

Application Elements
  SC 1/AFNOR: Vocabulary.
  SC 7/SCC: Design and documentation of computer-based
    information systems.
  SC 14/ANSI: Representations of data elements.

Equipment and Media
  WG 2: Instrumentation Magnetic Tape.
  SC 10/UNI: Magnetic disks
  SC 11/ANSI: Flexible magnetic media for digital data
    interchange.
  SC 13/DIN: Interconnection of equipment.
  SC 15/SNV: Labelling and file structure.
  SC 17/ANSI: Identification and credit cards.
  SC 19/UNI: Office equipment and supplies.
  SC 23/JISC: Optical Digital Data Disks.

Systems
  SC 2/AFNOR: Character sets and coding.
  SC 6/ANSI: Data communications.
  SC 18/ANSI: Text preparation and interchange.
  SC 20/DIN: Data cryptographic techniques.
  SC 21/ANSI: Information Retrieval, Transfer & Management
    for Open Systems Interconnection.
  SC 22/SCC: Application Systems Environments & Program-
    ming Languages.

FOOTNOTES

1. National Information Standards Organization [Z39]. *Directory of Standards Committees 1984-85.*

Glossary

Terms are defined as used in this book. Information on ISO members is taken from the 1984 *ISO Memento.*

ABNT: Associacao Brasileira de Normas Tecnicas. Founding member (1947) of ISO, representing Brazil. Secretariat for two ISO subcommittees and one working group.

AFNOR: Association Francaise de Normalisation. Founding member (1947) of ISO, representing France. Secretariat for 29 ISO technical committees, 121 subcommittees and 243 working groups.

AIA: Aerospace Industries Association.

AIChE: American Institute of Chemical Engineers.

ALA: American Library Association.

ANSC: American National Standards Committee.

ANSI: American National Standards Institute. The overall organization for voluntary standardization in the United States, and the U.S. member of ISO, the International Organization for Standardization. ANSI does not develop standards, but serves as an accrediting agency, clearinghouse and publisher. ANSI was formerly ASA, the American Standards Association, and USASI, the United States of America Standards Institute. A founding member (1947) of ISO; secretariat for 14 ISO technical committees, 62 subcommittees and 194 working groups.

ARI: Air-Conditioning and Refrigeration Institute.

ASA: American Standards Association, the successor to the American Engineering Standards Committee as of 1928. Succeeded by *USASI.*

ASC: Accredited Standards Committees. American National Standards Committees have either become Accredited Standards Organizations, Accredited Standards Committees or have ceased to exist.

ASCII: American Standard Code for Information Interchange. Formally stated as ANSI X3.4-1977, ASCII assigns standard meanings to combinations of binary digits so that information can be exchanged. Any computer that uses ASCII will treat "01000010" as the letter "B."

ASHRAE: American Society of Heating, Refrigerating and Air-Conditioning Engineers.

ASME: American Society of Mechanical Engineers.

ASTM: American Society for Testing and Materials.

AWS: American Welding Society.

Accredited Standards Agency: Group that meets ANSI requirements for carrying out the process of developing voluntary consensus technical standards.

Active Standard: A technical standard that is established prior to, or together with, emergence of a new technology. Active standards are designed to prevent problems rather than to solve them.

Actor-Oriented: Defined in terms of the people and programs that initiate and moderate activities, rather than in terms of either the information being manipulated (*Message-Oriented*) or the manipulations (*Process-Oriented*).

American Engineering Standards Committee: Agency formed by ASTM and four engineering societies; eventually became ANSI.

American National Standards Institute: See *ANSI*.

Audiocassette: See *Compact Cassette*.

BASIC: Beginner's All-purpose Symbolic Instruction Code. The most widely used programming language on microcomputers. Originally developed at Dartmouth.

BCS: Bureau of Ceylon Standards. ISO member since 1967, representing Sri Lanka. Secretariat for one ISO subcommittee.

BDS: State Committee for Science and Technical Progress. ISO member since 1955, representing Bulgaria. Secretariat for one ISO subcommittee.

BDSI: Bangladesh Standards Institution. ISO member since 1974.

BEMA: Business Equipment Manufacturers Association. Precursor to *CBEMA*.

BISAC: Book Industry Standards Advisory Committee, a group that formulates industry standards and proposes consensus standards for the book industry.

BSA: Komiteti i Cmimeve dhe Standarteve. ISO member since 1974, representing Albania.

BSI: British Standards Institution. Founding member (1947) of ISO. Secretariat for 23 ISO technical committees, 88 subcommittees and 285 working groups.

BSR: Board of Standards Review. The ANSI board that verifies that organizations have followed the proper process and achieved consensus. BSR actually approves ANSI standards at the ANSI level, but does not pass on the technical content of standards.

Beta: Originally Betamax; Sony Corporation's name for its system for video cassette recording.

Biblid: Bibliographical strip, a concise summary of bibliographic reference data intended for use at the foot of the front cover of periodicals. Developed by ISO and defined by ISO R30-1956. Not widely used in the United States.

Bit: A single unit of information in data processing. Short for *B*inary Dig*it*. A bit has two values usually represented as "0" and "1." All digital computers work with data made up of collections of bits.

Bit Sequencing: Order in which bits of a character are transmitted or stored.

CAMAC: Computer Automated Measurement and Control, a set of standards for traffic measurement and control embodied in ANSI/IEEE Camac-1982.

CAS: China Association for Standardization. PRC member of ISO since 1978. Secretariat for one subcommittee in 1984.

CBEMA: Computer Business Equipment Manufacturers Association. Secretariat for ASC X3.

CD: See *Compact Discs.*

CD-4: Name for a completely discrete four-channel recording system popularized by RCA and used by Warner Brothers and others. Unique among the three four-channel LP processes used in the early 1970s, CD-4 could actually reproduce four discrete channels.

CERTICO: ISO's Committee on Certification.

CLR: Council on Library Resources. One of the funding agencies for ANSC Z39 from 1961 to the early eighties.

CNLA: Council of National Library Associations. The secretariat for NISO.

COBOL: *CO*mmon *B*usiness *O*riented *L*anguage, the most widely used high-level programming language on large business computers. One of the oldest programming languages, and one of the first to attempt to make programs roughly resemble natural language.

COPOLCO: ISO's Committee on Consumer Policy.

COSQC: Central Organization for Standardization and Quality Control. ISO member since 1964, representing Iraq.

COVENIN: Comision Venezolana de Normas Industriales. ISO member since 1959, representing Venezuela.

CP/M: Control Program for Microcomputers. The industry standard operating system for 8-bit microcomputers based on the Intel 8080 and Zilog Z80 CPUs. A product of Digital Research Incorporated.

CPU: Central Processing Unit, the heart of any computer. Distinguished from memory, clock, input/output and display.

CSK: Committee for Standardization of the Democratic People's Republic of Korea. ISO member since 1963.

CSN: Urad pro normalizaci a mereni. Founding member (1947) of ISO, representing Czechoslovakia. Secretariat for one ISO technical committee, four subcommittees and eight working groups.

CYS: Cyprus Organization for Standards. ISO member since 1979.

Classification Standard: See *Grading Standard*.

Code Extension: Adding new characters to an existing repertoire. ANS X3.41 specifies techniques for adding characters to ASCII.

Community Standard: Any technical standard other than an internal standard. Usually used to refer to standards which are not formal consensus standards.

Compact Cassette: Original name for the audiocassette, developed by Philips of Holland and promulgated as a licensed standard.

Compact Discs: 12cm discs containing digital signals, played back using lasers. Compact Disc encoding and playback standards were established by the consortium of companies (primarily Phillips and Sony) that developed the medium, allowing the new medium to develop rapidly on a base of solid technical standards. Also called *Digital Audio Discs*. Abbreviated CD or DAD.

Consensus: General agreement. In the standards field, consensus is assumed to mean that no critical objections exist. Consensus for technical standards does *not* mean unanimity; ANSI regulations require that any standard receiving a 2/3 positive vote be forwarded for adoption.

Cutter Number: Alphanumeric identification for a book within an LC or Dewey class. Named for Charles Ammi Cutter.

DAD: Digital Audio Disc. See *Compact Disc.*

DB-25: Common connector for RS-232C interfaces. A connector with 25 pins arranged in two rows, 13 pins on the upper row and 12 on the lower.

DCE: Data Communication Equipment, equipment that communicates information. Modems and computers are data communication equipment.

DEVCO: ISO's Development Committee, concerned with standardization in developing countries.

DGN: Direccion General de Normas. Founding member (1947) of ISO, representing Mexico.

DGQ: Direccao-Geral da Qualidade. ISO member since 1949, representing Portugal. Secretariat for two ISO technical committees and two working groups.

DIN: Deutsches Institut fur Normung. ISO member since 1951, representing the Federal Republic of Germany. Secretariat for 26 ISO technical committees, 104 subcommittees and 263 working groups.

DINT: Direction de la normalisation et de la technologie. ISO member since 1978, representing Ivory Coast.

DRI: Digital Research Incorporated. Software company that developed CP/M.

DS: Dansk Standardiseringsraad. Founding member (1947) of ISO, representing Denmark. Secretariat for four ISO technical committees, three subcommitees and 19 working groups.

DTE: Data Terminal Equipment, equipment expected to be the end-point (terminus) of data communications. Printers are data terminal equipment.

De Facto Standard: Apparent standard arising through common practice without any formal agreement. De facto standards may be more apparent than real, or may be attempts by one agency to preempt a field.

Defective Standard: A technical standard that fails to serve the proper purposes of a standard.

Derived Search Key: Key to access bibliographic records, formed by taking groups of initial letters from two or more words of a field or fields. OCLC author, title and author/title keys are derived search keys.

Digital Audio Disc: See *Compact Disc.*

Dominant-Agent Standard: See *First-Agent Standard.*

Dvorak Keyboard: A keyboard configuration considered by some to be much more efficient than the traditional *"QWERTY"* keyboard.

EBCDIC: Extended Binary Coded Decimal Interchange Code. IBM's standard coding for machine representation of characters. The major alternative to the formal consensus ASCII.

EIA: Electronic Industries Association.

ELOT: Hellenic Organization for Standardization. ISO member since 1955, representing Greece.

EOS: Egyptian Organization for Standardization. Member of ISO since 1957.

ESI: Ethiopian Standards Institute. ISO member since 1972.

ETB: End of Transmission Block, ASCII control character 17.

EXCO: Executive Committee of ISO.

FORTRAN: *FOR*mula *TRAN*slation, the oldest high-level programming language in wide use. FORTRAN is still the most widely used programming language for scientific and mathematical problems.

FORTRAN 77: Version of FORTRAN embodied in ANS X3.9-1978 . Not fully compatible with earlier ANSI FOR-

TRAN, abandoning full compatibility in favor of "good language practice." A controversial language standard.

First-Agent Standard: Standard established by the first major agent in a particular field. Functionally synonymous with *Dominant-Agent Standard.* When an early agent does a good or successful job, others are likely to follow that agent's lead rather than produce incompatible developments.

Formal Consensus Standards: Standards developed by an accredited standards agency following proper methods to ensure consensus among interested parties. The narrower meaning of "technical standards" is "formal consensus technical standards," those that go through the formal process. All ANSI standards are formal consensus standards, but some American formal consensus standards are not ANSI standards.

GOST: USSR State Committee for Standards. Founding member (1947) of ISO. Secretariat for ten ISO technical committees, 31 subcommittees and 14 working groups.

GSB: Ghana Standards Board. ISO member since 1966.

GW BASIC: "Gee Whiz" BASIC. The "advanced BASIC" used on most MS-DOS computers other than the IBM PC, and essentially identical to IBM's BASICA. Until recently, GW BASIC and BASICA represented Microsoft's most powerful BASIC.

Grading Standard: A technical standard that establishes defined grades for a product. Grading standards usually concern natural products or refined natural products; for instance, "SAE 10W-30" is a grade of oil based on a grading standard.

Guideline Standard: A standard that provides suggested practices but does not aim for uniformity or interchangeability. Many library-related standards are guideline standards.

Hollerith Card: 80-column paper card with 12 rows for rectangular holes. Also known as tab card, IBM card, punched card or 80-column card.

IAC: International Advisory Committee, a committee of ASC X3 which coordinates X3's work with activities in ISO, IEC and other international bodies.

IBN: Institute Belge de Normalisation. Founding member (1947) of ISO, representing Belgium. Secretariat for four ISO technical committees, 11 subcommittees and 24 working groups.

ICONTEC: Instituto Colombiano de Normas Tecnicas. ISO member since 1960, representing Colombia. Secretariat for one ISO working group.

IEC: International Electrotechnical Commission. The oldest international body for technical standards (founded in 1906).

IEEE: Institute of Electrical and Electronics Engineers.

IFLA: International Federation of Library Associations.

IIRS: Institute for Industrial Research and Standards. ISO member since 1951, representing Ireland.

INAPI: Institut algerien de normalisation et de propriete industrielle. ISO member since 1976, representing Algeria.

INFCO: ISO's Committee on Information.

INN: Institutio Nacional de Normalization. Founding member (1947) of ISO, representing Chile.

INNORPI: Institute national de la normalisation et de la propriete industrielle. ISO member since 1984, representing Tunisia.

IPC: Institute for Interconnecting and Packaging Electronic Circuits.

IRANOR: Instituto Espanol de Normalizacion. ISO member since 1951, representing Spain. Secretariat for four ISO subcommittees and six working groups.

IRS: Institutul Roman de Standardizare. ISO member since 1950, representing Romania. Secretariat for two technical committees, five subcommittees and one working group.

ISA: International Federation of the National Standardization Associations. Formed in 1926 to coordinate international standardization efforts. Abandoned during World War II.

ISBD: International Standard Bibliographic Description. Best known in terms of ISBD punctuation, the distinctive and controversial punctuation pattern used in most USMARC cataloging since 1974.

ISBN: International Standard Book Number, a standard numbering system used throughout the publishing world. Embodied in ANS Z39.21.

ISI: Indian Standards Institution. Founding member (1947) of ISO. Secretariat for five ISO technical committees, 15 subcommittees and four working groups.

ISIRI: Institute of Standards and Industrial Research of Iran. ISO member since 1960.

ISO: International Organization for Standardization. The international body for voluntary standards, with representation from national standards organizations.

ISSN: International Standard Serial Number. A standard number used throughout the world for serial publications. Embodied in ANS Z39.9.

ITAL: *Information Technology and Libraries,* divisional journal for ALA's Library and Information Technology Association (LITA). Began publication when the *Journal of Library Automation* ceased publication.

ITINTEC: Instituto de Investigacion Tecnologica Industrial y de Normas Tecnicas. ISO member since 1962, representing Peru. Secretariat for one ISO technical committee and three working groups.

Identifier: ISO equivalent name for subfield. Element within variable length data fields in ISO 2709/Z39.2 formats which identifies portions of the field. The length of the identifier is stated in the leader.

Implementation-Defined Portion: That portion of the directory within MARC (and other Z39/ISO 2709) records which can be defined within a specific implementation. USMARC does not allow for an implementation-defined portion.

Indicator: In MARC formats, character that appears at the beginning of variable length data fields and provides some information to assist in interpreting the field. USMARC formats provide for two indicators at the beginning of each field; other ISO 2709/Z39.2 formats may provide for zero to nine indicators per field.

Industry Standard: Apparent standard practice within an industry, not necessarily based on any agreement or even any reality. "Industry standard" is probably the most abused term in the standards field and is nearly devoid of any real meaning. Compare *De Facto Standard, Licensed Standard, First-Agent Standard* and *Consensus Standard.*

Interchangeability: Standardization intended to assure that all versions of one defined product can be interchanged in working with other products.

Internal Standard: Technical standard developed to establish consistency within an organization or group of one or more people.

International Organization for Standardization: See *ISO*.

JBS: Jamaican Bureau of Standards. ISO member since 1974.

JISC: Japanese Industrial Standards Committee. ISO member since 1952. Secretariat for two ISO technical committees, 12 sub-committees and 29 working groups.

JOLA: *Journal of Library Automation.* Quarterly journal of ALA's ISAD (Information Science and Automation Division), which became LITA (Library and Information Technology Association). JOLA was replaced by *Information Technology and Libraries* (ITAL) in 1981.

Julian Date: Day of the year, where January 1 is "1" and December 31 is either "365" or "366." Also called *Ordinal Date.*

KBS: Bureau of Standards. ISO member since 1963, representing the Republic of Korea.

KEBS: Kenya Bureau of Standards. ISO member since 1976.

LCCN: Library of Congress Card Number, a number assigned by the Library of Congress. The LCCN could be considered a standard number, although the Library of Congress makes no such claim.

LYSSO: Libyan Standards and Patent Section. ISO member since 1978, representing the Libyan Arab Jamahiriya.

Leader: In the context of MARC formats and other formats based on ISO 2709, a leader (or record leader) is a 24-character string at the beginning of a record which defines fundamental machine-processing aspects of that record, including its length, status and makeup of directory.

Length of Field: In MARC records, a portion of record directory elements indicating the length of a field.

Licensed Standard: An industry standard established by the process of licensing a protected process or product.

MSC: State Committee for Prices and Standards of the Mongolian People's Republic. ISO member since 1979.

MSZH: Magyar Szabvanyugyi Hivatal. Founding member (1947) of ISO, representing Hungary. Secretariat for one ISO technical committee, one subcommittee and seven working groups.

Message-Oriented: Defined in terms of information being sent, rather than in terms of the processes used to send and manipulate the information. Compare *Process-Oriented*.

MicroPro International: Microcomputer software company, best known for WordStar.

Microsoft BASIC: Name for any version of *BASIC* developed by Microsoft Corporation. Most microcomputers use some version of Microsoft BASIC. The many versions of Microsoft BASIC are not necessarily compatible with each other.

Minimal BASIC: A limited subset of BASIC designed to be easy to implement in a standard fashion on almost any computer. Defined by ANS X3.60-1978.

Minimum Quality Standard: A technical standard that establishes the lowest quality level acceptable for a product. The best minimum quality standards are *Performance Standards,* defining acceptability based on performance using standardized tests.

Modem: *Mo*dulator-*dem*odulator. A device to translate the binary (on/off) signals characteristic of computers into modulated tones suitable for transmission over phone lines and similar equipment.

NAPLPS: North American Presentation Level Protocol Syntax. A standard method for transmitting characters and graphics, to be used in videotex and teletext applications.

NC: Comite Estatal de Normalizacion. ISO member since 1962, representing Cuba.

NFPA: National Fire Protection Association.

NISO: National Information Standards Organization (Z39), successor to ANSC Z39. NISO (Z39) creates and maintains standards in the fields of libraries, publishing and information science.

NNI: Nederlands Normalisatie-instituut. Founding member (1947) of ISO, representing the Netherlands. Secretariat for five ISO technical committees, 15 subcommittees and 48 working groups.

NSF: Norges Standardiseringsforbund. Founding member (1947) of ISO, representing Norway. Secretariat for two ISO technical committees, seven subcommittees and 11 working groups.
Also: National Science Foundation. One of the funding agencies for ANSC Z39 from 1961 to the early 1980s.

NSO: Nigerian Standards Organization. ISO member since 1972.

NUC Code: National Union Catalog Code. An alphabetic code identifying a library or library-related agency. NUC codes have been in use for most of the century. NUC codes are not considered proper "standard identifiers" because they vary in length and, more important, use upper and lower case letters to distinguish between libraries.

Naming Standard: Any standard that establishes consistent naming conventions, including vocabularies and technical dictionaries.

National Information Standards Organization: See NISO.

OCLC: Online Computer Library Center, Inc. America's largest shared cataloging, acquisitions and interlibrary loan system, and one of the largest online systems in the world.

ON: Osterreichisches Normungstinstitut. Founding member (1947) of ISO, representing Austria. Secretariat for two ISO technical committees, five subcommittees and 11 working groups.

OSI: Open Systems Interconnections, a model for computer-to-computer communications design developed by ISO.

Operability: Ability to be used operationally, including self-checking properties and suitability for use with standard schemes.

Ordinal Date: See *Julian Date*.

pH: Hydrogen-ion activity, used to express alkalinity or acidity. A pH of 7 is neutral; lower values represent increasing acidity, while higher values represent increasing alkalinity. Technically, pH is the negative logarithm of the effective hydrogen-ion concentration in gram equivalents per liter.

PKNMiJ: Polish Committee for Standardization, Measures and Quality Control. Founding member (1947) of ISO. Secretariat for one ISO technical committee, five subcommittees and seven working groups.

PL/I: Programming Language One, a complex high-level programming language in fairly wide use. PL/I is widely used in bibliographic applications.

PLACO: Planning Committee of ISO.

PSA: Product Standards Agency. ISO member since 1968, representing the Philippines.

PSI: Pakistan Standards Institution. ISO member since 1951.

Parallel Transmission: Data communications technique in which more than one transmission channel is used to transmit more than one bit at a time. Most typically, eight or nine channels would be used to transmit the eight bits of a character (with the ninth channel carrying a parity bit). Compare *Serial Transmission.*

Parity: Equivalence or equality. In data storage and communications, "parity bits" are extra bits added to characters such that the sum of all "1" bits in the supplemented character is either even ("even parity") or odd ("odd parity"). Parity bits serve as a crude error-sensing mechanism: if any single bit of a character is misread, the parity will be wrong.

Pascal: A computer language developed by Niklaus Wirth. Pascal is touted as a modern, structured, standard and transportable language. It is structured but neither as standard nor transportable as adherents would claim. A standard Pascal does exist, but lacks sufficient power for most uses.

Performance Standard: Standard that defines a system or object by the end result rather than by means used to achieve that end. Some performance standards do include some "means" requirements that are fundamental to successful performance.

Process-Oriented: Defined in terms of processes taking place, rather than in terms of information being transmitted and manipulated. Compare *Message-Oriented.*

Pseudostandard: Something that appears to be a technical standard, but is not. Examples include single names for multiple incompatible "standards" and "standards" that are actually internal practice for a single agent, and subject to unilateral change.

QS: Quadraphonic/Stereo, a system developed by Japanese companies to encode four audio channels on a standard two-channel long-playing record. As with *SQ*, QS could not restore four discrete channels. QS showed good front-rear separation at the expense of full left-right separation.

QWERTY: Standard name for the most prevalent keyboard layout for typewriters and other alphabetic machines. Named for the top row of alphabetic keys, QWERTY was designed in the nineteenth century to keep frequently used keys well apart on the machines, reducing the frequency of jammed keys. QWERTY is generally considered less than ideal for keying efficiency, but continues to dominate.

Quadraphonic: Having four sound channels. Common term for the various surround-sound systems of the late 1960s and early 1970s.

REMCO: ISO's Committee on Reference Materials, which establishes suitability of references for citation in standards.

RLG: The Research Libraries Group, Inc. A consortium of universities and libraries to pursue common aims in library and scholarly fields. Operates *RLIN*.

RLIN: Research Libraries Information Network. Computer support arm of The Research Libraries Group, Inc. Includes a large shared cataloging and acquisitions system.

Reactive Standard: A technical standard developed because of perceived problems with existing situations. Compare with *Active Standard*.

Romanization: Conversion of other alphabets or non-alphabetic scripts to Roman letters.

SAA: Standards Association of Australia. Founding member (1947) of ISO. Secretariat for six ISO technical committees, four subcommittees and 23 working groups.

SABS: South African Bureau of Standards. Founding member (1947) of ISO. Secretariat for two ISO technical committees, two subcommittees and two working groups.

SAE: Society of Automotive Engineers, one of the earliest American standardization agencies, founded in 1910.

SAN: Standard Address Number. A standard number identifying addresses within the publishing and library industries, embodied in ANS Z39.43.

SANZ: Standards Association of New Zealand. Founding member (1947) of ISO.

SASMO: Syrian Arab Organization for Standardization and Metrology. ISO member since 1981.

SASO: Saudi Arabian Standards Organization. ISO member since 1974.

SCC: Standards Council of Canada. Founding member (1947) of ISO. Secretariat for five ISO technical committees, 23 subcommittees and 50 working groups.

SCISA: Standard Code Identification of Serial Articles. A numbering standard proposed in 1975 but not adopted.

SCSN: Standard Computer Software Number. Proposed by a NISO standards committee in late 1984, this number appears to be redundant since ISBNs are being assigned to computer software.

SFS: Suomen Standardisoimislitto r.y. Founding member (1947) of ISO, representing Finland. Secretariat for four ISO subcommittees and eight working groups.

SII: Standards Institution of Israel. Founding member (1947) of ISO. Secretariat for one ISO technical committee, three subcommittees and one working group.

SIRIM: Standards and Industrial Research Institute of Malaysia. ISO member since 1969. Secretariat for one ISO working group.

SIS: SIS—Standiseringskommissionen i Sverige. Founding member (1947) of ISO, representing Sweden. Secretariat for 11 ISO technical committees, 25 subcommittees and 71 working groups.

SISIR: Singapore Institute of Standards and Industrial Research. ISO member since 1966.

SMC: Secretariat Management Committee of ASC X3, X3's equivalent to a council.

SNIMA: Service de normalisation industrielle marocaine. ISO member since 1963, representing Morocco.

SNV: Association suisse de normalisation. Founding member (1947) of ISO, representing Switzerland. Secretariat for four ISO technical committees, 17 subcommittees and 19 working groups.

SPARC: Standards Planning and Requirements Committee of ASC X3. SPARC evaluates the need for new standards, audits standards development on functional and economic grounds and checks standards for conformance to objectives.

SQ: Stereo-Quadraphonic. System developed by CBS to store four channels of audio information within the two available channels on a standard long-playing record, using an algebraic matrix. Algebraic matrixes did not permit re-creation of four discrete channels. European recording companies continue to produce some SQ-encoded classical recordings.

SSD: Standards and Quality Control Department. ISO member since 1973, representing Sudan.

STACO: ISO's Committee on Standardization Principles, a forum for discussion of fundamental aspects of standardization.

STRN: Standard Technical Report Number. An unusual standard number consisting of alphabetic, numeric and mixed segments. Embodied in ANS Z39.23.

SZS: Savezni zavod za Standardizaciju. ISO member since 1950, representing Yugoslavia.

Safety Standard: A technical standard expressly intended to ensure safety.

Serial Transmission: Data communications in which bits are transmitted one at a time along a single communications path. Compare *Parallel Transmission.*

Simplification: Standardization through reduction in the number of varieties of a given product.

Specification Standard: A standard which establishes a definition rather than a name, symbol or grade.

Standard Kilogram: A metal ingot (or one of a limited number of copies) that had at its creation a mass of exactly one kilogram, within limits of available measurement techniques.

Starting Character Position: Element of a MARC record directory that, when added to the length of the directory and leader, shows the first character position in a field.

Symbol Standard: A technical standard that defines symbols. ANS X3.5: *Flowchart Symbols and Their Usage* is a typical symbol standard.

TAPPI: Technical Association of the Pulp and Paper Industry.

TBS: Tanzania Bureau of Standards. ISO member since 1979.

TCVN: Direction generale de standardisation, de metrologie et de controle de la qualite. ISO member since 1977, representing the Socialist Republic of Viet Nam.

TESLA: Technical Standards for Library Automation Committee of the Library and Information Technology Association of the American Library Association (ALA LITA TESLA). The professional committee most responsible for this book.

TISI: Thai Industrial Standards Institute. ISO member since 1966.

TSE: Turk Standardlari Enstitusu. ISO member since 1956, representing Turkey. Secretariat for two ISO subcommittees.

TTBS: Trinidad and Tobago Bureau of Standards. ISO member since 1980.

Technical Standard: An explicit definition that can be communicated, is not subject to unilateral change without notice and, if properly followed, will yield consistent results.

Teletex: One-way information services using television screens for display. Teletex services transmit a sequence of set screens or pages, over and over, with a user's selection being limited to choosing which pages to view. Distinct from *Videotext,* which provides for two-way communication. Teletex may be a broadcast medium.

Test Standard: A standard that specifies testing methodology.

Transliteration: Conversion of characters from one alphabetic system to another alphabetic system. *Romanization* is one particular form of transliteration, but also encompasses those cases where non-alphabetic languages are represented in Roman characters.

UCSD Pascal: Version of the Pascal programming language developed at the University of California, San Diego, and licensed by the Regents of the University of California. UCSD Pascal includes an operating system.

UL: Underwriters Laboratory, Inc.

UNI: Ente Nazionale Italiano di Unificazione. Founding member (1947) of ISO, representing Italy. Secretariat for two ISO technical committees, 32 subcommittees and 35 working groups.

UNIX: An operating system developed by Bell Laboratories.

UNSCC: United Nations Standards Coordinating Committee. Founded in 1943 to coordinate international standardization; led to formation of ISO.

USASI: United States of America Standards Institute. Successor body to *ASA* in the 1960s, succeeded by *ANSI*.

USMARC: Generic name for MARC bibliographic formats in the United States, principally LC MARC from the Library of Congress, but also OCLC MARC, RLIN MARC and WLN MARC (among others).

UTLAS: University of Toronto Library Automation Systems, a bibliographic service founded by the University of Toronto. UTLAS is now a commercial service.

VCR: Video cassette recorder.

VHS: Video home system. Name for the most popular system of video cassette recording. Originally developed by Sony, but passed up for the technically superior Betamax/Beta system. Sony sold the technology to Matsushita, which made VHS a commercial success.

Verification: Assuring that a product actually meets claimed standards.

Videotext: Two-way information services to provide pages of information on television screens, with requests and other feedback also being available. Compare *Teletex*.

WLN: Western Library Network, a regional bibliographic service.

WordStar: Popular microcomputer word processing system produced by MicroPro International.

YDNI: Badan Kerjasama Standardisasi LIPI-YDNI (LIPI-YDNI Joint Standardization Committee). ISO member since 1954, representing Indonesia.

Z39: American National Standards Committee Z39, formed in 1940. The standards committee devoted to libraries, information science and publishing. ANSC Z39 became NISO (Z39), the National Information Standards Organization, in 1984.

Z85: American National Standards Committee on Standardization of Library Supplies and Equipment. Secretariat is the American Library Association. ANSC Z85 created one standard, Z85.1: *American National Standard for Permanent and Durable Library Catalog Cards*. Z85 has since dissolved, with NISO (Z39) taking responsibility for Z85.1.

ZABS: Zambia Bureau of Standards. ISO member since 1984.

Selected Bibliography

This bibliography includes all sources examined or used in preparing this book, except for standards discussed in Chapter 1 and Chapters 10–12. Bibliographic citations for those standards are included with the discussions.

"American National Standard Committee Z39 X/C 34 on Code Identification of Serial Articles, Draft Code Proposal." *Journal of Library Automation.* 8(2): 154-161; 1975 June.

American National Standards Institute. *1985 Catalog of American National Standards.* New York: ANSI; 1985. 158 p.

American National Standards Institute. *1984 Progress Report.* New York: ANSI; 1984 May.

American National Standards Institute. *National Electrical Safety Code, ANSI C2-1977.* New York: IEEE; 1977. 345 p.

Avram, Henriette D.; McCallum, Sally H.; Price, Mary S. "Organizations Contributing to Development of Library Standards." *Library Trends.* 31(2): 197-221; 1982 Fall.

Brown, Thomas P. "Communication Standards for Online Interchange of Library Information." *Library Trends.* 31(2): 251-264; 1982 Fall.

Carpenter, Chas. *Dollars and Sense.* Garden City, NY: Doubleday, Doran; 1928. 256 p. (A diatribe against standardization as a tool of communism, railing against all government agencies and against "buying by specification." Lively, remarkable and an interesting relic of the early days of "unfettered capitalism.")

Carter, Ruth C. "Identifying Needed Technical Standards: The LITA TESLA Committee at Work." *Library Hi Tech.* 5: 37-40; 1984.

Coles, Tessie, V. *Standards and Labels for Consumers' Goods.* New York: Ronald Press; 1949. 556 p.

Crane, Rhonda J. *The Politics of International Standards: France and the Color TV War.* Norwood, NJ: Ablex; 1979. 123 p. (A fascinating and thorough account of France's use of technical standards to erect non-tariff protectionist barriers. Shows politics and economics at play in the field of technical standards.)

Crawford, Walt. "EBCDIC Bibliographic Character Sets— Sources and Uses: A Brief Report." *Journal of Library Automation.* 12(4): 380-381; 1979 December.

Crawford, Walt. *MARC for Library Use: Understanding the USMARC Formats.* White Plains, NY: Knowledge Industry Publications; 1984. 222 p.

Crawford, Walt. "Standard Fare: One We Don't Need." *LITA Newsletter.* 19; 1985 Winter. p. 4-5.

Davis, Charles. "Forward." *Library Trends.* 31(2): 189; 1982 Fall.

Dvorak, John C. "Inside Track." *InfoWorld.* 1984 October 8. p. 88. (Discussion of uproar over revised ANSI FORTRAN and apparent incompatibility with earlier ANSI FOR-TRAN.)

Electronic Industries Association. *EIA Standard Interface Between Data Terminal Equipment and Data Communication Equipment Employing Serial Binary Data Interchange, EIA RS-232C.* Washington, DC: EIA; 1969 August. 28 p.

Frase, Robert W. "Procedures for Development and Access to

Published Standards." *Library Trends.* 31(2): 225-236; 1982 Fall.

Guide to Submitting Standards to ANSI for Approval. New York: ANSI; [1984]. 5 p.

Harriman, Norman F. *Standards and Standardization.* New York: McGraw-Hill; 1928. 265 p. (Good early work with a careful, balanced view of the process and purpose of technical standards. A thoughtful work in an era when technical standards could be controversial (see Carpenter, *Dollars and Sense*).)

Hartmann, David C. "Standard Fare: Update on ANSC Z39 S/C D: Computer-to-Computer Protocols." *LITA Newsletter.* 13: 6-7; 1983 Summer.

Hemenway, David. *Industrywide Voluntary Product Standards.* Cambridge, MA: Ballinger; 1975. 141 p. (A good look at industry standards, with some emphasis on problems with standards and use of standards for anticompetitive reasons.)

Hickey, Thomas B.; Spies, Phillis B. "Standards for Information Display." *Library Trends.* 31(2): 315-324; 1982 Fall.

Houghton, Bernard, ed. *Standardization for Documentation.* Hamden, CT: Archon; 1969. 93 p.

Hurt, Peyton. *Bibliography and Footnotes.* Third edition. Berkeley, Los Angeles, London: University of California Press; 1968.

Index and Directory of U.S. Industry Standards. Englewood, CO: Information Handling Services; 1983. 2 v.: 547 p., 684 p. (Index to all ANSI and most other standards association standards, with numeric and subject indexes to the main list.)

International Organization for Standardization. *Information*

Transfer. Geneva, Switzerland: ISO: 1982. (ISO Standards Handbook 1). 522 p. ISBN 92-67-10058-0. Available from ANSI.

International Organization for Standardization. *ISO Memento 1984*. Geneva: ISO; 1984. 141 p.

Lagueux, Paul B. "Standards for Networks and the Identification of Some Missing Links." Markuson, Barbara; Woolls, Blanche, eds. *Networks for Networkers*. Indianapolis: Neal-Schuman; 1980. p. 174-184.

Lyons, Nick. *The Sony Vision*. New York: Crown; 1976. 235 p.

Moffett, Carol Willis. *More For Your Money*. New York: Public Affairs Committee; 1942. (Public Affairs Pamphlets #63). 31 p. (A brief, early consumer-oriented introduction to the value of technical standards.)

National Bureau of Standards. *Guide for the Development, Implementation and Maintenance of Standards for the Representation of Computer Processed Data Elements*. Washington, DC: NBS; 1976. (FIPS Pub. 45).

National Information Standards Organization (Z39). *Directory of Standards Committees, 1984–1985*. Gaithersburg, MD: NISO; 1984. 44 p.

National Information Standards Organization (Z39). *Directory of Voting Members, 1984–1985*. Gaithersburg, MD: NISO; 1984. 11 p.

National Information Standards Organization (Z39) Progress Report, 1984-1985. Washington, DC: NISO; 1985 April 30. 21 p.

Paul, Sandra K. "Library Standards: An Introduction to Organizations and the Standards Process." *Library Hi Tech*. 7: 87-90; 1984.

Paul, Sandra K. "Standard Fare: A Joy Forever." *LITA News-letter.* 17: 5; 1984 Summer. (Discusses BISAC and its decision to use Z39.2 as the basis for the variable-length ordering format.)

Paul, Sandra K.; Givens, Johnnie E. "Standards Viewed from the Applications Perspective." *Library Trends.* 31(2): 325-342; 1982 Fall.

Peters, Paul Evan. "Standard Fare: A Brief Discussion of Models." *LITA Newsletter.* 15: 11-12; 1984 Winter. (Commentary on James Rush's model for standards planning, initial suggestion for a higher-level model.)

Prigge, R.D. [and others]. *The World of EDP Standards.* [Blue Bell, PA]: Sperry-Univac; 1978 November. 165 p.

Reck, Dickson, ed. *National Standards in a Modern Economy.* New York: Harper & Row; 1956. 372 p.

Rush, James E. "The MARC Formats: Their Use, Standardization, and Evolution." *Journal of Library Automation.* 13(3): 197-199; 1980 September.

Rush, James E. "A Proposed Model for the Development of an Integrated Set of Standards for Bibliographic and Related Data." *Library Trends.* 31(2): 237-249; 1982 Fall.

Sanders, T.R.B., ed. *The Aims and Principles of Standardization.* [Geneva]: ISO; [nd]. 115 p.

"Second Draft Proposal to ISAD/TESLA." *Journal of Library Automation.* 10(2): 181-183; 1977 June.

Simplification, Standardisation, Specialisation: Case Studies on Variety Reduction. Volume 2. Paris: Organization for European Economic Co-operation; 1959 February. 97 p. (Detailed studies of economies achieved by reducing variety.)

Standardization Activities of Concern to Libraries and National Bibliographies: An Outline of Current Practices, Projects and Publications. London: IFLA Committee on Cataloguing; 1976. 36 p.

"Standards in Industry." *The Annals of The American Academy of Political and Social Science.* 137: 1928 May. 282 p.

Tannehill, Robert S., Jr.; Husbands, Charles W. "Standards and Bibliographic Data Representation." *Library Trends.* 31(2): 283-314; 1982 Fall.

Verman, Lal C. *Standardization: A New Discipline.* Hamden, CT: Archon; 1973. 461 p. (A careful, exhaustive work on technical standards in theory and practice. Written from an Indian perspective, it tends to favor governmental involvement and imposed technical standards, particularly for developing countries.)

Wall, C. Edward. "Microcomputer Software Indentification: The Search for Another Numbering Standard." *Library Hi Tech News.* 13: 1, 11-19; 1985 February.

Wellisch, Hans H. *The Conversion of Scripts—Its Nature, History, and Utilization.* New York: Wiley; 1978. 509 p. (Information Science Series). (Pages 245-309 discuss multiple standards for Romanization.)

Wood, James L. "Factors Influencing the Use of Technical Standards in a Nationwide Library and Information Service Network." *Library Trends.* 31(2): 343-358; 1982 Fall.

Index to Standards

285

General Index

ABOUT THE AUTHOR

Walt Crawford has been manager of the Product Batch Group in the Computer Systems and Services Division of the Research Library Group (RLG) since 1980. He began at RLG in 1979 as a programmer/analyst. Previously, he was a programmer/analyst in the Library Systems Office of the University of California, Berkeley, from 1972 to 1979. His experience in library automation began in 1968 when he designed and implemented a circulation system (based on punched cards) for the Circulation Department of UC Berkeley's Doe Library.

Mr. Crawford has been active in the American Library Association since 1975 and has been involved with the Technical Standards for Library Automation Committee (TESLA) of ALA's Library and Information Technology Association (LITA, formerly ISAD) since 1976. He was a member of that committee from 1978 to 1982, and chair from 1980 to 1981. In July 1985, Mr. Crawford became RLG's alternate representative to NISO (Z39). Mr. Crawford has served as a liaison from RLG to the USMARC advisory group since 1981, and became a member of the MARBI committee in 1985; he also began serving as editor of the *LITA Newsletter* in July 1985.

Mr. Crawford has published articles on MARC, library automation, technical standards and microcomputers in several professional journals. He wrote *MARC for Library Use: Understanding the USMARC Formats,* Knowledge Industry Publications, Inc., 1984.

He is currently working on *Patron Access: Issues for Online Catalogs*, to be published by Knowledge Industry Publications, Inc.